M000017532

BEYOND THE CLASSROOM

THE UNCONVENTIONAL EDUCATION OF AN ENTREPRENEUR

JOHN F. STANKIEWICZ

© 2020 John Stankiewicz

All rights reserved. Published in the United States of America. No part of this book may be reproduced or transmitted in any form or by any means, electronic or mechanical, including photocopying, recording, or by any information storage and retrieval system, without permission in writing from the publisher.

The information provided in this book is for general informational purposes only. This book is not to be used for business or financial advice. The author is not a financial advisor. The publisher and author are not responsible for any damages or negative consequences from any treatment, action, application, or preparation, physical, medical, or financial, to any person reading or following the information in this book. Some names and identifying details have been changed to protect the privacy of individuals. The events that are recorded in the book are those that I remember to the best of my ability, though others may have a different take on those events. There is no harm intended in anything that I say. Any use of this information is at your own risk.

Earning levels for Isagenix® Independent Associates that appear in this publication are examples and should not be construed as typical or average. Income level achievements are dependent upon the individual Associate's business skills, personal ambition, time, commitment, activity and demographic factors. For average earnings, see the Isagenix Independent Associate Earnings Statement found at www.IsagenixEarnings.com.

Isagenix products are not intended to diagnose, treat, cure, or prevent any disease. Weight loss should not be considered typical. For more information on the study, see IsagenixHealth.net.

ISBN (print, soft cover): 978-1-7346480-0-3
ISBN (print, hard cover): 978-1-7346480-1-0
ISBN (ebook): 978-1-7346480-2-7
ISBN (audiobook): 978-1-7346480-3-4

Published by Stankiewicz Ventures, LLC
www.JohnStankiewicz.com
Email: John@JohnStankiewicz.com

ISA FOUNDATION
Inspire. Share. Advocate.

CREATING POSITIVE CHANGE

Our mission is to create global, sustainable impact through volunteer efforts and charitable contributions focused on healthy nutrition and support for underserved children, wellness education for all, and aid for those affected by natural disasters.

- Every child deserves a healthy, nutritious meal.

- Every person deserves the education and empowerment to live a healthy life.

- Every family deserves the means to survive and recover from natural disaster.

The ISA Foundation is committed to providing resources to those who need them most and making a positive difference in the lives of people around the world.

10% of all book proceeds will be donated to the ISA Foundation.

CONTENTS

INTRODUCTION

"GO TO SCHOOL, work hard, get good grades, earn a respectable degree, find a secure, well-paying job, work forty hours a week for forty years, then retire and enjoy what's left of your life." And so goes the key to success as told by our family, teachers, friends, and peers.

If you are anything like me, the thought of that being your reality during the short time we have on earth probably makes you want to dig out your eyeballs with a dessert spoon. Unfortunately, that is the very route that most of us are encouraged to pursue by society. That is the route that I was encouraged to take. That is also why at the age of twenty-six I am writing this book for you.

I am here to tell you that a life exists where you call the shots, where you can live in foreign countries and use the world as your playground, where you can earn money from wherever you'd like without having to answer to a boss, and where you are the one who decides exactly what you do with your time. How do I know? Because I have been able to do just that.

Before I go any further, I want to make one thing clear. The purpose of this book is not to completely deter you from going to school. School is great for people whose dream is to become a doctor, lawyer, or engineer. I am a college graduate myself, and as you will see in the coming chapters, some of the most important lessons I learned came from my time in school. I am not here to attack school, but I am here to bring light to what is happening.

Times are rapidly changing. The opportunities we have today were not available five, ten, twenty, fifty, or one hundred years ago. Technology and the internet have completely changed the way we make a living; however, most of what we are taught in schools reflects what was necessary to succeed decades and even centuries ago.

We have a system where one size fits all. Every single person is unique and has their own special gifts to bring to the world. Too many students are being made to feel inadequate if they do not receive As on their ability to regurgitate memorized information onto a Scantron sheet. They are told if they ever want to be successful, they must figure out a way to get good grades.

So what about the C student? The kid who feels inadequate because he doesn't get straight As and isn't getting into the top colleges that will be crucial for his success? The kid who isn't intrigued by what he's being taught in school and is bashed for focusing on his passions because those will never get him anywhere? The kid who wants to travel, build a business, and live life on his own terms without checking into a cubicle nine-to-five every day for the rest of his life?

I am that kid.

That's why I am compelled to bring this book to the world to show you that I am just like you. Average in class, not excited about working for a corporation my entire life, and simply desirous of more. My goal is to show you my journey, the lessons I learned along the way, and how the success I have today is almost entirely attributed to the lessons I learned outside of the classroom from experience.

After a hard-fought mental battle, I decided the best way to convey this message to you was through my story. Some of the lessons you will encounter in my story will be more black and white, while some will be left up for interpretation.

As I wrote this book, my most important goals were to entertain you as a reader, inspire you, and shift your perspective as to what is possible in this world. I want you to see the importance of getting out there and going after whatever your gut says is right. I want you to understand that experience is the best teacher in life. I want you to know that you will get knocked down many times before you experience the sweet taste of victory!

Above all, after reading this book, I want you to get out there and pursue what your heart has been telling you to do. Maybe it's a business idea that you have yet to take action on because you fear judgment from your peers. It could be pursuing your childhood dream of being a singer or actor. Maybe you have always wanted to drop everything, pack a suitcase, and aimlessly wander the world. Whatever it is, my goal is for you to be inspired to take action. We get one shot at this life, and let me tell you, it is meant to be lived.

As you flip the page to what I consider the beginning of my journey to success, I ask one favor of you. Please read this book with an open mind to possibility. Forget about what your parents, teachers, or friends told you that you could or could not do. If at any point you are reading and an idea or passion surfaces that you buried due to fear of judgment or rejection, stop and write it down. If that happens, it is something that you were put here to pursue.

Now, I invite you to come along with me on my journey beyond the classroom.

1

WILL JOHN STANKIEWICZ REPORT TO THE MAIN OFFICE?

IT WAS THE final period of the day. My freshman year of high school was just about halfway through, with midterms right around the corner. As my teacher's monotone voice lectured about the importance of understanding how to solve quadratic equations for our upcoming test, I was daydreaming of carving through the fresh powder at the local mountain on my new snowboard.

Just as I was about to sail off the first jump of my run, an all-too-familiar announcement came over the intercom and snapped me back to reality.

"Will John Stankiewicz report to the main office, please? John Stankiewicz to the main office."

The entire classroom turned their heads and stared. My best friend Mike nudged me as I stood up, smirked, and made my way to the principal's office. This was nothing new for me. School had always been the place where getting a good laugh came first and education came second.

Whether it was swinging across the gym on the climbing rope like Tarzan and nearly kicking my classmate's head off or hiding in a cabinet for an entire period of science, I always had something up my sleeve and was no stranger to facing the music. It wasn't that I was an awful student, the content just bored me, and it never made sense to me why everyone cared so much about getting an A on their social studies homework.

For some reason, as I made the walk of shame down to the office, I had a bad feeling in my stomach. When I got there, the secretary had me sit and wait until the principal was ready to see me. I sat in the office for what felt like an eternity pondering what I possibly could have done this time. *Was it for putting Joe's shoe in the ceiling during science?* No, he wouldn't have told on me for that. Maybe my study hall teacher found out I stuck a paperclip in the outlet? I thought about the explosion of sparks that resembled a grand finale showcase on the Fourth of July. That one might be expensive.

Finally, the vice principal peeked her head out of the office door and waved me in. As I walked into the room, I realized that this must have been a big deal. The superintendent, principal, and vice principal were all sitting around a circular table and instructed me to pull up a seat. They wasted no time.

"Mr. Stankiewicz, do you know why we called you down today?" said the vice principal.

"Not a clue, but I'm sure there must be some reason," I replied.

"Earlier today a student made a bomb threat, if you remember being on lockdown fourth period. We brought the student in to assess why he might have made such a threat. We had an in-depth conversation with him about his time here at our school and some of the other things that he may have done wrong since the start of freshman year," the vice principal said.

"John, he told us that two and a half months ago he asked you if you could get him marijuana, and you ultimately sold him a bag of it for five dollars. We take this matter very seriously here and need to know the truth. We assure you that if you come forth and admit that you did this, everything will be much better off. It will all be okay, and we will be able to take steps to correct this incident, but we need you to tell us the truth," she said.

My heart rose into my throat. I immediately turned red and got lightheaded as butterflies rushed through my body. I could form no words. This was the last thing I expected. The exact memory hit me out of nowhere like an uppercut from Tyson. I was in history class when this kid asked me if I could get him a nickel bag of weed. Since

I considered him to be a friend and knew where I could get it, I decided to help him out. One time. Now here we were. I felt betrayed and foolish and like my back was against the wall.

"Mr. Stankiewicz?" the vice principal inquired as she glared at me sideways.

"We just want to figure out what happened, John. If you will just tell us the truth, we can work to resolve this. We all make mistakes. We want to help you," the superintendent chimed in.

Being fourteen years old and scared out of my mind, I had no idea what to do but trust them.

"Yes I did it. But I swear, it was only one time. I am not a drug dealer by any means. I promise this will never happen again, you have to trust me. My parents are going to kill me. They cannot find out about this. This will ruin my life."

After my panic-driven rant, they simply looked at each other, then looked back to me.

"Thank you so much for cooperating, John. We just need you to write down exactly what happened, sign the paper, and then we can work to correct this."

Trembling, I wrote my confession. When I was finished, I brought them the paper and asked, "What now?"

"Well, John, you possessed and sold illegal drugs on school grounds. This is no small offense. By policy, we are required to place you on a ten-day suspension. After that, you will have a hearing in front of the board of education to determine what happens next. We will definitely take the fact that you cooperated into consideration," the principal explained.

They notified my parents, and as far as I was concerned, my life as I knew it was officially over.

My mom was out of town for a business conference and had her trip turned upside down when the news was relayed to her. She had nothing to say to me. My stepdad picked me up from the school and brought me to his workplace down the street where he was building a stone wall.

He had no words for me either. I kept my head down, threw on a pair of gloves, and started to move piles of stone.

The next ten days were spent in a living purgatory. My parents drove me to my grandparents' house and made me tell them what

I had done. My grandfather shook his head in disbelief while my grandma just stared at the ground. I felt like a disgrace around my family and uncomfortable even being in our own home.

I spent most of the suspension in my bedroom, avoiding contact with anyone and basking in my shame. With all of this alone time, my thoughts began to eat away at me. The only glimmer of hope I held onto was the principal telling me everything would be okay since I had told the truth.

Two weeks later was the night that determined my fate: the board of education meeting. I showed up in a shirt, tie, and dress pants with a prepared two-page apology. When the doors opened to enter the meeting room, I felt like I was walking into the Supreme Court to defend myself against murder allegations.

Fifteen members of the board looked me up and down as I slowly approached the table to take a seat and learn my fate. They opened the hearing and asked me if I had anything I would like to say before they made their decision. I stood up and delivered my apology with the utmost sincerity, trembling the entire time. I took a look around the room, and not one person made eye contact with me.

"Mr. Stankiewicz, the board of education has decided that the most appropriate course of action is your expulsion from our high school for the remainder of the school year. However, if you complete 200 hours of community service before next fall, we will allow you to come back and attend the beginning of the next school year. We will provide you with tutors so you don't fall behind academically. Thank you for your apology."

Boom. And just like that, in January, during my freshman year, I was kicked out of high school.

All the worry and angst leading up to this hearing turned into a blank and emotionless feeling. I looked over to see my stepdad looking down at his folded hands. My mom had a small tear in her eye as she stared into her lap. Right then, I hit the biggest low point I have ever experienced in my life, and at the time, I thought there was no way I could ever recover from it.

That night I laid in bed without sleeping for a single minute. I just stared up at my ceiling, wondering.

People who get kicked out of school amount to nothing. What will I do with the rest of my life? Will anyone ever forgive me for this?

How am I supposed to get into college? If I can't get into college, I am doomed for sure. What else can I possibly do? Work at a fast-food restaurant? Is there any way I can ever succeed in life now?

These questions tore me to pieces because I did not have answers for any of them.

I was living in the rural town of Goshen, Connecticut, where the most exciting event of the year was the annual diesel truck pull at the local rodeo, so the news of what happened spread like wildfire. Stories were all over the newspaper and local news stations with headlines like "Freshman Drug Dealer Caught in High School Drug Bust."

Although what actually happened was the furthest thing from that headline, the media never missed an opportunity to sell their paper. Every parent from my school and every person in my town knew what I did.

The girl who I liked was forced to stop talking to me because her mother did not want her daughter talking to a drug dealer. Families who did not know me prior to the incident did not want their kids hanging out around me. I was dealt blow after blow. After a couple of weeks of moping around the house, my parents sat me down at the kitchen table.

My mom said, "John. You have definitely broken our trust. Nothing about this situation makes us happy or proud. We are just as embarrassed as you are. We realize that this is a rock-bottom point for you. But you need to understand this. You are fourteen years old. You are a kid. Kids make mistakes. Yes, this mistake is much bigger than most kids make, but what is done is done. It is definitely going to take time, but eventually this will be behind you."

Mom went on, "I know you feel like your life is over right now, but you don't even understand how much time you have ahead of you. You can continue to mope around, or you can face your actions like a man. The bright side is that the only place you can possibly go from here is up."

I still had my doubts, but I knew they were right. Moping around was doing me no good. I had to figure out a way to power through this and get back on track. There were two options. I could let this make me or I could let it break me. I knew it would not be easy, but I chose to make this a defining moment.

As the months passed, I focused on doing what I had to do to get back on track with my life. This included going to the homes of my family and friends and delivering an in-person apology for what

I had done. Fortunately, everyone that meant a lot to me accepted my apology. Things at home began to return to normal, and I felt comfortable being around my family. Their forgiveness made me feel like a human again.

In regard to my academics, I was assigned individual tutors for all of my classes. Each of the teachers went above and beyond to make sure I not only stayed on track but excelled in each subject. I went to all of my tutoring hours and received top grades in all of my classes. Their sacrifice and belief in me helped rebuild my belief in myself.

I spent four hours every morning at the local church stuffing envelopes, painting fences, making pies, weeding gardens, and doing whatever tasks they needed to complete my 200 community service hours. The people of the church were extraordinarily appreciative of my work and restored my sense of purpose.

I spent many hours alone thinking about what happened and what I could do moving forward. Although I thought my life was over at first, I decided that it was just beginning. I made the decision that I was going to be a success. I did not know what I was going to do exactly, but I knew for a fact that I was not going to let this be the end of me.

Eight months later, it was time for me to return for my sophomore year of high school. As it turned out, the school had conducted my expulsion with an extreme lack of professionalism. They were under heat.

Although I already served my sentence and they could not change the past, they could change the future. They erased the expulsion from my record. I knew what I did was wrong, and I knew that people would still have their opinions about me, but this was an enormous moment. This was my second chance.

It was time for me to show the world that I had what it took to be successful.

2

THE BURGER FLIPPING EXTRAORDINAIRE

I WALKED THROUGH the hallway toward my first class as an exonerated high school student. My best friend Mike, a six-foot-four beast and the star athlete of the school, led the way with a shirt we had gotten customized that read "Stankiewicz Security."

My friends ran up yelling "Welcome back, Stank" as they patted my shoulders and laughed at the scene we were creating. Other students rolled their eyes, and teachers simply looked in the other direction. It felt weird being back at first, but the warm welcome changed the energy.

As we entered the history classroom, I picked a seat toward the back. The whole class watched with a smile as I made my triumphant return. As soon as I sat down, the teacher's voice boomed and immediately erased everyone's smile, including my own.

"Mr. Stankiewicz, you will be sitting right here," he said as he pointed to the desk at the front and center of the room.

"Mr. Bigbert, can I just sit here? Everyone else picked their seat?"

"MOVE NOW. Unless you want to start your year back with a trip to the office," he yelled as he stared directly into my eyes. The entire classroom fell silent waiting for my response. Anger rushed through me, but I bit my tongue, gathered my stuff, and moved to the front of the room.

I quickly realized that I was on a short rope with the school's staff. I played into their game for the first semester back. Half of this was because I wanted to prove them wrong; the other half was because of soccer season. If I got in trouble, I could not play. That was motivation enough for me. I stayed out of trouble and focused on getting good grades. This was crucial for me to get on the path to being a success.

At first, this plan worked well. But as high school went on, I started to not care about class again. I still maintained average grades even when I was hardly trying, but I knew something was off. The content bored me. I could not relate to the teachers. I could not even relate to many of my peers. They put so much time, energy, and focus into perfectly translating a paragraph about themselves into Latin. I asked the teacher why I should bother wasting my time learning a language that is no longer used in the world. I got sent to the office for challenging authority.

I had many questions as to why we were learning concepts I would never use in my life. The answer I often got was that I needed to learn them so that I would get good grades, get into a good college, get a respectable degree, and get a good job with a company that would pay me well and provide me with good benefits so that after forty years of work I could retire.

I asked about the people who did not go to college who had massive success. The actors, singers, business leaders, and athletes who were making millions of dollars, and some did not even complete high school. I was told that these people were lucky, born with something that I did not have, and to stop being unrealistic. As a young kid, you sort of just trust that these people must be right. They are the adults after all.

Little did I know that they most likely were not happy with where they were in life and unknowingly had these limiting beliefs instilled within them.

The only option I had was to continue on this educational path that bored me to death. It was the only way for me to have so-called true success. Otherwise, I would end up working as a cashier for the rest of my life. Suffering through schooling seemed like a much better option.

Already I was experiencing what life would be like if I did not get a fancy degree. Growing up on a farm and having a stepfather who is a stonemason gave me an early taste of hard labor. From tearing down stone walls by hand, digging fifty-foot foundations with a hand shovel, splitting wood, and shoveling chicken shit out of our chicken coop, I quickly decided that was not the life for me.

My family always worked hard to make sure they could provide for us to the best of their ability, but we did not live a life of excess. As soon as I turned sixteen, I was told if I wanted a car to drive, it was time for me to get a job. I decided to try another route that would not leave my hands full of splinters and blisters.

My first job was at the local ski area working in the kitchen. They assigned me a value of $8.25 an hour. I did not have much leverage seeing that I was sixteen with zero work experience, so I gladly accepted. I got off to a great start and quickly moved up the ranks.

First I was scooping clam chowder, then manning the fry-o-lator, then I got upgraded to the prized position: the burger flipper. I was doing such a great job that my manager pulled me aside one day and told me that they were going to move me up to the high-class restaurant on the mountain.

I was ecstatic. This restaurant was known for being less work, and employees would walk away with over $100 in tips per shift. I started visualizing all the things that I could do with that kind of money and was motivated to get to work.

The next day was New Year's Eve. When I arrived, my manager said, "All right, Johnny. We are sending you up to Pine Lodge today. Do you mind bringing these two buckets of chili with you on your way up?"

"No problem," I replied. "Am I taking the quad or snowmobile to get up there?" I always saw the managers driving around on them and was pumped that I finally got the opportunity to start using them too.

He laughed. "Do you know the trouble I could get in with the insurance company if something happened? Absolutely not! You have to walk up."

Well, it could be worse. At least the extra money I make will be worth it.

I grabbed the five-gallon buckets of chili and made my way up the mountain. Unfortunately, my skateboarding shoes had zero traction left. During my climb, I was flailing around in an attempt to keep my balance and prevent slipping on my ass and sliding to the bottom of the mountain. In doing so, the scorching hot chili started spilling all over my pants. *It will all be worth it*, I kept repeating to myself.

Finally, after what felt like an ascent up Everest, I reached the restaurant. I was not so pleasantly greeted by the head chef. Her six-foot-tall big-boned stature glared down at the chili all over me, and I could instantly tell that someone had defecated in her Cheerios that morning.

"Why are you wearing the chili we are supposed to sell? Whatever, we are already slammed. We need to get to work." She threw me right into the battlefield.

I spent the next thirteen hours running around the kitchen doing whatever order this overly stressed lady barked at me. The entire day she was freaking out, and it was clear that I was there to be used as her verbal punching bag. By the end of the day, I was exhausted both physically and mentally. The only thought that kept me going was the fat paycheck I would get for the abuse.

At the end of the night, all of the customers left the dining room. I saw the waiters and waitresses compiling their tips for the day. Each one left the restaurant with a huge stack in their hands. I could not wait to get my cut. After every customer left, the manager in charge of the money said, "Normally we don't split tips with the kitchen staff, but since it's New Year's Eve, we all decided to pitch in for you guys." He handed me a twenty-dollar bill.

I can hardly describe the flurry of emotions that went through me at that time. Pure rage would probably be the most accurate, but I remember distinctly thinking to myself, this is not how I am going to live my life. At the time I did not have many options. From what all my teachers told me, this would be how my life played out if I did not get good grades and a good degree. If that's what it was going to take, that is what I had to do. This path of hauling sloppy chili up a mountain was definitely not the life for me.

I had a talk with my manager and was moved back down to the main lodge after just a few shifts in that hellhole. He knew he threw me into a war zone and understood why I was so frustrated. I finished off the season and was on to my next job.

My new job was at a local ice cream shop and restaurant. Although I did not get paid much, this job was actually a positive learning experience for me. I was able to work with another one of my best friends, Christian. We worked hard, long hours in a scorching hot kitchen, but we always made the best of it and kept each other laughing.

The only issue was that as I flipped burgers and tried to keep up with the never-ending incoming orders, the same thoughts went through my mind. This is not the life for me. I was put here for more and I am capable of more. Still, I did not know exactly what it would be. The only way I knew at this point was trading time for money. That is how you make a living. I figured as I got more educated, I would be able to trade my time for even more money. That thought kept me going.

In the kitchen of the ice cream shop and restaurant where I worked with Christian Anderson (left) and Jeff Peck (center) in 2012.

At the time I didn't think much of it, but I remember sitting at school one day with an energy drink that I bought for $2.50 at the gas station. My friend walked over and offered me $5 since they did not sell them in school. It was a no-brainer and I accepted the offer. This sparked an idea.

The next week, I came to school with a case of energy drinks that I purchased for an even greater discount. I started to sell them for $5 a can from my locker until a teacher caught onto my endeavor and shut down the operation.

I managed to break even and particularly remember the overjoyed feeling of locking in a profit. Still, I was in no position to test more teachers, so I decided it would probably be best to scrap the venture and try to focus on school.

As I entered my junior year of high school, I started thinking about college. I decided that the best direction I could take in life would be to become a physical therapist. After seven years of school, I would be able to earn $100,000. Six figures, baby! The work seemed somewhat interesting, too, since I was always into sports. I was ready to buckle down and go after this lifelong career path.

Immediately I was met with extreme scrutiny from my peers and teachers. They told me I should rethink my career plans. My guidance counselor told me I had a 2.7 GPA. No respectable colleges with a physical therapy program would accept that. I got in too much trouble in school. No colleges want a student who spends more time in the in-school suspension room than in history class. I was told to look into a community college or possibly a trade school. I had better chances of making that work.

This lit a fire under me. I knew my grades did not reflect my intelligence. I decided to throw AP chemistry and AP English on my plate. I started paying attention in class, and my grades skyrocketed. I took success to a new level that impressed everyone, including me.

Unfortunately, I decided to kick it up a notch too late. It was time to start applying for colleges, and my piss-poor freshman and sophomore grades were what schools would pay attention to. Nevertheless, I began applying and began hearing back.

I only applied to four schools. The University of Vermont put me on a wait-list. The University of Connecticut accepted me to their branch location five minutes down the road but rejected me from the main campus. The University of Hartford accepted me into their physical therapy program, and the University of Rhode Island accepted me into their general studies program.

After weighing my options, I decided to attend the University of Rhode Island for a few reasons. It seemed like a decent enough school, and I loved the idea of getting the hell out of my small town to an entirely new state. It would be a fresh start and a big step toward becoming successful. As high school was coming to an end, I was on cloud nine. I bragged to everyone about going off to school and smirked at the people who doubted I could do it.

Life was starting to come together.

3

NOTICE OF INSUFFICIENT FUNDS

I CAN HARDLY describe the excitement running through me as I tossed my cap up in the air on graduation day. Part of it was because I was so ready to move on to the next chapter; the other part was because I knew I had successfully pulled off an elaborate senior prank that involved farm animals freely roaming the school's hallways without having to face the consequences.

Other than getting away with this final prank, I was also excited for what was next. I consider high school an awesome part of my life where I learned some of my greatest lessons; however, I was more than ready for the next chapter. I was ready to meet new people, live on my own, and start the process of sprinting down my path to success.

I quickly learned that once you have committed to success, the universe will begin to heave obstacles directly onto your trajectory to see if you are cut out for it. I was dealt with a major hurdle. Next to my expulsion, I consider this matter to be one of the most important events that ever happened to me.

The University of Rhode Island was set to be the place for me to begin making my mark in the world. I was so pumped for the education, the fun, and the experiences that would come with this stage of life. I went to orientation, met hundreds of people who would be part of the incoming freshman class with me, and was ready for this next chapter. I told all my friends, family, and teachers. Everybody. I had all the gear and even signed up for classes. Everything was in place.

One month out, it was time to pay for my first semester of school. The out-of-state tuition was steep, over $40,000 for one year. I really did not think much about this part of the equation. My mom is a classic hustler who did it all from owning a bakery, operating a home-cleaning business, and at the time was working in direct sales for a company that sold delicious appetizers, spices, and dessert mixes.

On top of that, she helped my stepdad operate our organic vegetable farm as well as his stonework business. Because they were entrepreneurs and business owners, I sort of knew there were slow seasons where my parents struggled, but I really had no clue what our financial situation was like. Growing up, I almost always got the things I asked for, and they did everything they could for my brother, sister, and me to have a good upbringing.

When the bill came for school, my mom and I had to have the conversation. Typically when I saw her, I was greeted with positivity and the youthful energy of her blond curls, big blue eyes, and perfect smile that made her look thirty instead of fifty. This time, however, the look on her face made it clear that something was wrong.

"There is just no way we can afford this, John," she said. "We don't have the money and the bank won't lend to us. You are not personally able to take out student loans this large for your first year of school, and you neglected to apply for any scholarships."

"What are you trying to say, Mom?" I could tell where the conversation was headed.

"The University of Rhode Island is out of the question, John. The absolute best we can do is send you to the University of Connecticut branch school. It is only five minutes down the road from us, so you can commute from home for the first year. I spoke with the financial aid people, and you will be able to get a student loan for that. I know how excited you were, but there is nothing we can do. I'm so sorry."

I felt as if I had been hit by a bulldozer. I was absolutely devastated. I did not say a word, ran to my room, and slammed the door. I did not speak to anyone in my family for almost two weeks. I was so embarrassed and did not know why this was happening to me.

Once reality set in, I had to start telling my friends the news. I was so embarrassed by the reasoning that I made up an entire lie as to why I was no longer going. I told people that the school messed up my housing and screwed me over. The truth was neither myself or my family could afford it. At the time I played the victim card wondering why the world hated me so much and why this would happen to me. In reality, this was a blessing in disguise.

Once I got over the wallowing, I had a decision to make. Similar to my expulsion from high school, this situation could do one of two things—make me or break me.

I decided that finances would never have to dictate the decisions I made in my life from that point forward. I did not know the power of this thought at the time, but now that I have undergone so much personal development, I understand that this event created the foundation of my "why."

The pain from this event was so unbearable for me and it lit a fire inside of me to take 100 percent control of my life. I decided that finances would never be an issue for me, my future family, and generations to come after me. I made my why much larger than myself.

I had no idea what exactly I would do to accomplish this. Still, the plan was to go to school and make that six-figure income after seven years of education. I had no idea that by declaring this I had sent an enormously powerful signal out to the universe, and the opportunities to take control would start attracting into my life.

I spent the year commuting to the local branch down the road, working at the local restaurant, and spending a lot of alone time reflecting on where I was and where I wanted to go. I occasionally traveled on the weekends to visit my friends who were away at school to get my fix of the partying I was missing out on as well. The time seemed to drag by, but the year finally was coming to a close, and I had a trick up my sleeve to finesse the system and get out of my house.

I got nearly all As my first year of college, was on the dean's list, and could use this as leverage to go away to a real school. Typically, people were at the branch until all their prerequisites were completed. This took about two to three years and then you got an automatic transfer into the main UCONN campus. I found a way around this requirement.

I realized the major of athletic training only had one year's worth of prerequisites offered at the branch school. I did not want to be an athletic trainer, but I decided to tell my counselor this was the course I was passionate about following. I showed her my need to transfer for the upcoming school year, and although they did not normally do so, she agreed and approved my transfer to the main campus after one year at the branch.

I was finally on my way to attending a real college. One more summer stood between me and my dream of actually pursuing physical therapy.

4

ONE DAY, YOU WILL THANK ME

THE SUMMER OF 2012 was coming to an end, and we were finishing it off with our traditional family trip to the Outer Banks in North Carolina. We always went with different family or friends, and this year we were splitting a vacation home with the Walter family. The story of how this family came into our lives is a powerful example of the universe working to create alignment.

My mom is one of the most inspirational women I have ever met. In her book *The Lemonade Diet*, she does a beautiful job of teaching the reader how to turn life's lemons into lemonade. She had very little growing up and tragically lost her father at the age of sixteen. For her, attending college was completely out of the question. After high school, she had no choice other than to get to work.

She kept up working multiple jobs until she met and married my father, became pregnant with me, and decided to open a bakery with him to pursue her passion for baking. She quickly realized she was ball and chained to the business, spending nearly every waking hour at the bakery just to pay the bills.

After a few years, they decided to sell the bakery and ended up getting a divorce. Although the venture was a failure (as was the marriage), the bakery opened her entrepreneurial spirit. She started a cleaning service, but this ended once she fell off a balcony and broke most of the bones in her body. After recovering, she took up multiple home-based sales businesses. She succeeded, but once she had my younger brother and sister, she needed to spend more time at home to deal with our mischievous antics. Her life changed when she met Cyndi Walter.

My mom met Cyndi at a friend's home where Cyndi was hosting a party to sample a product line of appetizers, desserts, and different seasonings for cooking. Cyndi was the company representative who was leading the party.

Cyndi had grown up in our area of Connecticut but had since moved to Ohio. She came back just to host this event. At the very end, my mom and Cyndi had a conversation. My mom remembers Cyndi specifically telling her that she would be fantastic at what she does and that Mom should join her sales team. My mom was not so sure at first, but Cyndi has an extraordinary ability to radiate belief and uplift people, so my mom trusted her and they partnered up.

Cyndi, like my mom, has been a ball of youthful and positive energy ever since I met her. Her big green eyes, pristine smile, and pure soul instantly boost the attitude of everyone she encounters. It was no wonder they hit it off immediately and went on to become best friends and business partners.

After about six years of building that business together, both my mom and Cyndi were top producers in their company. They were getting recognized on stage, sent on free trips, and even put in the trade magazines. From an outsider's perspective they were absolutely crushing the game. However, there were two issues.

Neither Cyndi nor my mom was making a six-figure income even though they were top producers. They were doing events in people's homes three to four times a week, lugging around the product and setting it up. Whatever they did not sell would have to be loaded back up and brought home with them. Also, the products that they sold slowly grew out of alignment with their identities.

Both had started running marathons, and my mom suffered from some health issues, so she decided to embrace a vegan diet. Even though cheese balls and cinnamon muffins may taste delicious, they certainly aren't the best foods to put in your body. Eventually, my mom was using none of the products herself. Her integrity became compromised, she was burned out from the grind this business involved, and she decided to step away.

Cyndi was devastated but decided to continue on for the next couple of years. Eventually, she hit the point where she was no longer in alignment with the company either and released her team. However, being the world-class entrepreneur she is, she was not done just yet.

Going into this Outer Banks vacation, Cyndi had told my mom about a new opportunity she found that would change their lives. She wanted to show her in person, so she said that they would wait until they arrived to discuss it further. My mom was so exhausted and burned out that she wanted nothing to do with the conversation, but since Cyndi is her best friend, she told her she would listen.

We arrived at the beautiful beach house that was three stories tall, fully equipped with a hot tub, pool, and even an elevator. My mom wanted to relax after a long twelve-hour drive, but Cyndi insisted that she take a look at this opportunity. They compromised and decided to have their talk in the hot tub.

Hours passed and there was no sign of Cyndi or my mother. All of a sudden, they emerged from the hot tub deck like they had been hypnotized by the entrepreneurial gods. My mom went from completely uninterested to fully sold on the opportunity. Even worse, she immediately attempted to cast the spell on me.

"John, you have no idea what this is going to do for us. You have no idea what this is going to do for YOU! This is incredible. I've never seen anything like this before in my life. I am so excited for us to do this. Our lives are never going to be the same," she proclaimed with confidence.

"Mom, I have no idea what you're talking about, or what you two did in that hot tub, or why you think I would want to be involved. You and Cyndi do your thing. Christian and I are headed to the beach."

Christian and I laughed as we grabbed our skim boards and ran out of the house directly to the ocean. We both had been working over thirty hours a week behind the grill and fry-o-lator together all summer and were not going to allow anything to disrupt our week of freedom.

As the vacation went on, I continued to hear more and more about this opportunity. I heard about these nutritional systems that were sourced from the most premium ingredients on the planet. I heard about this compensation plan that was allowing people to make six- and seven-figure incomes, all from their phone and computer. I continued to hear my mom tell me how this would change our lives forever.

I had no idea why she thought I would do this with her. I really had no idea how any of it could possibly apply to me. I was focused on going away to college, getting my degree, and making a large income that way.

I remember her telling me, "I am getting you involved. You do not have to do anything right now, but one day you will thank me for this."

I still had no idea what she was talking about. I kept a closed mind to the opportunity and disregarded it. At least for the time being. Now, I have shared this exact story to thousands of people about my first exposure to the industry of Network Marketing.

As the summer came to an end, it was finally time for me to go away for my first semester at a real college. I was so pumped to get out of my house and start living on my own. The year of hell was finally over. I could finally get back on track with all of my friends and start to experience the amazing opportunities college had to offer.

5

WHERE ARE THE GIRLS?

JUST LIKE THAT, it was move-in day. I said my goodbyes to my family, packed up my mom's car, and headed out to start my new life.

Even though UCONN is the largest school in my state, I hardly knew anyone who attended it. I only had one person I considered to be a good friend who went there. He already had been there for a year and had plans to live with friends he had met, so I elected to get random roommates. I was completely cool with this option and thought it would be a good way to meet new friends.

Arriving on campus was exactly what I envisioned it would be. In the middle of nowhere in Central Connecticut, the campus was an entire community of its own. The brick buildings built when the school was founded in 1881 stood tall above the perfectly groomed landscape that was in peak bloom.

Even more beautiful were the packs of college girls exploring the campus with smiles ear to ear, as it was likely their first time being free from home as well. We drove by multiple houses with shirtless bros drinking Natural Lights on their lawn chairs, scoping out the new freshman talent. I fell in love with the environment and energy surrounding me. This is where I was supposed to be.

I realized that I got very lucky with my living situation. I was originally supposed to live in an old dorm with three other guys in one room. I received a Facebook message from some kid asking if I would switch places with him. He told me he was living in Garrigus Suites, which included two rooms that housed three people each, and it even had its own bathroom. The building was newer and typically only juniors and seniors had access to it because of its desirability. He knew the kids I was supposed to live with and wanted to be roomed with them. It seemed like a win-win to me, so I gladly switched.

I took the elevator to our fourth-floor suite, and my roommates were already there. I could tell we would all get along, but one kid in particular and I clicked immediately. He was standing there in gym shorts and a UCONN T-shirt as if he had just left the gym, and I was particularly perplexed by the fact that for being about 5 foot 8 he had calves the size of footballs. He also was rocking short hair with the sides faded that had become my signature look, although his hair was blonde instead of black.

As he told me about his passions to become an athletic trainer, I could tell that he was smart, driven, and an extremely well-spoken individual. Go figure, his name was John as well.

Just as I finished unpacking, John told me he was going to play basketball with his fraternity brothers and invited me to come with him. I had always heard the word *fraternity*, but I genuinely had no idea what it meant. I also was terrible at basketball at this point in my life, but I accepted the invite anyway.

His friend pulled up in an old Honda Accord, and we packed four of us into the backseat—something I would get used to throughout my time there. When we got to the court and started playing, I realized I was way out of my element. His friend Jordan, who frankly looked like he had not an ounce of athleticism within him, started raining threes and putting me to shame.

I suffered through the game, and even though I had a disastrous performance, the guys were really cool and told me I should come out and "rush." I had no idea what they were talking about, but I said sure.

I had missed out on the party scene during my entire first year of college while I was living at home, and I was determined to make up for it. My good friend Sean invited me to come pregame at his dorm and to go to this huge house party his friends were having. I always had memories of Sean being a taller, good-looking dude who was a part of the cool crowd from my rival high school, so I could not wait to see how he was living in the big leagues. It sounded like the perfect way to get my feet wet in the scene, so I gladly accepted and headed over to his room to get the show started.

Sean lived in a room setup similar to mine, with two rooms that each had three beds and a bathroom connecting them. When I showed up, the room was completely full, and 95 percent of the population were dudes, but it was full nonetheless. I started meeting all of his friends and began the process of building my college network.

A few hours went by of chugging beers, drinking games, and conducting pure debauchery until an RA made everybody leave the dorm. It was time for my first college party.

We walked across a dewy field behind the building that must have been at least half a mile long. After we completed the trek across the field, we continued another mile down the road until we arrived at the party. It was hosted at a small, white, beaten-down house that probably would have collapsed like a house of cards if you kicked it the right way. People were flooding out of all entrances into the lawn and driveway, and, once again, it was men as far as the eye could see.

They had people monitoring who was entering the party, and they had the audacity to charge us each five bucks to enter. I looked at the scene and begrudgingly slapped a Lincoln into his hand. After beating our way through the mob of incoherently drunk party animals, we were able to squeeze through the back door into the house. We were received with more men sweating, spilling, shoving, and screaming. I really was not into what was going on, but I figured the more I drank, the better it would get. That's how college works, right?

We had been there for about a total of ten minutes and decided to start a game of beer pong. Halfway through the game, I noticed a metallic object launch through the window on the other side of the room and skid across the floor. Shortly after, a few people on that side of the room began coughing. Then, everyone in the room was coughing. Once my nose started to feel like someone was holding a blowtorch to it and my eyes began pouring tears, I was out of there.

I threw my shirt over my face and sprinted for the door to get outside, shoving down everybody in my path. After breaking through to the nontainted outdoor air, I looked toward the road and saw a squad of cop cars fit to take down a small army. We realized what was going on. They had tear-gassed the house. We were absolutely livid, lost our buzz, and decided to call it a night. My first college party lasted an entire fifteen minutes, and just like that, it was over.

I began the hour-long walk to get back to my dorm from the party house and was absolutely furious. This is not how college was supposed to be. There were supposed to be girls everywhere, parties that went until the sun came up, and strictly good vibes. So far, all I saw was a plethora of men, sweat, and the need for a gas mask if I wanted to make it past midnight without being subdued by tear gas. There had to be a better way.

The next day I was venting to my roommate John about the night before. He simply laughed at me and said, "Yeah, dude, unless you're in a fraternity, it sucks here. That's why I joined Pike. Otherwise, you'll just be going to parties with a ton of dudes that get shut down by the cops before they even start."

I still had no idea what this fraternity thing was, but if that's what I had to do to have fun, I was in. John seemed to know a ton of people and have the nightlife scene on lock, so I asked him how to get involved. The next day, he introduced me to the rush chair who was in charge of recruiting new members, and so it began.

I will never forget my first interaction with the rush chair Nick. We exchanged a few messages through Facebook, and he offered to bring me to the first rush event. I waited outside of my dorm building for him to pick me up, and he made nothing short of an unforgettable first impression. An FJ Cruiser pulled into the wrong entrance, which only allowed one-way traffic, flew up the hill kicking up clouds of dust behind it, and pulled over the curb into the lawn in front of my dorm.

"John, get in, bro," he yelled out the window over the deafening EDM music blaring in his vehicle.

I hopped into the car and was greeted by a good-looking Greek guy who was short but absolutely jacked with tan skin and a million-dollar smile. This guy could sell water to a drowning fish, and in hindsight, it was no wonder the fraternity picked him for the rush chair.

"So what's up, bro? You pumped to rush or what, dude?" Nick asked me.

"To be honest, I don't really even know what this rush thing or a fraternity is. I just went to a party across campus last night that got tear-gassed then had to walk an hour back to my dorm and it sucked. My roommate told me that if I want to go to good parties and have fun, I had to join a fraternity, so I figured I'd check this out," I replied.

"Dude. GDIs are losers. I can't believe you would try to go to one of their parties. Fraternities run this school and the party scene. You want parties? Girls? Alcohol? Look no further. We got you covered, man. If you join Pike, you won't have to worry about any of those things ever again," Nick proclaimed.

"Sounds pretty legit, man. I'm excited to go check out this event," I replied.

I still had no idea what a fraternity was, but I was sold. We got to the rush event, and Nick started to introduce me to the brothers. All of them were telling me how much fun it was, how it was the best decision they ever made, and how I had to join. As I talked to more and more of the guys involved, I started to get a better idea of what fraternities were all about.

First, I came to find out that GDI stood for God Damn Independent, which referred to people who were not affiliated with a fraternity. Apparently GDIs sucked. Nothing good came from being a GDI.

More importantly, I finally found out what a fraternity actually is. A fraternity is simply a brotherhood or a social group for men who share similar interests and experiences. In the case of college, similar interests tend to be partying and hooking up with girls. In the macro picture, it represents so much more.

They explained to me how, once college was over, we would have this huge network of guys who go on to become doctors, lawyers, engineers, businessmen, dentists, politicians, and much more at our fingertips. The relationships and connections we would form through the fraternity would serve us for the rest of our lives. That turned on a lightbulb for me.

There were about twenty different fraternities at UCONN, and I could tell Pi Kappa Alpha was the right fit for me. All of the guys were ex-athletes or current athletes and preferred gym shorts and sneakers over pastel shorts and boat shoes. I got along with the majority of them and managed to stay strong through the rest of the rush events, which essentially were just a bunch of bros flirting with each other.

As rush was coming to an end, it was time to see if they would give me a bid to become a new member of the fraternity.

And here's what happened: It was almost midnight the next Tuesday night, and I needed to get to bed so that I would be well rested for my biology lecture at 8:00 a.m. Classroom attendance and getting good grades would be crucial if I wanted to be a physical therapist and earn that six-figure income.

My twin-sized bed let out a loud squeak as I hopped underneath the covers. As soon as I closed my eyes, I heard a pounding on our door. I walked over, shirtless and in my boxers, and cracked it open. Nick and the president of the fraternity kicked it in the rest of the way and ran inside screaming.

"CONGRATULATIONS, GUYS! WE ARE HERE TO OFFICIALLY OFFER YOU A BID TO JOIN THE PI KAPPA ALPHA FRATERNITY AS A NEW MEMBER!"

They slammed a bottle of Jack Daniels into my chest and suggested I take a shot to celebrate receiving the bid. It would have been rude to decline, so I took a rip. I then passed the bottle to my other roommate BJ who had been rushing with me and was offered a bid as well. We signed our bid to officially begin pledging for the fraternity. I had no idea what was in store or how insane the rest of the semester would be, but I was excited about this new experience.

We were instructed to meet outside the Visitors' Center on campus at 8:00 the following night. There we would meet the rest of our pledge class and officially begin the process of joining the fraternity. After they left, I went to bed and promptly attended my lecture the next morning ready to learn.

The following night marked the beginning of one of the most memorable three-month spans of my life. All twenty-three of the pledges congregated outside the Visitors' Center. Up until this point, we really did not know each other outside of our awkward encounters at the rush events. We introduced ourselves to each other and began mentally preparing for what was ahead.

To protect the integrity of the fraternity, I will not get into the specifics of exactly what took place over those three months. However, I will tell you this:

I formed a bond with each of the guys I pledged with that could not be replicated with any other individual. We did everything together. We went to class together, the dining hall, gym, "pledge inspections," sorority houses, socials, fundraising events, house parties, each other's dorms, and much more. There were guys in the beginning that I felt like you could not pay me to be friends with. Some of those same guys turned into my closest friends today.

By the end of pledging, I felt as if I had it figured out. I came there knowing nobody and now had hundreds of close relationships. I no longer needed to put on hiking boots and a hazmat suit to attend a party. We had exclusive events every weekend that you would never want to miss. What began as a platform to meet more girls and go to more parties, which definitely was a success in and of itself, turned into an abundance of relationships that has been one of the most valuable assets to serve me to this day.

6

THE ORANGE CAN OF DREAMS

FINALS WERE RIGHT around the corner and I had some serious studying to do. I was at the desk in my dorm, nose deep in a microbiology book, when I saw the notification on my phone. It was Christian. I opened up the message.

"We need to get on a Skype call, bro. I found something that is absolutely crazy."

I could only imagine what it was. I looked at the phone for a moment as I thought about my relationship with him. We had met in sixth grade at a weeklong getaway called Nature's Classroom. Our middle and high schools were regional, so they combined students from three small towns in our area. Before we went to middle school, Nature's Classroom was the place they sent us to meet all of our new classmates for the first time.

My memory of it is clouded, but this particular piece is crystal clear. We had just settled into our cabins, which had about thirty kids stuffed into bunk beds. Christian and I were on opposite sides of the room, each on top bunks. Being young boys, as soon as the adult overseeing us left the room, we began to throw any object we could get our hands on at each other. For me, this was a beanie.

With all my might I launched it across the room at Christian. I overthrew the beanie and, instead of hitting Christian, hit the wall a few feet above his head, and it stuck there. Christian, with his potato head and long surfer hair, looked up at the beanie stuck to the wall, then slowly looked back at me with his big blue eyes, and his jaw dropped to the floor.

After that, the battle ceased, and we put all of our collaborative efforts into sticking everybody's clothing to the walls and ceiling. Our chaperone came back and damn near had a heart attack.

As our relationship formed, I noticed a key trait about Christian. He was hands down the best storyteller I had ever met. When he started to tell a story, everyone would fall dead silent just waiting for his punchline or zinger that would have everybody in tears. All of the attention would turn to him when he entered the room, no matter where we went.

He went around telling this tale that he called the butterfly story. Essentially, he told an overly in-depth story about this adventure he went on in California that had a recurring butterfly motif. He made it so suspenseful and engaging that after bringing people on an absolute fuck-around for sometimes close to ninety minutes, he would bring it to a close with, "And I get back home. I walk into the bathroom and turn the light on. I look down at the sink and twist the faucet, and you know what came out?"

"Oh my god. The butterflies came out of the sink?" would be the response he got every time.

"Nope. Just water," he would say as he pulled out his phone to check his missed messages. Everyone would lose their shit once they realized they sat and listened to an hour and a half of him babbling for no purpose whatsoever.

I hope I never have to sit through that story again.

So his text triggered my memory. I laughed thinking about all of the hysterical times we had together growing up and more recently working together in the kitchen. We quickly caught up on everything that was going on in our lives, a few crazy college stories, and then got into it.

"So, dude, Spencer hit me up the other day with the craziest opportunity, and I can't sleep thinking about what we are going to be able to do with this," he began.

We had met Spencer in high school. We immediately hit it off and, as a result, were invited to all of the parties that Spencer's high school friends had. Spencer is the type of person that everyone wants to be around and is always the life of the party.

"Spencer moved to California with Nic this past year. They met these guys who are twenty-two years old and make six figures through this company that sells these healthy energy drinks." He placed an orange can of energy drink in front of the webcam.

"You remember when we went on vacation and your mom and Cyndi were freaking out about that new opportunity they found? It's the exact same type of company, except for people our age. We can absolutely crush this. We know so many people, bro."

Up until this point, I didn't know what my mom and Cyndi were really doing after that hot tub conversation in North Carolina. I knew they were helping people get healthy, and I had even started using some of the products. However, I did not understand the business model at all. I asked Christian to explain to me how the entire business worked.

"This is an entirely new way of making money. It isn't the typical job where you are trading your time for money. We are going to be self-employed and able to earn as much money as we want. With Network Marketing, we are going to make residual income—money that comes in while we sleep. Let me show you."

He showed me how, in a typical retail business, a large portion of revenue is invested into getting their products out to the world. This includes commercials, billboards, sponsoring athletes, brick-and-mortar stores, and all outlets that go into generating awareness around the brand. Take Nike, for example. Nike gave LeBron James a deal that could pay him over $1 billion during his lifetime, all for bringing awareness to their brand by wearing that check on his chest.

In Network Marketing, these traditional outlets are not used. You will not see Network Marketing products on store shelves, on billboards, or in commercials. Instead, they take this large portion of revenue and handsomely reward their distributors for getting their product out to the world by building a network of customers via the most effective form of advertisement there is: word of mouth.

Then he explained to me how, as humans, we are always referring people to products and experiences. We see a movie we love, we tell our friends to go watch it. We go to a restaurant and have a great experience, we make sure our family and friends go there. We go on an awesome vacation, we tell our friends they should go too.

Unfortunately, if we refer someone to a restaurant and they go and rack up a $300 bill, even though we are the reason they went there, you don't get any of that money. In Network Marketing, we would be using a product we love and get paid for referring other people to it. Even further, once the people we referred used the product, we would get paid when they referred people as well, to a never-ending degree.

He pulled out a whiteboard and began drawing the structure of this company. He told me to imagine if we just refer five people to these energy drinks. Then those people refer five people. Then those people refer five people. Then those people refer five people. If that's all we did, we would have 625 customers in our organization and get paid off every single one of them. All from telling five people.

After he showed me how this would be something that grew exponentially, he went on to show me what residual income was.

The best way to describe residual income is money that you earn long after the initial work has been put in. I love to use the example of J. K. Rowling writing Harry Potter. She put in countless hours coming up with the idea, writing all the different drafts, and editing—and the entire writing process leading up until the final product was ready to hit the shelves.

During that time, she was broke and earned no money. Once the book was on the shelves, we all know what happened next. Harry Potter became a worldwide phenomenon, and that book continued to sell regardless of if she worked another day in her life. Now she is earning piles of money all from that initial grind she put in.

Unfortunately, I was only a muggle and did not possess the abilities to create the magical wizard land that Rowling did so beautifully. Further, I barely had any money to my name and would not be able to earn a residual income from traditional investments in stocks, real estate, or businesses. Christian was showing me an opportunity where the average person with above-average goals and dreams could earn a residual income.

After he explained this opportunity to me, my mind expanded to new dimensions. I was so fascinated by residual income and could not believe they never taught me about this in school. Why would I ever want to trade my time for money when I could earn money in my sleep?

"These guys have built gigantic networks in this company and some are earning $2,000, $5,000, $10,000, and even $50,000 a week,"

Christian told me. "They are dropping out of school, traveling all over the world, driving foreign cars, and rocking diamond watches all from sharing this energy drink and teaching other people how to create an income with the opportunity. There is absolutely no reason that we cannot be doing that as well. What do you say, man, are you going to do this with me or what?"

I was so excited by the end of our video call and told him I was all in. I just needed to wait for my final exams to be over and get together the $600 required for my initial investment. I told him we would get together over winter break to get the ball rolling.

That night as I attempted to go to sleep, I could not. I had never been this excited about something in my entire life. A new universe was unlocked that I never even knew existed. I started to dream. I dreamed of the tremendous impact we were going to make with this new business. I dreamed of the freedom I would have to travel the world. I dreamed of earning my money residually and exponentially rather than linearly. I dreamed of taking my life by the horns and being my own boss. I dreamed of how this could be the vehicle that took me down my path to success.

As the sun came up, I still had not slept. I could not stop envisioning numbers multiplying in my head and how massive a network we were going to build, the residual income, and how different our lives would be from this point on. I had a few more exams in my way. Then I would figure out how to get the money to get started.

After my last exam, my mom picked me up from my dorm. I stayed low key about my plan to join this different company. We proceeded with catching up and discussing her business and how my first semester at school went. I knew she would be disappointed that I was planning on doing this different business, and that is the last thing I wanted.

I truthfully just thought that there was no way I could successfully build with her company. They did not have the young people that I could relate to and build a thriving organization with. In my mind, I was making a wise choice, and I would not have been able to be told otherwise.

It was great to be back home. It was the longest time I had ever gone without seeing my family and dogs, and it was nice to be around them after a crazy first semester. Still, my mind was racing a million miles a minute, and I needed to see Christian.

Although I had not started yet, I still wanted a game plan so I would come out of the gate strong. He told me the California guys were in town and having an event surrounding the opportunity, and I was pumped to check it out. I headed to his house and to my first official Network Marketing presentation.

I sat there for hours as I learned more about the products, the company, and the industry. I saw my buddy Spencer for the first time since high school sharing how ecstatic he was about this opportunity. They had brought their friend Antonio who had introduced them to the company and was making an absolute killing. He shared his story about how at just twenty-two years old he was able to earn a six-figure income, drop out of college, and build this business full-time. His Louis Vuitton duffel bag caught my eye. He told me he always packed it half full so that he could make new purchases while traveling the country building his business.

I was in awe and still in disbelief at how amazing this opportunity was. I could not believe how simple it was. All I had to do was share healthy energy drinks with people and show them how they can earn money in a totally new way. After conversing with everyone at the event, we retreated to Christian's to figure out how I could get going ASAP.

While we were at his house, I figured out the solution. Before every semester, my grandparents would give me $500 for textbooks and school-related expenses. Needless to say, textbooks would be put on the back burner for the first few weeks of the upcoming semester. This business was way more important to me. Besides, my textbooks were not allowing me to earn a residual income. I've actually never officially told my grandparents I did this, but at this point, I think we can agree this was one of the most important decisions I've made in my life.

Christmas came. I got the check for books from my grandparents, and I officially was in business. When I made my order, I decided it was time to tell my mom. She called me from her company's New Year's kickoff conference, ecstatic. She told me there were thousands of people there; the energy was through the roof; and she could not be more excited about where the company was headed. She went on to tell me how they just released a new all-natural energy shot and how she was so excited for all the young people we would bring into the business with this new product.

I proceeded to tell her I actually just joined a different company with all-natural energy drinks and I had $600 worth of them on the way to our front door. She was certainly not happy with my decision at all; in fact, I think she would have strangled me through the phone if it were at all possible. Nevertheless, she decided to support my decision. She started to plug me into the world of personal development and all of the resources that would help me succeed in the industry.

I began devouring any resources I could to help me succeed. Information about the company, information about the industry, books, podcasts, and YouTube videos. You name it and I consumed it. I had about a week left of winter break before I would go back to school and officially launch my business.

I decided not to tell anyone what I was doing until I got back to school so that I could dive all in. I started to plant some seeds with my fraternity friends about this amazing opportunity and said that we had to meet up as soon as we returned. Christian and I spent most nights of that break together strategizing so we would be ready to dominate.

Finally, the day came to go back, and I loaded up my mom's car with all my clothes, belongings, and six cases of energy drinks. When we arrived, John offered to help me unpack the car and bring my belongings up to the room. I had hinted to him about the opportunity when I first talked with Christian, and he was somewhat interested, but not completely sold like I was.

When he came down to the car and saw the stack of energy drinks in the trunk, he started to laugh but was open to hearing more once he saw my level of belief. My other roommate completely laughed at me as I brought them upstairs, claiming I was an absolute idiot and just lost all of my money in a pyramid scheme. I was unfazed.

That night, I pulled John aside and told him the deal. I said to him, "Look, dude. I'm doing this. We know so many people here and you have what it takes to do it with me. I'm not going to force you into it, but you're going to regret not having joined me once you see me blow this up. I want to work with you and make this happen, but at the end of the day, it's your choice. I just wanted you to be the first person I talked to."

He was in. We immediately began inviting people to our dorm to hear about the opportunity. The first day I signed up eight new distributors and earned back my initial investment and then some. I was sharing the story of the company, the opportunity we had, and why this product worked so well for our generation—over and over and over. I had so much genuine passion and determination that people could not help but be excited themselves. We generated some serious buzz, especially among our fraternity, and people had mixed reactions about it.

After hearing our presentation, most people would join or at least understand why we were so excited, even if they ultimately decided it was not for them. There were also some people who absolutely did not agree with what we were doing at all. I was called Bernie Madoff, a scam artist, and even had some people I considered best friends trying to discourage me completely. Whenever I would talk about my excitement, they would sigh and try to change the topic. I persisted nevertheless.

My sole focus was building this business, and I did whatever I had to do. I was constantly holding meetings in our dorm, on video calls with potential business builders, and training my growing team. We continued to build our organization, and it started spreading to other college campuses.

Once our team started to grow on other campuses, we began doing events there too. I did not have a car, so I had to borrow one from a girl who lived on my hall. On Saturdays we would drive to the other campuses and hold opportunity events in dorms, classrooms, or out in the courtyards if necessary. We were dedicated to showing the younger generation that there existed an alternative and better way to take control of their lives. There were no excuses, and I was determined to make it happen by any means necessary.

My focus was so intense that I started to lose complete interest in my classes. I was enrolled in some of the hardest prerequisites for the physical therapy path, and I could not stay engaged for the life of me. I was constantly on my computer checking the growth of my team. I would be texting people and leaving lectures early to share the opportunity with them on the phone. Sometimes I'd skip the lecture completely because I saw more value in building my business.

I had discovered the world of entrepreneurship, and from that point on my perspective of school and classes were permanently changed.

At the six-month mark of relentlessly building this business, I took a step back and reevaluated my long-term stance on the company. My goal this entire time was the residual income. The time freedom. Building a long-term asset that would pay me for years to come. The patterns I was noticing were troubling, to say the least.

Our business was a revolving door. People were quitting just as quickly as they were joining. The whole way for this to work was to have a network of customers who introduced new customers that reordered the product monthly. After making their initial purchase, most people never bought again. Nobody cared about the products. I personally really enjoyed the energy drink, but the only reason people were purchasing it was because of the opportunity that I was painting for them.

I also noticed that people were only joining after hearing me speak. Almost 99 percent of our customers who joined did so after a call with me or hearing me speak at an event. I had an unparalleled dedication and passion surrounding the business. People would get excited after hearing me, join the business, talk to a couple of friends on their own who would say no, and then that person would fall off the face of the earth.

Few people stayed true to the long-term vision and quit after the slightest amount of adversity. They would revert right to the safe path. In a business that was supposed to be built off a little bit of effort from a lot of people, I felt like a one-man show.

My belief started to fade, and that's when I had a phone call with my mom. She and Cyndi had thousands of people joining their organization, all having fantastic health transformations and earning significant incomes.

"Mom, I'm doing everything I can to grow this business, but it's just not going the way I planned. I'm doing absolutely everything the people who are succeeding at a high level are telling me to do, but everyone is quitting. I'm starting to doubt this company. Everyone is flashing their Mercedes, designer clothes, and all these material items to get people to join, and it's starting to make me uncomfortable. It's almost like I know when I'm talking to a new person that they are going to scrape up the money, order for a month, then quit because they are not rich. I'm starting to doubt that the company will be here for the long run. I don't know what to do," I told her.

Mom told me this: "Listen, John. It's awesome that you guys have all these young people who are building this business. It's really cool to see how motivated and ambitious you all are. But here's the thing. Nobody cares about energy drinks, nor are they life-changing. Sure, college kids are using energy drinks, but I highly doubt most are consuming a case per month before they join your company. Plus, I hate to say it, but your compensation plan sucks. With what you've done so far, you should be earning a six-figure income. Now that you understand this industry better, you really should take a look at what we are doing with my company. You are going to be blown away."

I sighed. She had wanted me to work with her from the beginning, and of course she thought her company was better. But she had some good points. This energy drink was not changing any lives. There was no emotional connection to the product that kept people around. And as for the compensation plan, I could not really say because I hadn't looked at any others yet, but the bonuses were not all that great. The possibility for long-term residual income was there, but nobody was sticking around for that to happen. I decided I had nothing to lose by looking at her company.

The spring semester came to an end. My first full year away at college. As I packed up my dorm, I knew I was faced with a big decision to make going forward. As soon as I got back home, I sat down with my mom and went over what her business had to offer.

She pulled up her back office and started to show me her organization. I was blown away. She had thousands of people in her organization, and only introduced about one hundred of them personally. This is how it was supposed to work. This was residual income. I asked her what the difference could be.

She began rifling through hundreds of transformation pictures. People who lost ten, twenty, fifty, and even a hundred-plus pounds using their nutrition systems. People were using these products and having life-changing transformations. Why would they stop ordering and using a product that makes them feel amazing? Plus, the fact that the products work so well makes them that much easier to share.

When one of her friends lost fifty pounds on a nutrition system, all their friends asked them what they are doing and wanted to join them. The business model and products worked together seamlessly with her company.

On top of that, the compensation plan was infinitely more generous. She claimed it is the best in the industry, and that's a huge reason why Cyndi chose the company. Of course, I thought she was just overly passionate about what she was doing, but the numbers didn't lie. My mom had never graduated from college or earned a six-figure income her entire life. Going into her second year of the business she was on track to earn six figures.

My mind was blown and now I realized why she was so fired up about what she was doing. I now understood her excitement when she first learned about the company on our Outer Banks trip. It was a difficult decision, but at that moment I decided if I was going to be building a Network Marketing organization, her company would be the one I would do it with.

My first order of business was to tell Christian I would be leaving the energy drink company and working with my mom. It turned out that he was having the same doubts about the longevity of the company and no longer felt that he aligned with the integrity either. The second order was to tell my upline leader I was stepping away. That phone call still drives me today.

I dialed up the phone. Antonio picked up. We had a short typical conversation, and then I dropped the news on him.

"Look, Antonio, I just don't see it anymore. I've worked my ass off for the past six months and I'm starting to have my doubts," I said.

After a short pause, he replied, "What do you mean you don't see it anymore?"

"I don't think this company is going to be here for the long run. I mean everyone is quitting as quickly as they are joining, and everyone is in it for the wrong reasons. Everything revolves around all this materialistic shit and the integrity is all out of whack. I had a talk with my mom and took a look at her company. Since she enrolled me when she started, I already have hundreds of people in my organization and I know they will be there for the long run. I am in this to build a long-term asset, and I decided I'm going to put my efforts there," I explained.

Hell's gates unleashed upon me.

"You think that you are going to quit here and go succeed somewhere else? I have news for you, that's not how it works," he exploded. "You are never going to be successful in any other business if you quit this. You are making a terrible mistake and will regret this for the rest of your life."

His words triggered a tidal wave of ambition inside me. I turned his doubt and negativity into pure motivation.

Now came the time to tell the few remaining people I still had in my organization. I thought it would be a no-brainer for everyone to switch over to this new company. The products made sense, the compensation plan was amazing, and the company was doing everything right. This is when I hit one of my biggest moments of adversity.

Nobody would switch with me. Everyone I talked to had lost faith in me. I shared the first business with every person in my network with such passion and certainty, and now doubt had fully set in among them. The people who were a part of my organization at one point or another were burned out and wanted nothing to do with Network Marketing anymore. Even worse were the people who were not in my organization.

"We told you, dude. These pyramid schemes will never work for you. Get back to reality."

"We don't want to hear about any more of your scams."

"You stole everyone's money already, why do you think you can do it again?"

It went on and on. Throughout building my first business I never let the negativity from small-minded people get to me. Now it was. My belief in what was possible with Network Marketing was still there, but I did not know how to handle this tidal wave of rejection. I took it personally, and it took me out of the game.

After attempting to build this new business for about a month, I decided that I needed to put it on the back burner. I continued to share with people casually but did not put myself out there like I had the first time around.

This was my first real failure and I faced a dilemma. This newly found entrepreneurial spirit was ignited inside of me through Network Marketing. It opened up a world I never knew existed.

When I entered Network Marketing, I entered the realm of personal development. When I first started, my mom sent me the book *Rich Dad Poor Dad* by Robert Kiyosaki that presented ideas I had never before heard of, but they made so much sense. I became addicted.

In my free time, I would read books that challenged the conventional way of thinking. Books that showed me the power of your mind and that your only limitations are self-imposed. I learned about the law of attraction. I learned that we are in control of our destinies. People are so accustomed to accepting the constraints society puts on them, and I realized this was complete BS. We are divinely powerful beings with no caps on our potential.

Even though Network Marketing was not working out at the scale I wanted it to as quickly as I wanted to, I knew that I was destined for much more in life than checking in forty hours a week at the cube farm. I made the decision that my degree was not going to be my destiny anymore. I switched my degree to applied mathematics because math had always been a breeze for me and I knew it would not take much effort. Additionally, I decided that whether it was Network Marketing or another venture, I would find my success in the world of entrepreneurship.

7

OPERATION PAINT THE CAMPUS ORANGE

One Semester Earlier

I WAS SITTING in my dorm, at my desk, diligently studying for my final exam the next morning in accounting. With our energy drink business in full swing, all I could think about was growing my team. I could not care less about the class, but I knew I had to suck it up and get the exam over with. Just as I started getting into a good studying zone, my door violently swung open.

It was one of our friends who lived on our floor, Sanjay. When we first moved in, Sanjay would bust in our door regularly, sit down, and fire up NBA 2K12. At first, it was rather intrusive and weird, but over time we realized we had a similar mindset and that he was a really good connection to have.

Sanjay was a smaller Indian guy who possessed the hustle mentality as well. He was a true genius and always up to something whether it was trading stocks or pursuing a new business opportunity. When he told me he was nearly kicked out of high school, too, I could not wrap my head around how such an innocent person could manage such a feat. It made a lot more sense to me when he revealed that the reason was because he hacked into the school's grading system to alter a grade for a girl he liked. Where he went wrong was showing his friend how to get in, who proceeded to change multiple people's grades from Cs to As. That is when local detectives came knocking on their doors.

Naturally, we brought him our energy drink business right off the bat, but he felt that it would not be a venture he would succeed at. He still supported us and loved to hear all of our victories along the way. John and I ended up getting so close with him that we decided to all move into an apartment together for the upcoming school year.

This particular invasion was not to come in and BS. This time, Sanjay meant business. He came in with this black scanning device in his hand and ripped my accounting book off the desk. He scanned it, read his screen, and threw the book on the floor.

"What the hell are you doing, dude?" I yelled at him.

"That book is worthless. What else do you have?" he said without skipping a beat.

"What do you mean it's worthless? I have an accounting exam tomorrow. It is absolutely not worthless. I need it," I shouted at him.

"Ah here's a good one." He grabbed a psychology book off my desk. "I can give you $40 for this."

I had finished the final and did not need the book anymore. I was still confused, but I sold him the book. As he forked over the cash, I realized that Sanjay had a business opportunity up his sleeve.

"What's the deal here, man. Why are you buying these textbooks?" I asked him.

"Actually, we could probably do something really big with this. Finals are almost over but let's talk next semester when we are all living together. We could do this as a team and all make a ton of money together."

The Following Semester

The end of the semester was approaching, and John and I finally pinned down Sanjay to figure out what the hell he was doing with these textbooks. We gathered in the living room of our new apartment, and Sanjay gave us his business presentation.

"Guys, here is what's going on. There's a large-scale transfer of textbooks that happens every finals week. Students pay hundreds of dollars for their textbooks at the beginning of every semester. Once the classes for that semester are over, they have no use for those textbooks. So they resell those books for a fraction of the price they paid."

He went on, "When the students sell their books back to the school, Amazon, or whoever, those people take those books, jack up the prices, and then resell them to new students who need them. They are literally printing money and making an absurd amount off such a simple concept. So why can't that be us who's making the money?"

My intuition made sense of it, and that was all I needed. I told Sanjay I was in. John saw the vision as well and decided he wanted in on the operation. Sanjay also recruited his friend Kyle. We got to work.

One of the issues we faced was that textbooks were expensive, and we had little capital. Sanjay already had a solution. He found a company that recruited college students to go around their campuses buying textbooks. They would provide us with unlimited capital, advertising materials, and book scanners, and they would give us money for every book we purchased. For outdated books, it would be only a dollar, but for current books, they offered much more. With unlimited capital and no risk at our fingertips, we had nothing to lose.

There were multiple parts of the operation. As soon as the school released the schedule for final exams, the first phase was initiated. This was the research phase. We needed to find out every course that our school offered that semester, what textbook was required for it, how much money we could buy/sell the textbook for, and when/where the final exam was taking place. We made a gigantic spreadsheet that laid out all of this information. Now we knew exactly what we were looking for.

The next part was the advertising phase. We called this Operation Paint the Campus Orange. We had 10,000 orange flyers printed. On them we stated that we purchased all textbooks and had a website for students to make an appointment for us to come to their dorm to buy them, and a number they could text the ISBNs to in order to get an instant price quote. We launched this portion of the operation the weekend before finals started, and this is where the hustle would begin.

UCONN has about 20,000 students, and we would not be satisfied unless every single one had a flyer in their hand. Sanjay, John, Kyle, and I took out a map of the campus and strategically divided up the dorms we would paint orange. None of us had a car, so we were on foot. We loaded up our backpacks with flyers, split up into two teams, and got to work.

John and I partnered up for the flyer mission. We started on the bottom floor of our old dorm building. Every single door got a flyer under it with no exceptions. Well, we decided on one exception.

After we completed our old building, we went to the freshman dorms that were next door. We had no access to the building, so we would have to wait until a student was walking in and sneak in behind them. We started on the top floor this time and worked our way down. I approached a door on one side of the hallway that had a big fancy bulletin board stating it was the RA's room.

Sanjay's voice saying "No person left unflyered" played through my mind. Since RAs were people, too, I flung an orange flyer under their door. I made it two more doors down the hall when I heard the door burst open behind me and the screams of an extremely irritated RA.

"What do you think you're doing? Is this service campus approved? If not, I will bring it to the dean's office and have you kicked out if you guys are students here. Tell me!" he yelled at us.

John and I looked at each other and without hesitation sprinted down the staircase, out of the building, and retreated to the dining hall. We sat there for a minute, collected our breath, and then I shook my head.

"There are five more floors in that building that did not get flyered. We are going back," I said. He grinned and we headed back to the building. This time we implemented the exception: no flyers under RA doors.

This part took two nights and would take about eight to ten hours each night to flyer the entire campus. Mostly it was a boring and repetitive process with an excessive amount of sweat and a sore back from lugging around fifty pounds of flyers, but we knew the grind would be worth it in the end. Plus, there was always excitement.

A common occurrence was students ripping out of their room once the flyer came shooting in. Normally they would scream at us for soliciting them, tell us to fuck off and get out of their dorm, or crumple up the flyer and throw it into the hallway. We encountered RAs pretty often, and to make the experience more exciting, we would always run away and then just come back in through a different entrance.

We also had people who thought our service was awesome and thanked us. Then there were the people, although very few, who would light up because they understood the grind, and it fired them up. Those are the people you want to bring into your circle.

After the campus was successfully painted orange, the buying began. Our appointment system would start pinging nonstop. An overwhelming amount of text messages would flood in from people looking for quotes on their textbooks. This is where the division of labor became so important.

John was in charge of the appointment system and doing all of the meetings. Sanjay took care of the text message quotes, manned a table in the middle of campus, and helped wherever we needed someone. Kyle was in charge of the accounting of books and money. Other than that, I don't really know what his purpose was. He was always just bitching, overwhelmed, and couldn't understand how the rest of us always wanted more and more business. He thought we had plenty.

As for me, I had a job that helped form me into the person I am today. My job was to go to the final exam lecture halls we researched that had the most profitable books, stand outside with a stack of cash, and buy as many textbooks as I could get my hands on. Everyone decided that I was the most personable and my pitch would result in the most success. It definitely felt like the toughest of the jobs, but I've always been down to play the role that will lead to the most success for the team as a collective, so I was in.

Exam day one rolled around and it was game time. Our schedules for the week would be absolute hell. Keep in mind we were students ourselves and needed to prepare for and take our exams as well. This meant every day we would wake up at 2:00 a.m., study until 8:00 a.m. when the exams started, buy books or take exams from 8:00 a.m. to 11:00 p.m., and then go to bed and repeat. To this day it's one of the toughest yet most rewarding grinds I've endured.

The first exam on my spreadsheet was a 200-person physics class. We could get $90 for the book, so I was offering $50 cash. The exam started at 8:00 a.m., and at 9:00 a.m. students started finishing up. As I was sketchily pacing around the hallway of the musty scented and outdated building, I noticed the first student walk out of the lecture hall.

I walked up to him empty handed and proceeded to say, "Hey, dude. I'm uh ... actually uh ... buying textbooks. Can I ... buy yours?"

He looked at me like the biggest weirdo on the planet. He replied, "I'm good," and kept moving. I awkwardly approached the next two people, and they avoided me like the plague. I watched as a group of five more students walked out and did not even try to approach them.

I was pissed off. They gave me the worst job and knew I would look like a dumbass trying to buy textbooks all day. They knew I was destined for failure. I left the lecture and found Sanjay at his table in the brand new union building letting all the business come to him.

"Dude, this sucks. No one wants to sell their books. I'm wasting my time. I don't want to do the lectures anymore," I told him.

"How did you go about it?" he asked me.

I told him about my miserable attempts.

"Change your approach, man. You are one of the most confident people I know. Think about how you were when you were presenting your energy drink opportunity. You just aren't comfortable doing this yet. I know you got this. Try again at the next lecture."

As I walked to the next lecture, I already felt more confident just from the belief Sanjay poured into me. It reminded me of when I first took up the sport of baseball. I was in my awkward stages, slightly chubby, average height, and had never swung a baseball bat in my life.

The first year I played I was nine and got placed by default into the AAA league where I was an overwhelmingly average player. The following year it was time to try out for Majors where most of my friends with experience were already playing.

During my tryout, I had a very average showing. I made an error when fielding a ball, I whiffed at a few pitches, and it was clear I was far from the best pick for a team.

That night, I received a call from Jim Keller, the coach for the Orioles. He informed me that he drafted me to Majors for the upcoming season and explained how excited he was to have a player like me join the team. I was beside myself and fired up that I would no longer have to be in *The Bad News Bears* league anymore.

Coach Keller took me in and held me to a standard that I thought would be impossible for me to live up to. Even though I began average, he radiated an unwavering belief in me that I could become one of the best players in the league. From the beginning, he treated me like a superstar and kept his confidence in me even when I made foolish mistakes.

Coach Keller's belief in me translated into my building a tremendous amount of belief in myself. During practice, I would have ice in my veins and clobber every pitch he threw my way. I became a brick wall behind home plate as a catcher. In games, I could be a little jumpy and nervous as I stepped up to bat. He would always look at me with confidence and say, "John, it's just batting practice."

For the next three years, we went on to become one of the best teams in the league. Coach Keller's vision came to fruition, and I became a weapon on the team. I even was selected to the league's All-Star team to compete for the Little League World Series for two years in a row. I became a leader on the team who the younger players wanted to be like. The player I became was a product of the unshakable belief Coach Keller had in me, because it gave me a reason to believe in myself. Self-belief is the first step and bedrock foundation for succeeding.

Sanjay's belief made me feel the same way Coach Keller used to. I was still slightly aggravated, but I knew he had a point. I was extremely uncomfortable going up to random people trying to buy their books. I decided to change my attitude toward it, try a new approach, and this time believe in my ability to make this business happen.

The next lecture was a philosophy exam. There were 250 people in this class in one of the newest lecture halls on campus. Plus, there was only one hallway out, meaning they all had to pass by me once they finished. I researched the book and saw we could sell this one for $90 as well. I decided to offer $40 cash if I was going to be putting myself out there like this. Forty-five minutes in, the first person walked out of the exam holding their textbook. I approached him with a big smile, holding an orange flyer and a stack of Jacksons.

"What's up, man? I hope you crushed your exam. I'm actually doing textbook buyback and can offer you $40 cash for that philosophy book," I said.

He looked at me, looked at the cash, looked at his book, and paused.

"Sure why not, I don't need this stupid book anymore anyway. Here you go. Can I sell you my other textbooks too?"

I handed him a flyer and told him to text his ISBNs to our instant quote system. This small victory fired me up beyond belief, and I approached every single person walking out of the lecture hall with equal enthusiasm. By the end, I had purchased twenty-five textbooks, which was $1,250 of profit for one hour of getting extremely uncomfortable. This means that 225 people rejected me in some way, shape, or form.

Some people did not have their textbook; some wanted to keep it; some were selling it to a friend; some wanted to check and see how much money they could get for it elsewhere. They were not saying no to me as an individual. They simply did not want to part ways with their book at the moment. The mass amounts of rejection did not bother me anymore, because I knew I only needed a small percentage of people to say yes.

I was on top of the world. I loaded up the bags of textbooks and brought them back to Sanjay at his table and smacked them down. He gave me a huge grin, and said, "I knew you'd kill this."

As the week went on, I became more comfortable standing outside lecture halls buying textbooks. Sometimes one of the team members would be free to join me, which would make it even more fun, but, overall, I was good on my own. The thousands of nos I would receive didn't bother me at all. We were printing money, and I knew just a 5 to 10 percent success rate would lead to a pretty payout.

Every now and then I would run into people I knew coming out of the lecture halls. The reactions were always mixed. Some people recognized the grind and thought it was cool. Most people would take the opportunity to trash me.

"Dude, don't you think you should be more worried about studying for exams and your future rather than buying textbooks?"

"Times must be tough, huh, Stank, standing outside lecture halls desperately trying to make a buck?"

People would laugh. People would question my motives. People would make fun of me. The fact of the matter was people simply did not understand. They did not understand why I would put my focus on any area other than getting perfect grades on my exams. To them, good exam grades meant a good GPA, which meant a solid job once they graduated. They were scared of what would happen in the world if they didn't have the grades to get their steady paycheck job. For me, I was scared of the very world they were striving for.

One of the best moments for me was toward the end of the week. I had a final exam for my economics class, but there was a dilemma. The textbook for that class was one of the top five books we were looking to buy. Everybody was busy during the time I was taking the final, so it was up to me to complete my exam, then immediately begin purchasing books.

My alarm went off at 2:00 a.m. I woke up, hopped in an ice-cold shower to wake myself up, and hit the books. I studied straight through until the 10:00 a.m. exam time with more focus than I ever had in the past. I actually enjoyed economics because I found it to be applicable, but I also would be leaving a lot of money on the table if I was not the first student done.

I got to the lecture hall and took my seat among 200 students who were nose deep in their books. I was scoping out all the exit points in the room and trying to determine which would be the best to stand outside since I was a one-man show. I made my decision, and the professor handed out the exam. I began rifling through it.

Twenty-five minutes passed, and I was on the last few questions. I skipped over a few to go back to since I was not positive about the answer. Out of the corner of my eye, I saw a girl walk up, hand the professor her exam, and exit the room holding her textbook under her arm. Another guy finished up and left the room holding his textbook as well. My focus was completely destroyed. I took educated guesses on the few questions I was unsure of and ran to the front of the room.

As I handed my paper to the professor, he asked, "Are you sure you don't want to double-check your work? You still have an hour and a half."

I saw another girl finishing up.

"Nope, I'm good. Have a great break," I replied as I scurried out of the room.

I picked my exit and the real economics exam began. The first five people who walked out of the room sold me their textbook. A trend I noticed in this business was when students saw you already bought a bunch of textbooks, they were more inclined to sell you theirs. Conformity at its finest. I had nearly thirty textbooks in my pile with a half hour left of the exam. I was running around like a madman and not exactly using my indoor voice, which must have been carrying into the classroom, so the professor came out to see what was going on.

He came out and recognized it was me. He looked over at all the books I purchased and all the cash I was holding. He looked at me for a few seconds, nodded, and said, "You've got it figured out, my friend. Just keep your voice down."

He went back into the classroom and I finished strong. Over $1,500 in profit and confidence that was through the roof. I texted Sanjay to come help me transport the mountain of books back to our apartment. Lugging the bulky books was always the worst part. I never understood how people could string together so many words to create those paper bricks.

After six days, the week of craziness came to an end. All the exams were finished, and it was time to see the final numbers. Even though all of us were running off minimal sleep, we all gathered to see the final tally.

Our apartment looked like a textbook bomb went off. There were piles of books on every square inch of the floor, every closet, every table, all over the kitchen, and even in our beds. Food delivery boxes littered our apartment that looked like a post-apocalyptic disaster. Complementing our newly acquired library were piles of cash. We threw on *The Wolf of Wall Street* as we started to account for the books and money and to figure out what our final profits were.

I will never forget the feeling as we crunched the numbers while sipping a celebratory beer. I looked around at our crew and knew what we were doing was special. Right then we were just buying books, but what would this lead to in the future? We all thought differently and hustled like I had never seen before.

That one week I had proven so much to myself. I entered an entirely new realm of discomfort that caused me to grow beyond belief. I dealt with so much rejection that I became desensitized to it. More importantly, I committed and saw the venture through while most of my "friends" were telling me to quit. My levels of fulfillment were through the roof.

*Piles of textbooks and food delivery boxes covered every square
inch of our apartment and looked like a post-apocalyptic disaster.*

Kyle looked up from the computer with the final number. He
announced it to us, and it felt like we had just won the NBA Finals.
John started pounding his chest screaming. Sanjay started laughing
uncontrollably. I had an ear-to-ear grin on my face as I beamed John in
the chest with a stack of twenties, and they exploded all over the room.

Let's just say from one week of giving it everything we had, we
earned far more than any of our friends would be making the entire
summer at their internships. I did not even feel the fatigue anymore,
and we decided it was time to celebrate. Our favorite way to celebrate
was to multiply some of the money we earned at the casino.

We each took a portion of our proceeds, hired a driver, and went
straight to Mohegan Sun. Our first move was $420 on the roulette
table on black. The dealer looked at us funny, but we were still on our
high from the humongous win that week. He spun the little white
ball into the wheel. It clanked around and picked its slot: 15 black.

8

THE WOLVES OF WEED STOCKS

Since the textbook operation was a venture that could only be conducted twice per school year, I had to find different ventures to earn money. That is why when I saw Sanjay installing multiple computer screens with moving charts in his bedroom, I was naturally inclined to inquire about what he was up to.

"Medical marijuana stocks, dude. This stuff is insane, Stank. I made $500 yesterday just trading them. I'm literally printing money out of thin air."

Until this point, I had no clue how the stock market operated. My parents never invested in it or talked about it, and none of my classes ever taught me how it worked. All I knew was rich people did it, so there must be some substance. That, parlayed with Sanjay's excitement, had me willing to learn more.

He sent me all of the material he had learned from so far. He paid an absurd amount of money to access this course. Apparently the developer was a guru when it came to day trading stocks. Sanjay spoke very highly of him, and I trusted Sanjay's judgment, so I decided it was worth diving into.

Before I started going through the courses, Sanjay pointed out a specific stock that he thought was poised to blow up. They were a company out of Canada that produced the equipment used to grow medical marijuana. The investment guru was all for it, and it seemed like a promising company. This was 2013, and the laws were still strict surrounding the use of marijuana. Since this company did not actually produce weed, they would not have many legal restrictions. Plus, as the industry grew, more and more equipment would be required.

I loved the idea and kept my eye on it. I also have to admit that the idea of making money legally from marijuana this time around gave me a sick sense of delight.

I dove into the course and was consumed right away. Everything the guru taught was speaking my language. There is an inner math nerd within me, and I found all of the lessons so fascinating. On top of it all, I loved that trading was essentially a form of gambling. It was us versus this imaginary giant that represented the market of people trading. We profit, we win. We lose money, he wins. My competitive edge loved it all.

As if adopting an entrepreneurial mindset wasn't bad enough for my attention span in the classroom, this completely put the icing on the cake. I didn't listen to a word any of my teachers were saying. I was glued to my computer studying charts, indicators, and the wisdom of investing gurus.

Every waking moment was spent studying or practicing trading skills in a simulation market. After a couple of weeks, I had enough of the simulations and was ready to get some skin in the game. I thought I knew it all and that I would take this game by storm. In the beginning, I was right.

A new semester began and with it came my refund check from student loans. I needed some of it to pay for food and school-related expenses, but I had an extra $1,000 that had no place to go. I loaded it into an E-Trade account and prepared to try my hand in stock trading.

The medical marijuana stock Sanjay was watching had gone from $0.10 to $0.25 per share since he first informed me about it. He had more than doubled his money and was convinced it was not going to stop any time soon. The entire time fear of missing out was killing me, so at last, I was finally able to participate in the money printing.

I was a little bummed I missed out on the initial profits Sanjay made, but we were sure the stock would still soar. I purchased $1,000 of stock at a $0.28 share price and held on for dear life. Now that I had money on the line, that was technically a loan, I was emotionally invested.

I would read every article regarding the medical marijuana sector as soon as it was released. I tracked every single statement our investor teachers had to say about the stock. Even more obsessively, I watched the charts move every minute from 9:30 a.m. to 4:00 p.m. for not only my stock but every single one in the sector. I was hooked.

At this point, Sanjay had about $10,000 invested in the market. His entire bedroom was lined with computer screens and looked like a Wall Street satellite office. He was barely going to class and had become a full-blown addict. I was going to class, but not a word that was said made it through to me. All I focused on were the share prices increasing and decreasing and what news was being relayed.

In physics lab where I was not allowed to have my computer, I had my phone under the table where it looked like a disco ball of flashing green and red lights. Figuring out the angular momentum in inelastic versus elastic collision was not making me any money.

Finally, after the price raised to $0.36 cents a share, we had our explosion point. I remember sitting in class thirty minutes before the closing bell watching the stock soar upward. I could hardly control myself. I was watching the green line on the graph taking off like a SpaceX rocket toward Mars. I ran out of the classroom, got on the phone with Sanjay, and started freaking out as the final bell rang. It finished up 52 percent on the day, and it was all the talk within the medical marijuana sector. We had picked a winner and could not be more confident in our future with trading. It was too easy and too much fun.

Over the next few days, the stock kept exploding and eventually got all the way up to the $0.70 range. I had turned $1,000 into over $2,500. I certainly was not rich, but $1,500 of profit was a lot of money to me, especially at the time. One of the investor guru's most important principles was to lock in your profits. I decided to cash in my chips and look for the next play. I already had money in an assortment of other medical marijuana stocks from my personal savings because the entire industry was on fire, and I wanted a piece of it all.

My friends started to notice me in the library doing absolutely no schoolwork and studying stock charts on my computer. People were intrigued and asked me what I was doing and how they could get involved. I never made promises, but I always told people exactly what we were doing and what we envisioned.

A bunch of people decided to get in and start trading as well. It's funny to me how people will put their cash into an opportunity they think will make them rich quickly without second thought; however, when you bring them a legitimate business opportunity where true wealth can be built, they think it's a scam or too risky.

Many of our friends invested into the particular stock that we made a killing on. When I cashed out on the stock, I told my friends I had sold but many still wanted to hold. It was a money multiplier, so why would they want to get out of it?

Shortly after I sold, I ran into one of my old roommates, BJ. He was raving about going to Panama City Beach for spring break, which was only five days away. I had never been on spring break, and the year prior everyone went to Cancun, but I could not afford it. I thought about the $1,500 I had just made.

I asked BJ what his plans were and if they had room for an extra. He laughed and thought I was messing around. I told him I was completely serious and wanted in on the trip. He called his friends whom he was staying with, and they said I was more than welcome to come. I bought a plane ticket right on the spot.

A few days later we were off to Florida. Because I had not experienced a spring break yet, I was prepared for an absolute shit show. I imagined it must be like a scene from *Girls Gone Wild* where there were no rules and maximum degeneracy. My excitement for the experience was at legendary heights; however, I still could not take my mind off the market.

We boarded the plane at JFK, and right before we took off, I was studying the charts of a few other weed stocks we were following. One, in particular, was poised to blow up, and we had been following it for months. I double-checked with all my sources, evaluated the indicators, and decided I was in. I purchased a large share right before the flight took off, and it began going up immediately.

By the time we landed in Florida, I could not be more eager to check my phone. As soon as we hit the ground and cellular service returned, I went straight for my E-Trade app. I was up $200 dollars already. A smug feeling of accomplishment rushed through me. With all these wins I was experiencing, I was ready to get the party going.

The next week was one that definitely took a few years off my life but was worth every single day I lost. We barely slept, spending the entire day at beach parties and the entire night at various clubs. One day on the beach I took out my phone, saw I was up $500 on my most recent move, and cashed in. To top it off, during our time there, UCONN also began its run that eventually led to both the men's and women's basketball teams winning NCAA National Championships. The energy could not be paralleled, and I felt like life could not be better.

When we got back and the rioting calmed on campus from our meteoric run to championships, reality smacked us in the face. It was only a few days after my return that the notification popped up on my phone. The stock that I made all the money from trading originally had been halted for investigation by the FTC due to suspicious activity.

This was not a huge deal for me because I already sold my holdings, but both Sanjay and John still possessed a large number of shares. Not to mention multiple friends whom we told about our venture had their money tied up in the mess as well. Their money was frozen with no guarantees of getting it back.

Sanjay and John kept their cool, and our investor guru assured us there was nothing to worry about. He even said he had plans of buying more shares once it became unhalted because it would come back at such a discount. I liquidated all of my holdings and decided to hop on the train. It only made sense the stock would go up after it resumed trading.

Two weeks later, the FTC decided to cease its investigation. No foul play was detected, but the stock still opened at 25 percent of the price it was trading for when it was halted. I put the remaining money I had left in my brokerage account into the shares with confidence knowing I had just taken advantage of a fire sale. I wish I had been right.

Over the next few days, we watched the price of our stock continue on a downward trend. It continued to fizzle away until it was only worth a couple of pennies. I was down over 90 percent on the transaction, and all of my profits that I did not use for Florida were gone. I felt that everything I had learned, studied, and listened to was for absolutely nothing. I spent so much time, effort, and energy trying to figure out the market, and, just like that, my money was gone. I realized that I was not a huge hotshot and that I was not invincible to the crushing forces everyone else faces who plays in the market at one point or another.

Following the gigantic loss, John decided that he was spending too much of his energy and focus on the market and that he needed to focus on school. He always was into the entrepreneurial grind, but at the same time, he cared a lot about his degree and maintaining his perfect grades. His goal was to be a doctor, and all the money-making activities were just hobbies in the meantime.

Sanjay's account diminished to a fraction of what it was at its peak. He decided to stay in the game and keep going after it, but to cut back on the intensity and overwhelming focus.

For me, I decided to stop completely. The market was not a healthy influence in my life. There are other ways to make money, and certainly other ways where I would have much more control. I had beginner's luck and thought I knew everything about trading. It is not until you take a humbling blow that you realize you really aren't shit.

Having decided that trading life wasn't for me, I closed this chapter of my career in entrepreneurship. What has always held true for me is when one chapter ends, another exciting chapter always begins.

Although it was not exactly coming in wheelbarrows, money began coming in from my Network Marketing business on a weekly basis. Even if it was just $50 a week, it was still helping me fund my college lifestyle. This definitely had my attention. Also, I did not know quite yet, but the next business venture was right around the corner. It was always just a matter of time with this squad.

9

THE WHEELS ON THE BUS GO FLYING OFF

THE DYNAMIC AMONG Sanjay, John, and me was unique to say the least. We were always talking bigger picture and new business ideas, watching *Shark Tank*, and discussing opportunities. It simply never stopped. We were obsessed with growth and figuring out how to succeed at the highest level.

One night Sanjay came back surprisingly late, so we asked him where he was. He told us he just left a meeting with the Student Entrepreneurial Organization. He explained that it was a group of students who were passionate about business and side hustles. They met weekly to put their creative energy together and discuss making various business opportunities happen.

John and I gave him shit because we found out he had been attending these meetings for a year and just now thought to tell us about them. Sanjay always had mysteries about him that were perpetually being unveiled. He had no mal intention, but we could not believe that he did not tell us about the group earlier. After we gave him some slight verbal abuse, he invited us to the next meeting to check out the group.

The next week when we walked into the meeting, we knew right away that we were at home. There were about ten students there who all shared an identical mindset and spoke the same language as we did. The true entrepreneurial mindset is rare to come across, and I knew this group was special.

At our first meeting, we decided to get out a whiteboard and free flow ideas. We split into a few different groups and wrote down every idea that came to our minds. An on-campus laundry service. A homework helper's service. Selling pizza slices as people left happy hour at the bar.

I even joked around and said we should not be building a business; we should just buy as much Bitcoin as we could get our hands on. At the time Silk Road had just been shut down, and all we kept hearing about was Bitcoin. We thought Bitcoin was an interesting idea, and Sanjay even considered using his student loan refund check to purchase some, but after we watched it tank to a hundred dollars, we steered clear. We all laughed and kept brainstorming.

When we were finished, we gathered around the conference table and compiled all of our ideas. As we were going down the list and collectively discussing each business, one in particular stuck out to us: a service to bus students to off-campus parties and events.

The president of the organization, Miller, said that a few years ago a couple of guys started a similar business. They would charter buses and find the best concerts and organized parties off campus to bring students to. Apparently, they had a ton of success, but they graduated and no one was there to keep the business going. We decided it was worthwhile and that we wanted to pursue it. Right then and there we decided to take action.

Six of us were down to go all in on this business. There was Sanjay, John, Miller, Frankie, and Nishant. We needed a good amount of cash to get the ball rolling, so it was necessary for us to have a decent number of partners. We also knew there would be a ton of liability attached to this sort of business, so we had to take care of the legal matters. We all decided to meet up the next day to figure out how we would get the business rolling.

We congregated at our apartment the next day when everyone was done with classes. Everyone did their due diligence regarding what would be required for us to get our company in motion, so we sat down and put it all on the table. We decided that $1,000 each would be enough to get started.

We needed an LLC. There was an immense amount of risk attached to this. We knew that we would essentially be babysitting a mob of inebriated college kids, and if anything were to go wrong, we did not want to be held responsible. We decided upon the name WeDot for our LLC, and under WeDot, we would operate as WeBusU. We figured we would have many more business ventures in the future, and we could use WeDot as the umbrella.

Next, we needed a division of labor. Miller self-appointed himself as CEO—his justification being he was the president of the organization. Most of us did not agree but also did not care enough to put up a fight. John was in charge of event coordination. Frankie took the lead on marketing. Sanjay was in charge of sales, IT, and basically all miscellaneous activity. Nishant was the funding chair and looked for as many different ways to obtain more capital.

I was the CFO. With my math background, I felt comfortable handling all our finances. In the end, it was an equal partnership, and we would all end up helping across the board anyway.

After we got the framework in place, we needed waivers drawn up to eliminate all liability. We reached out to a few lawyers who tried to take us for our entire bank account. We were on a strict budget until we actually started generating some cash and were trying to keep it as low cost as possible.

This is when Miller chimed in. "You know, the original owners who graduated have already done this. They have all the paperwork necessary. It could save us a whole lot of time and energy if we can make a deal with them to acquire it all."

We agreed it was worth looking into. Miller said that he would reach out and see what they would do for us.

Two days later he came back with an answer. For $2,500, all assets and paperwork they had involving the business were ours. Operating agreements, liability waivers, established connections, their assistance and much more. Miller went on and on about how much value they were bringing us at such a low cost.

"Low cost? Absolutely not! This is a robbery. All of this was worth zero until we called them and now they are trying to cash in. We don't need them. Let's just make an event happen," Sanjay angrily replied.

"It's too big of a risk, Sanjay. We could lose the entire business if we don't do this properly and something bad happens. I'm not willing to risk it. If we don't get these assets, then I'm out," Miller said.

Frankie, John, and Nishant were indifferent but also felt that we should get the protection. I felt the same way, but I knew these guys were taking us for a ride. They were working in their office cubicles, had us hit them up about their company, and now saw dollar signs. I suggested negotiating to half the price, but Miller refused. He said it was a fair price and we needed them. After a heated debate, we decided to purchase them.

With most of our money already spent before we even began, we decided we all needed to throw in an extra $500 each. This would give us a little more padding. I collected the money from the new investment round and set up a business bank account. Now that the entire infrastructure was in place, it was time to get out and make some money.

We met in our apartment to decide what our first event would be. We were looking through concerts, sporting events, parties, and any events that resembled some sort of fun. Anything would be better than the same two bars on campus that people went to four nights a week.

After hours of scouring, we decided upon the Barstool Blackout Tour. A massive shit show of lights, foam, lasers, and pounding EDM music. It was sure to be a hit among the student population. Plus it was forty-five minutes off campus, so people would need transportation. We locked in the event.

Sanjay wanted to go check out the venue and thought it would be a good idea to try and get some tickets at discounted prices. That way, we could offer a package deal so people could get both the event ticket and transportation with one purchase. Fortunately for us, that semester John had his sweet 2000 Hyundai Elantra with him on campus. No longer did we have to borrow cars or take on the world by foot. We all hopped in and headed to Hartford.

We pulled up to the venue. Smack-dab in the middle of the hood. Homeless people littered the streets, and the venue was covered in graffiti. Thankfully, the inside of the building was much nicer than its surrounding environment. The only thing in the lobby was a ticket counter, so we approached it and knocked on the plexiglass pane. A minute or two passed, then a middle-aged man with a cigarette stench hobbled out of his office to figure out what the hell we were doing there.

"Excuse me, sir, we have a business where we bus students from UCONN to off-campus events. We are very interested in partnering with you guys for your upcoming Barstool Blackout party. Would you mind showing us around the venue?" I politely asked.

He looked at us like we must have been lost, then slowly motioned for us to follow him inside.

The place was enormous and was split into two sections. The elevated area toward the back had a large island bar that was surrounded by a lounge area with ample seating for people to hang out. The front lower level had a large, open dance floor in front of a towering stage. I envisioned foam cannons unleashing their contents upon a sea of students as they temporarily put their ambitions to be a doctor aside and reverted to their primitive nature. Within sixty seconds, I knew this was it.

"This is perfect. We are locked in," I told the worker whose body language showed he was taking us a bit more seriously.

"Cool. So how many people are you guys bringing?" the man asked.

I went to reply, but Sanjay cut me off.

"Two hundred. We want to make a deal with you. Since we are going to be packing this place out, we were wondering if you would sell us some discounted tickets," Sanjay boldly stated.

The worker laughed in our faces.

"If you boys really think you are going to bring through 200 people, then absolutely. But you have to buy all the tickets right now."

"All right, well—" I got cut off again.

"Done. It says on your website tickets are $50 each. How about $20?" Sanjay asked.

The guy started to take us seriously again and thought about it for a few seconds.

"Sure. Only if you have cash."

Sanjay ran outside to an ATM to get the cash. I followed him out.

"Dude, are you out of your mind? We haven't even said a word to anyone about this yet. And you're just gonna buy 200 tickets? What the hell are you thinking?" I yelled at him.

"Stank. We are going to make it happen. Don't worry about it."

I shook my head.

"All right, man. The guys might not be too happy about this one, but let's go for it. We've got some serious work to do," I said.

We got back to campus and told the guys about Sanjay's latest business move. Miller damn near had a heart attack, but Nishant and Frankie were cool with it and saw it as a whole new source of revenue. Now we had a lot on the line and only two weeks until the event. We had to start getting the word out there. We decided to do it the best way we knew how to: Operation Paint the Campus Orange.

Sanjay and Frankie designed some catchy flyers and printed them at the local shop we used for the book business. We advertised $50 for the event and bus ticket, which would earn us a profit from both the bus and the event. It would not be a ton of money, but we were more focused on building the brand and helping people have a great experience. With more manpower than the textbook operation, we split up in teams of two and tackled the campus.

The flyer designed by the WeBusU team that was distributed throughout the entire campus for our first and only event.

After we successfully launched our advertising campaign, we realized that we needed to get buses in place for the event. We had no idea how many people we needed to accommodate, so John made sure we were overprepared.

There were a couple of bus companies to work with, but the previous owners told us they had a great relationship with one in particular. John got them on the phone and explained our entire operation and plans for our upcoming event. The guy seemed to really love it and offered to work with us. The price was definitely steeper than we anticipated, but the manager explained how much risk was involved with our business. We accepted and hoped that he would decrease costs moving forward as we brought them more business.

With about a week and a half until event time, we were less than enthused by the response we got from our flyers. We distributed at least 5,000 flyers and only sold twenty spots. Doubt and uncertainty started to sink in as tension rose among our team. People were pointing fingers and dishing out blame, especially toward Sanjay for his ticket purchasing stunt. We had no idea how we were going to fill up one bus, let alone sell 200 tickets.

We called for an emergency team meeting at our apartment the night before the event. We had thirty ticket packages sold. We still had 170 tickets left. We tried to productively brainstorm, but once again everybody started pointing figures and blaming each other.

Somewhere during the blame game, we heard a ding on Frankie's computer. He looked down at the screen to find a Facebook notification. It was in the UCONN Buy or Sell page. More often than not it was used as a forum for pouring gasoline on the fire of whatever controversy was happening at our school at the time. Nonetheless, the community did stick to the main purpose and allowed students to offer to buy/sell anything.

"Wait a minute guys, check this out," Frankie said as he turned his computer toward us.

"Who is going to Barstool Blackout in Hartford? Tickets are sold out. If anybody has an extra, I would be willing to pay $60 for it."

As we were reading this post, another one popped up.

"SOS. Need a Barstool Blackout ticket. If you are selling one HMU ASAP!"

We all looked at each other. Sanjay had monopolized the market and now nobody could purchase tickets from the venue. We had them all. At that moment, we decided to pivot.

No longer was the concern to fill up buses to make our money back. We would flip our tickets. Sanjay grabbed the computer from Frankie and started to respond to the posts and arranged meetings with the people requesting tickets. We had less than twenty-four hours to offload 170 tickets, and now we had an idea of how we could do it.

We found the buy or sell groups for surrounding colleges and finessed our way into them. Low and behold, these people were looking for tickets to the party as well. We spent all night scouring the pages for any posts of people inquiring about tickets and responding to them. We put up our own post for the next day.

"Selling Barstool Blackout tickets. Will be in the student union all day to meet up. Message us for pricing."

The bickering and blaming ended. We put all our energy into ticket sales and were pressed to make them happen. It is in these moments when your back is against the wall that you have no choice but to perform and execute.

The entire next day was spent scalping tickets to students from UCONN and our enemy campus. Even people from Hartford were driving to Storrs to buy our tickets because they had no other choice. We also noticed our sales were going up through our website for the ticket and bus bundle. We got to fifty-five sales and had to cut it off because we had filled the entire bus. It wasn't 200 combined tickets like we had hoped, but this was a much prettier scenario than the one we faced the night before.

We needed what we called bus jockeys to make sure this event went smoothly. Since it was our first event, we decided it would be best if one of us took the jockey position. That way, we could save money and also learn how to effectively do it. Then we could teach people in the future. Again, everyone agreed that I was the most social and outgoing and elected for me to take the spot. I was a one-man show and everyone else decided that they would meet us at the venue.

We had a stack of waivers that we made every student sign to ensure no liability would fall on us if anything went wrong. As students started arriving at our meeting spot, I realized I was in for an interesting night.

We had a "no alcohol" policy, but we knew that these were college students we were dealing with. There was no way they'd be going to this event sober. Students began to approach the bus and it looked like a scene out of *The Walking Dead*. People were already assisting each other with basic bodily motions, laughing uncontrollably, stumbling, and shouting.

When I asked if they had alcohol, everyone laughed and said no. I was blown away by how responsible the group was. Weirdly enough, everyone had bottles of water. I could not tell them that they weren't allowed to hydrate.

One by one, we loaded up the bus. I took a head count and told the bus driver we were ready for departure. Before the party began, it was my responsibility to go through a list of announcements to make sure we were all on the same page. I took a firm stance in front of the bus with my clipboard and began to debrief the group. It was over before I even began.

"You the man, bro! Come take a shot!" shouted a bro in the back of the bus.

"Do you have a girlfriend?" a drunk sorority girl yelled to me.

I looked down at the paper and realized there was no point.

"Well, try to not end up in the hospital, guys. Let's have a night," I said.

The bus erupted in cheers. I asked the driver if she could turn the music on. She had an aux cord, which one of the students immediately took over. As soon as Drake came over the speakers, the bus turned into a mobile fraternity house.

I looked around and couldn't help but have a feeling of accomplishment. This is exactly what we envisioned. Students having fun and getting away from our cow farm of a school. It was great to see the event finally under way after the preceding weeks of uncertainty we faced. I was curious to see how the night would unfold if it was already starting off this hot.

I took a seat in front of the bus and contacted the crew.

"This is insane. Everyone is going crazy right now. I'm actually kind of jealous I'm not partying with them," I texted the group.

"Do NOT have any drinks, Stank. Everyone signed the liability form, right?" Miller asked.

"No promises, Miller. Yeah, all the forms are signed," I replied.

"This venue is crazy right now! There's a line around the block already. I'm trying to see if we can get our students priority," John chimed in.

The bus ride continued, and so did the party. I spent most of the ride conversing with the bus driver. I wanted to make sure we didn't destroy our relationship with the bus company. That was the key to our business moving forward. Without that, we were screwed. She was really cool and seemed to be fine with the debauchery going on, so I figured we were fine.

As we pulled up to the venue, we were dealt with our first curveball of the night. I got off the bus first and instructed everyone to hold on a minute while we tried to get them priority in line. I met up with John and Sanjay outside the front entrance. We went inside, but our ticket guy from a few weeks ago was nowhere to be found. There was just an angry bouncer the size of Schwarzenegger who could not care less about any deal we made. He said everyone had to wait in line.

I returned to the bus to instruct everyone to get off and into the line, and I saw one of the kids from the bus lying on the sidewalk. There was puke all over the place, and his friend was standing over him in disbelief. The bus driver was also standing outside of the bus extremely irritated. I came over to figure out what was going on, although I already had a hunch.

"He's been drinking since three p.m., man, but this always happens. He's a champ. Just give him water, a quick snack, and he will be right back in the game," his friend pitched to me.

I looked at the kid on the ground who was near motionless and curled up next to a pile of vomit. I knew he was TKO'd. I just was not sure how to handle the situation. I didn't want to put him back on the bus because if he puked in there, it would surely ruin our relationship with the bus company. I also did not want to call an ambulance because I knew we would be screwed. What would happen to our company if we had a student sent to the hospital at the first event? My options were limited.

The friend convinced me to give him a shot. He hoisted up his corpse of a friend and carried him into the lobby of the venue to get some water and snacks. Not even five minutes passed before John and Sanjay waved me over to the lobby. I looked inside and our friend was sprawled out on the floor of the lobby with more puke. Management was freaking out and threatening to call the police.

At that point, I was completely fed up and left with no options, so I called an ambulance and sent him on his way. I knew that we would have to deal with this later on, but for now, it was the only option I had.

For the next hour, we made sure everyone got into the venue safely. After all the students were in, we had a few hours to kill. We had about twenty tickets left over, so we tried selling them on the street. We flipped a few, but it was getting too late for anyone else to even want to go in. We decided to use the remaining tickets to go inside and check it out.

The venue I saw a few weeks prior was almost unrecognizable. Foam and paint were dripping from every square inch of the place, and it was an absolute zoo. The students tried to get us to join the partying, but we politely declined.

I always enjoyed going out, but I need my space and prefer conversation rather than being engulfed by a mosh pit of humans in barbaric form. Besides, I hate EDM music and crowded places with people shoving, sweating, and stampeding to see who can get closest to the strobe light that would probably initiate a seizure. We left after about fifteen minutes and got ready for the task of making sure everyone was accounted for at the end of the night.

As could be predicted, making sure everyone got back on the bus was a shit show. We agreed upon leaving at 1:00 a.m. We had people coming out at 11:30 p.m. shit faced demanding that the bus take them home, which of course was not possible. Then, we had people who did not want to leave. We gathered most of the people before the 1:00 a.m. mark and waited fifteen minutes for a few stragglers who never showed up. We texted them numbers for cab companies to get home, and we headed back to UCONN. A few of the guys decided to join me on the ride back, and we recapped how we thought the event went.

Overall, for the impending doom we were facing just twenty-four hours earlier, we agreed that everything went pretty well. We ended up making a profit due to flipping the tickets. The biggest issue was that the bus driver became progressively agitated, especially on the way home as the party continued. We figured we could smooth talk our way out of it. I spent the rest of the bus ride chatting with her in damage control mode. By the time we got back to campus, I thought I succeeded.

We finally went to bed around 4:00 a.m. and decided on meeting the following day to figure out our next steps.

The next morning, I woke up to John on the phone. I could tell the call was not good. He was pacing around the apartment and pulling every card he could to please the person on the other end of the line.

"We made sure the bus was cleaned up as soon as we got to the event, and as soon as we got back to the campus," John was saying.

"Yes, I understand but the kid did not puke anywhere on the bus. We got him an ambulance because he was attracting so much attention. We got word that he's fine now," he said.

"But, sir, nothing went wrong other than that. I swear we will make sure we monitor it better next time. It was a mistake that was completely out of our control."

"I understand. Have a good day," John said as he hung up the phone.

At that point, I was listening on the edge of my bed. As soon as John got off the phone, I was down his throat trying to figure out what just happened.

"The bus company says we are way too much of a liability for them to work with. The manager said we left the bus trashed. The driver was beyond upset with what she put up with and said they won't do business with a ravaging party company. He told us we can no longer use their buses for our events."

Sanjay had hopped out of his room and joined in. There was one other bus company we could talk to, but we already blew them off because their prices were outrageous and left us with no room to profit. Sanjay called them, and they raised their prices even higher. They knew we would be back.

We assembled the team and started discussing our limited options. After we went over the numbers from the previous night, I saw we had broken even from the initial investment we all put in. We had about $10,000 in cash. I saw this as a major win due to the fact that nothing went the way we expected it to. Coming out ahead is always a victory regardless of the convoluted path you may take to get there.

Unfortunately, we could not collectively decide on a solution moving forward that involved the continuation of the business. That was one of the biggest cons of having six equal-weighted decision-makers. It is not easy to come to one solution where everybody is happy. To add to the mess, three of the six partners were graduating in a few months. Thus, after one event, WeBusU was added to my list of failed ventures.

When we decided the business was a failure, I started to think about what failure really meant. Just because we shut the business down, does that mean we really failed? We ended up in the green. We learned how to mass advertise. We figured out a way to pivot when situations were going south. We bit off way more than we could chew and figured out a way to swallow.

I learned so many skills and lessons through this venture that ultimately failed. So was it a failure after all? My perspective shifted and I began to realize that all these failures—business and nonbusiness alike—were equipping me with the skills and lessons that brought me to the next level.

These so-called failures were teaching me lessons that I could not have possibly learned otherwise. They were helping me grow exponentially as an individual. I realized that these failures were, in fact, building the foundation necessary for success. I decided to fully embrace and fall in love with failure and, more importantly, to keep failing forward.

10

WHO KNEW THAT CHAINSAWS COULD FLY?

My SECOND YEAR away at school was officially complete. Coming off a wild year of business endeavors, growth, and learning while living with John and Sanjay, I needed to figure out a way to make some good money over the summer. We capped the year off with record profit numbers for our textbook business, made a little on the failed party bus venture, and my Network Marketing business was bringing in money every week, which I was grateful for, but it was not enough. I needed more.

Upon returning home, I had a talk with Mat, my stepfather. Mat is a stonemason and has completed beautiful projects all over the state of Connecticut. He is well known for being a master of his craft and for the red suspenders he always wears. One stone wall that he built took him nearly ten years on and off to complete all by himself. It was his claim to fame in our town, and we refer to it as the Great Wall of Mathew Wheeler every time we drive by it. The wall must be five football fields long. It is an incredible piece of art and an absolute masterpiece.

All of Mat's clients were people who experienced high levels of success in their life. The man for whom he built the great wall was an extremely successful businessman. Mat suggested that I could work at this man's property for the summer. His estate consisted of an elegant white Tudor-style home surrounded in gardens and a large piece of land with ponds, barns, large lawns and wooded area.

Mat talked to him for me and asked if he could use a helping hand while I was home for summer. I imagine he immediately lit up when he thought about all of the projects he could start up around his property and told my stepfather to send me over.

Mat gave me all the warnings I needed ahead of time. The guy was an absolute loose cannon. However, Mat referred to him as his best client because he provided a never-ending pipeline of work. Whether it was new work or repairing what the boss had just destroyed, there was always work to be done.

He told me no matter how stupid or convoluted the instructions I was given to complete a project were, follow them exactly. The boss wanted all tasks done his way, even if there was another way to complete them ten times more efficiently. He told me never to offer suggestions because if I did, this would send him over the edge and cause him to berate me. Essentially, just do exactly what the boss tells me to do and it will be smooth sailing.

I started the job and did my best to stick to this strategy. The boss would give me instructions on how he would like a project completed. When I started to work on it, I would realize that what he told me to do was going to result in the need to do ten times more work. I remember the first time telling him the problem I foresaw. He flipped out on me and asked me who the boss was. He told me it was his way, or I could go home.

This went on for the entire summer. Other than tasks where not much could go wrong such as weed whacking, I ultimately did much more damage than good. I broke the tractor and various attachments multiple times due to using them for jobs far beyond the scope that they were built for. I broke multiple chainsaws.

One time it was from cutting logs that the boss was swinging through the air in the clasp of his excavator. I was absolutely terrified, but I kept sawing away. Eventually, the chainsaw got pinched between logs. When I attempted to dislodge it, he jerked the excavator and the saw went flying fifteen feet into the woods. I saw the entire script of my life flash before my eyes.

He laughed and said, "Who knew that chainsaws could fly?"

After breaking all of his equipment, I would spend days repairing the equipment I had broken. It was a vicious cycle. I would complain to Mat about how ridiculous it was, but he always pointed out that the guy was paying me much more money than pretty much any other job I could get.

When I received my weekly pay, it would all be in $100 bills and rounded up to the nearest hundred. That part was awesome, but after a certain point, I had a realization.

I was earning plenty of money, but I was not producing any results. There was zero fulfillment from what I was doing because I was making no progress with any work I did. It was one step forward, two steps back for every single project.

Up until this point, I thought I would be happy simply making a ton of money. From this experience, I learned an extremely valuable lesson. I realized that I was not motivated by money alone. In order for me to feel fulfilled with my work, I needed to be producing results. More importantly, I needed to be producing value. Collecting a paycheck for meaningless work, to me, is depressing. It feels like my time was washed down the drain.

To fulfill my entrepreneurial side that summer, I started up a little side hustle. While on spring break in Florida earlier that year, I had made a connection that had access to wholesale pricing on sports jerseys. At first, I thought it would be cool to get some cheap jerseys to wear, but after doing a little market research, I realized that there was money to be made.

It was around the time of the World Cup. After a long day of destroying and repairing, I began to scroll through eBay. I noticed that the prices of World Cup jerseys were through the roof, especially for the US team. They were selling for anywhere between $80 and $100 apiece and people were actually buying.

I reached out to the guy I met down in Florida to inquire about getting a large order of jerseys. I could get any of the US team's jerseys for just $20 apiece. At that price point, I would make four to five times my money just from flipping them on eBay. It seemed like a no-brainer to me.

He put me in direct contact with his connection, and I ordered ten jerseys on my debit card.

About a week later, the DHL man pulled up our driveway with a decent-sized package. I eagerly ripped open the package. The jerseys were immaculate. Every little detail was perfect from the stitching and patches down to the tags hanging from them. I decided that one would be kept for myself and the rest would go straight onto eBay.

I turned our family kitchen into a production studio. I covered the kitchen island in a white bed sheet and brought in extra lights to make sure the photographs of the jerseys were perfect. I took pictures of each individual jersey from every angle that a buyer would be interested in seeing. After that, I set up a special eBay account specifically for this endeavor.

Then I individually listed each jersey. It recommended the seven-day auction option, but I was way too impatient for that. I listed them for a three-day auction, with a starting price of $39.99 and a "Buy It Now" price of $69.99. I figured that those prices were both far under what everyone else was asking, and if they went at that rate, I would still have a solid profit margin. The listings went live, and it was up to the market to decide if my venture would succeed or plummet.

Sure enough, within a few hours, I started receiving notifications on my phone. "US World Cup Soccer Jersey Ready to Ship." People were going straight for the "Buy It Now" option. After three of them sold, I realized that I undervalued the price. I raised the "Buy It Now" on the remaining jerseys to $100 and left the auction price the same. Nonetheless, I knew that this was working. I decided to place another order so that I could get more inventory on the market.

I put in an order for fifteen more jerseys. This time I ordered ten World Cup jerseys and five random NBA jerseys that were unique and I thought were cool. As I waited for them to arrive, I was thrilled to have sold every single one of the original jerseys I purchased. The sales ranged from $50 to $100, which was great seeing as how each one cost me only $20.

The inner hustler in me loved the entire operation. I loved the jerseys. I loved the flipping. I loved the idea of creating money out of thin air. I loved it all.

I anxiously awaited the arrival of the next batch of jerseys—not to mention, my new credit card with a higher limit. Now that I was aware of the money to be made, I could not stand being on the sidelines.

In the meantime, I carried on business per usual at the madman's house, narrowly escaping death day by day. That week I was weed whacking around his pond on a steep embankment. I had my headphones in, listening to a podcast, when all of a sudden I felt as if my hand was on fire. I looked down and realized that I had just shredded a yellow jacket nest into dust.

Unfortunately, I did not shred all of the yellow jackets with it. They arose from the ground like a fleet of black hawks, except instead of missiles they had stingers, and I was the target. The first one stung my hand and actually entered the inside of my glove and went to town. The next one that I saw had my forearm fully mounted, stinger inserted in my flesh.

When I realized what was happening, I dropped the weed whacker, which went directly into the pond, threw off my gloves and took off. I sprinted up the embankment, screaming my lungs out as the killers continued to mutilate me. Hands, arms, head, everywhere that skin was exposed. I ran as fast as I could, swatting and screaming until I finally reached the barn about two hundred yards away.

I ran inside and slammed the door, and even though there were no more hornets, I was still in a full-blown panic. The pain was unbearable and it actually felt as if they were still stinging me. The other guy I worked with came over, made sure I was not allergic, and got me some ice to put on some of the welts. I physically felt ill and decided that it was best for me to go home.

The next day I came back and my boss was there. I told him what happened, fully expecting him to be pissed off about my dropping the weed whacker in the pond or over the fact that I left three hours early. At the end of the story, a big smile came on his face.

"What did ya think? That the weed whacker was a fishing pole?" He laughed and continued on with his daily chaos and destruction. I shrugged and went on with the day. You really can't make this shit up.

As I was contemplating bailing on all my ventures to start up a business strictly to eliminate all life forms with wings and stingers, the DHL man pulled up my driveway. This time, the package was slightly bigger. I tore right in and laid out my merchandise. The jerseys were immaculate.

I set up my photo studio, took all the pictures, and posted the jerseys again with the same pricing strategy as the first time. Again, the World Cup jerseys flew off the shelf. However, the NBA jerseys did not do nearly as well. A few of them did not sell at all, and the others went for just $40 or less. I realized that just because I thought they were cool did not mean that there was a current demand for them.

It was the middle of the summer and no one was thinking about the NBA. People were thinking about the World Cup, and nothing is trendier than going all out in supporting your country in an event this big. Hence, people were willing to pay top dollar to show their pride now.

One issue I foresaw: our team was a far cry from being the best in the tournament. Once they lost, the demand would spike to zero. I had to capitalize while I could.

Within a few days, my new credit card came. I placed a $500 order for mostly World Cup jerseys. The rest were orders for friends whom I let pick jerseys that they wanted. For these orders, I did not try to profit much. Just enough to make it worth it for my time.

Right as I was expecting them to come, the whole US was ecstatic for the men's team. They just finagled their way out of the group stages after a win, a tie, and a loss. They made it to the round of sixteen and everyone wanted to show their support. There could not have been a better time for me to have placed this order.

The DHL man rolled up my driveway four days before the game. This time the package was the size of a hay bale. I ran inside, bear-hugging the huge block and slammed it on the counter. I ripped it open to lay the newly acquired jerseys out. As soon as the goods came pouring out, I noticed something was completely off.

Half of the jerseys were fine, but half were not the same jerseys I had been getting. These were piss-poor knockoffs that looked like they came from a sketchy stand on Canal Street. Furious, I went right to the computer to berate my supplier. I typed up a long email about how the experience had been great up until this point. I demanded a refund for the subpar jerseys that were shipped to me. On top of that, I demanded free goods because I was going to be missing out on the opportunity to capitalize on the World Cup hype. I sent the email and slammed my computer shut.

In the meantime, I listed all the jerseys that were of high quality. They sold right away. As badly as I wanted to purchase more to flip, I was hesitant. I was hesitant because I had just gotten absolutely fucked, and I was also hesitant because once the US lost, it was all over. I decided to wait until my supplier responded to figure out what my next action should be.

Later that night I received an email. I was told that a refund was not possible. I was also told that it was my error and that I selected that style of jersey. They also came with a pair of shorts, which was why there was a compromise in quality since it was the same price. The supplier did, however, agree to send me a free pair of sneakers with my next order to make up for the misunderstanding. Not exactly what I was looking for, but it was better than nothing.

A friend had been following my venture, and I informed him about the low-quality jerseys. He offered to take them off my hands at the price I paid to try and flip them himself. Since I did not feel comfortable selling them, I gladly accepted and offloaded them to him. People would probably still buy them, I just did not want my name attached to a product of that low quality.

I waited until the next game to decide on the future of the jersey business. It turned out to be a wise decision after Belgium beat the US 2–1. The demand died out immediately for World Cup jerseys. I searched through eBay to find another market to capitalize on, but no other jerseys were hot at the moment. The inventory I had access to was selling for double the price I could get it for at best.

Although I was still upset with my supplier, I decided to carry out the venture throughout the summer. I stuck with basketball and football jerseys for the most part. There was not a ton of money to be made, but it still earned me a few hundred extra dollars a week. Plus, I loved having the side hustle going on.

By the end of the summer, I decided to shut down the operation. It would be too much of a pain to carry on at school. I would be living off campus the next semester and did not have a car to make the post office runs. Plus, by the end of it, I lost faith in my supplier. I started to question their integrity and no longer felt comfortable doing business with them. However, from earning thousands of extra dollars, building my credit, and learning how to make money out of thin air, I was happy with the overall outcome of the operation. It was another failure where I learned a new set of skills and grew tremendously as an individual.

This so-called failure taught me that there is always a way to make money. You can always find a market inefficiency in one place and then capitalize on it in another. Whether this is from a garage sale, the dollar store, a connection, online, textbooks on a college campus, or even in your own closet, there is always a way to take an item and sell it for more.

People bitch and complain that they do not have enough money or that they do not know how to make more. With platforms like eBay and Amazon, there is always a way to start a side hustle and make a few extra bucks.

This venture also opened my eyes to the importance and power of credit. Most consumers in the United States are irresponsible with credit and buy items they do not need with money they do not have, and then they are stuck paying monthly minimum payments at astronomically high interest. People view credit cards as a way to spend money they do not have. Through this venture, I realized what wealthy people do with credit.

They use it as leverage.

They leverage someone else's money to make themselves money. Once I got my new credit card, I was able to buy inventory with someone else's money. Then, when I flipped the jerseys and made a profit, I simply paid off my credit card balance. This resulted in my earning rewards, getting access to a higher credit line, and building my credit score. Once you build your credit score, you start gaining access to so much more: credit cards with amazing perks, low-interest loans, the ability to rent your own apartment, the ability to buy a car, access to more of other people's money that you can leverage to make more money for yourself.

This was the first time I realized the power of credit. I could not believe it took me until I was twenty to find out how great a tool credit is. Not one single teacher ever educated me about it. All I ever heard was about how people were in horrifying amounts of debt from credit cards and how terrible they were. Maybe if they taught a class about how to build wealth with credit cards in school, people would be using it to win instead of drown. This whole venture jumpstarted my understanding of credit, which has grown to be beyond valuable today.

With more priceless lessons in the books, it was time for me to return to school. Sanjay was going to be away doing a Semester at Sea, so the trio disbanded. John and I decided to move into a house with six of the guys in our fraternity. We found the perfect house and mentally prepared for what would be a much different dynamic for the upcoming year.

11

WARNING: YOU ARE ENTERING THE COMFORT ZONE

I SAT DOWN in our newly furnished living room, exhausted from moving all of my belongings from the U-Haul into my new bedroom. We did a drawing for room selection, and I lucked out. I received the second pick and chose a large corner room on the main floor of the house. There were only three legitimate bedrooms in the house, so we were forced to get creative.

Next to my room was another large bedroom and a master bedroom. Those were occupied by John and my boy Colt. Colt and I grew up in adjacent towns and met during high school. We also attended the branch school together during my first year of college and kept each other sane through our time there. The three of us referred to ourselves as The Upstairs Boys.

The Downstairs Boys received the shit end of the stick. The best of the three rooms was a large room with a fireplace. This one was a pretty cool setup, just not an actual bedroom. My older brother within the fraternity, Sal, occupied this room.

Brent's room was more or less a crawl space underneath an addition that had been made to the house. There was no more than six feet of clearance and exposed two-by-fours all over the ceiling with protruding nails. We referred to it as The Cave.

Carson's room was the basement/laundry room. It did not have any utility that comes with a real bedroom. He simply nailed a sheet to the beam at the midway point of the basement and threw a carpet down. It made no sense that he and Brent were paying the same amount of rent as the rest of us. I have no idea how we decided that it was a fair arrangement.

We decided as soon as we settled in that it was only right that we had a housewarming party. This turned out to be an absolute disaster.

It was approximately 3:00 p.m. on a Wednesday afternoon. Our roof was covered in about twenty fraternity bros who were catching up after a long summer apart. Our house was in a residential neighborhood, and one or more of the neighbors must not have appreciated what we thought was an acceptable housewarming party. Two campus police officers pulled up and knocked on our door.

None of us wanted to deal with the situation and refused to get the door. Finally, Brent decided to take charge since nobody else would. He walked out to the front yard to see how he could be of assistance.

Brent, an extremely muscular African American with an assortment of tattoos, approached the police with his shirt off and his newly acquired pet ball python coiled around his neck. When I realized that's how he went out, I fully anticipated that we would all be arrested. I took a seat on a glass table as we observed how the interaction would unfold.

As soon as Brent somehow seemed to convince the police the situation was under control, a deafening explosion turned everyone's head as I fell through the shattered glass table. The cop ran over, saw me sitting in a pile of glass, and shook his head in disbelief. The result was a $250 ticket and a threat that we would be evicted if they received any more calls. We were not off to the best start.

I realized early on in the year that it would be a much different experience than my previous two years in college. John was in his last year of school and had an intense schedule that demanded a lot of his focus. The rest of my housemates were extremely ambitious, but they were fully committed to the school path to achieve their success.

This, alongside Sanjay being somewhere in the middle of the ocean, left me feeling like a lone wolf. It simply was not the same returning to the house as it was to an environment of electric entrepreneurial energy.

That year we also brought on multiple new distributors into our Network Marketing business. These people were high level, saw the vision, and hit the ground running with the business. My residual income levels took a leap, and I was earning more than I ever had before in my life. I had enough to cover all of my college expenses with a surplus to pretty much do whatever the hell I wanted to. This resulted in me slipping into one of the most dangerous places a person can be—complacency.

The money was coming in regardless of my efforts. I convinced myself that I did not need to hustle or create any side ventures that year. I just turned twenty-one. I should enjoy life, right? I had been grinding so hard up until that point in college that I barely enjoyed the social scene. What was money if I did not spend it? I decided that the income I had from my Network Marketing business was enough and that it was time to have some fun.

I started going to the bar multiple nights per week. I was attending every house party and fraternity event that we threw. We started to rent out top-floor penthouses at the casino and throwing exclusive parties. This was great, until the fifth time we did it.

At one party at the casino's penthouse, the place was jam-packed with our entire fraternity and sorority girls dressed as if they were attending a party at Jay Gatsby's mansion. The marble floors and gold-trimmed chandeliers gave off an essence of pure elegance. We had enough booze to incapacitate a small village, and everyone was having the time of their life.

I was off to the side, chatting with my boys when a commotion in the corner of the room caught my eye. One of my fraternity brothers, whom I will refer to as Crazy, was walking out of the master bedroom with an ironing board hoisted above his head. He was a shorter guy, and next thing I knew he disappeared into the crowd. The only reason I could locate him was because of the ironing board floating above the crowd of people dancing.

At this point, he had our full attention. We knew that there was absolutely no way he was going to do something responsible with it, but we decided that we would not be the ones to intervene. As we tracked the floating ironing board, we realized he was making a beeline to the balcony. As soon as he was within a few feet of the balcony's edge, he heaved the ironing board with the strength and grace of an Olympic athlete. My group went silent as he turned around pumping his fists up and down in the air like he just threw a pass for the game-winning touchdown.

Because we were thirty-eight floors up, it took a few seconds, but sure enough, the ironing board landed directly on a glass sculpture on the ground level. I was never able to see the aftermath myself, but apparently the sculpture was obliterated. Thousands of dollars of fines later, the casino completely changed the rules for penthouse rentals and has never allowed a party of that magnitude to happen again. It's always one person who has to ruin it for everyone.

Do not get me wrong, the parties were an absolute blast. I always have and still do love to go out and socialize. I also made some of the best memories of my life during that year. However, as time went on, I would be out at the bar and look around wondering what I was doing there.

The scene started to get redundant. It was the same place with the same people week after week after week. Everyone was taking full advantage of their glory years, because, after this, it was on to the real nine-to-five world, working the rest of their lives. People were using alcohol and partying as an escape mechanism to forget about the impending doom they faced. I felt like I was losing my edge and conforming with the masses.

I was trading in my obsession with business and success for partying and girls. I was losing my relentless desire to be as successful as possible. I justified it all because I was making a substantial income. Because of this, I even started to feel as if I were better than other people.

For so long I had felt the need to prove everyone wrong about me, and now that I had my first taste of success, I started to rub it in people's faces. I was flaunting designer clothes, blowing money unnecessarily, and making sure that everyone who ever doubted me knew I was succeeding.

The money I was earning put a magnifying glass on an enormous subconscious insecurity I had. I needed everyone to know that I was significant and successful. I started to actually believe money and material possessions were all that mattered. I thought I held the key to life, and no one could tell me otherwise. This damaged a lot of relationships and left a terrible taste in people's mouths.

As the school year went on, I started to realize that I was in a place of complacency. My income was still increasing, and, with that, my reckless behavior increased: nights that went to 6:00 a.m. at the casino, flying out to Vegas and staying at a penthouse in the Bellagio, "balling out" every moment I got a chance. I was fully comfortable. It was not doing myself or anyone around me any good.

I needed some type of change that would get me out of my comfort zone so that I could grow again. The truth was, I did not feel great. I felt much better when I was actively pursuing a challenge and growing as an individual. I thought of what the best options would be and knew I needed a different type of experience—one that would really shake me up and alter my perspective on life. One that would help humble and ground me. I decided that for the upcoming summer, I would take action on something that I desired my entire life.

I always dreamed of traveling the world.

My family typically went on our annual trip to the Outer Banks in North Carolina and to visit friends in California every few years, and my grandma brought us to Disney World to celebrate her retirement once. Other than that, I did not do a ton of traveling. I saw my friends traveling to exotic islands, Australia, Europe, and more and always wished I could enjoy those luxuries.

I had started traveling a bit throughout college, but most of it was domestic. I was extremely grateful to experience these new places, but, still, the farthest place I made it out of the country was to the Cozumel port in Mexico for a twelve-hour stop on a cruise. I wanted true cultural immersion and to experience an extended stay in a different country. I decided that I was going to study abroad. That upcoming summer would be my best chance to make studying abroad happen.

Initially, I wanted to go to Spain. The thoughts of a huge city, the beach, beautiful women, and the Spanish culture had me captivated. I scheduled a meeting with a counselor in the study-abroad office. I explained that I was an applied mathematics major and was looking for a summer program where I was most interested in traveling and experiencing another culture. The academics would be secondary for me. I learned that the options were nearly nonexistent for me to go to Spain. I was pretty bummed, but she had another suggestion for me.

"Have you ever considered Italy?" she asked.

"Eh, not really," I replied.

"You should look into the program we have in Florence. It is six weeks, and most students who go are in the same position as you. They just take random classes and use it as a way to get over there, travel, and have a great experience. You should just submit the application. It's due in two days. I think this would be your best bet."

What did I have to lose? I filled out the application knowing absolutely nothing about Italy. I did not know a single word of the Italian language, and, to be honest, I did not even know one fact about Florence. I had a few friends who studied there in the past and loved it, but other than that I was clueless.

Exactly two weeks later I got a letter saying I had been accepted into the program. At this point, I had made up my mind that if I got accepted, I would be off to Italy. All of the logistics were taken care of by the school, and the program required minimal effort on my part. Everyone I talked to kept raving about how awesome Florence was and how it was the best time they've ever had in their life.

About a month before the end of the spring semester and our departure date, we had our orientation for the program. We gathered in the large lecture hall in which I had pulled off my economics textbook purchasing stunt. I smiled to myself thinking about the memory.

I looked around and saw a few familiar faces, but nobody that I had any real relationship with. Half of me was excited to go on this trip without knowing anyone; the other half desired to have one of my boys to go through the experience with. It's always more fun going places with your best friends. At the same time, doing what I was about to would require some serious stepping out of my comfort zone, which would result in the largest amount of growth. That is exactly what I needed.

When they finished going through the orientation material, it was time to select which classes we would take. I was all in with putting a minimal effort toward my academics, so I signed up for a drawing class and another about the Florence experience. I assumed this meant walking around the city, eating Italian food, drinking wine, and eating more food. Seemed to me as if I would be able to handle this workload with ease. With orientation in the books, I was officially ready to head overseas for the experience of a lifetime.

12

JOHNNY FOREIGNER

WE HAD BEEN flying for over ten hours and were finally getting close. The pilot just announced we were passing over the Swiss Alps, so I groggily rolled up my window shade to check out the view below. Massive, rolling snow-capped mountains for miles on end. I could only imagine the other intriguing sights and scenes I would see in the upcoming six weeks.

Upon our arrival in Florence, we were all experiencing a cocktail of emotions. We were exhausted, uncertain, excited, uncomfortable, and anxious. Thankfully, we had multiple coordinators from our Florence school waiting at the airport to make sure we got to our apartments safely.

This process took quite some time, but finally, I was put together with one of my new roommates who also went to UCONN named Jack. We got along right off the bat. We had a lot in common so I knew we would form a great friendship.

Our coordinator gave us our apartment information, put us in a taxi, and instructed the driver where to drop us off. As we drove away from the airport, Jack and I got our first taste of culture shock. On the outer limits of the city the drive started off normally, but as we got into the city, we saw absolute pandemonium.

The taxi driver was on his cell phone the entire drive, screaming in Italian at both the person on the other end of the phone and the pedestrians in the street. The road became so narrow that we thought we were driving on a sidewalk. To top it off, there was absolutely no civil order with people walking around the street as they pleased, bumping into our car, and completely obstructing traffic.

Our taxi flew down a narrow cobblestone street when all of a sudden a structure appeared that towered above the rest of the city's buildings. I ducked down to get a better upward view out of the taxi's windshield. I had never seen anything like it. Intricately handcrafted marble blocks extended up into the sky that stretched as far down the street as I could see. The structure was complemented with a gigantic octagonal brick dome whose orange color stuck out against the white, green, and red marble.

"What is this building?" I said as I looked over to Jack.

"Dude you've got to be kidding. That's the Duomo, one of the largest churches in Italy and the biggest attraction in Florence. You must really not know a thing about this place, huh?"

It was funny because I actually knew nothing about Italy. I made no attempt to learn about the city or country I would be living in. I just showed up ready to embrace whatever was about to come my way.

We crossed over the Arno, the olive green river that divided city. To my right was a bridge covered in what appeared to be shops and small buildings. I later found out this was Ponte Vecchio, another one of Florence's most famous sites.

Only one block from the river was our apartment. The streets of the quaint neighborhood were lined with casual restaurants below pastel-colored Renaissance-style apartments that all seemed to be complemented by green or white shutters. The sounds of an organ echoed down the narrow and curving alleyway that was lined with Vespas and Smart Cars.

The aroma of fresh pizza radiated from the corner restaurant. I could feel the same energy that every "plan your next vacation to Italy" commercial makes you feel as you are watching from your living room. We were told we really lucked out because we were placed in one of the nicest and most authentic neighborhoods in the city. I immediately fell in love.

Another guy who worked for the school greeted us on the street, brought us into the apartment, and let us know the rules. We got our bags and walked up the narrow, ancient stone staircase to the top floor where our apartment was. The guy pulled out a skeleton key and unlocked our wooden door. I could not believe the key worked, nor did I believe they were even used. I thought they were just used in movies for hidden treasure chests.

We walked into the apartment and were greeted by our other three roommates. John and Nick were from Penn State and already good friends, and Joe was there alone from the University of Virginia. We all sat down, talked for a while, and realized we would all get along perfectly. My Italy adventure was off to a fantastic start.

We continued to get to know each other over a few bottles of wine they picked up from the local grocery store. They raved how each bottle only cost two euro. Dirt cheap, great quality. It was crazy how quickly the nerves of uncertainty were settled. After only thirty minutes we felt as if we had known each other our whole lives.

The next day we had our official orientation. Typical protocol, safety, do not buy drugs or let random Italians into our apartment. The usual. We began to meet our classmates, and I was blown away by how outgoing everybody was. It seemed like most people came alone and were looking to make new friends through this experience.

After our orientation, they gave us our class schedules and classroom locations. I glanced at my schedule and was a bit confused. My drawing class was there, but then the second slot said intro to the Italian language. I brought it up to an orientation leader and told her there must be a mistake, I signed up for the Florence experience.

"*Sì!* This is the Florence experience. Learning the Italian language," she replied.

Well, if I'm going to be here, it will be cool to know some of the language, I decided. I was a little disappointed I would not be strolling around eating Italian cuisine for class, but I was confident I could take care of that on my own time.

We all had different schedules and availability due to classes, so we did our best to coordinate our weekend travels around Europe. Crazy enough, the squad did not go on one trip together as a whole the entire time we were there. But we did make sure at least two of us were together for every destination.

For my trips, I decided on the Amalfi Coast, Cinque Terre, Lucca and Pisa, Venice, Rome, Croatia, and Barcelona. I made sure I would see as much as possible. As I locked in the purchases, I started to dream of how amazing it was going to be to experience all of these new places and cultures.

Now that the important stuff was out of the way, it was time to start going to class. This was truly my last priority, but it had to be done. My first class was the hoax of the century in the name of the Florence experience. The classroom was a tiny white box with twelve students and an angry Italian man standing at the front of the class. He began to aggressively introduce himself and spoke only in Italian as if we all were fluent in the language after being in the country for less than forty-eight hours.

After what I assumed was his introduction, he jumped right into a lecture on Italian grammar. He went straight through until our dismissal time and sent us on our way with a stack of homework. I was off to a terrible start on the academic side, but I held onto the hope that my next class would be better.

I walked downstairs into a gorgeous art studio that resembled a museum. I could not get over the level of detail of the self-portrait that was nearing completion on an easel of a man with a single finger up to his mouth. I was amazed at how the palette sitting next to the easel with a concoction of blended paints and a paintbrush created the masterpiece.

One painting that stood out to me in particular was a five-foot-wide recreation of the Ponte Vecchio that boldly projected its beauty across the entire room. The whole room was well lit by a wall of windows and gave off an invitation to create. I felt like the next Michelangelo in the making. I looked around and the class was entirely female except for one other guy.

The short and tan instructor walked in dressed as if he just left a GQ photoshoot. He introduced himself as Tiziano. He had crazy hair, and the moment he started talking to the class, I knew he was a ladies' man. His accent was thick, and his English was certainly understandable, but far from fluent. He made the funniest jokes—most of the time completely inadvertently—and after just one class period we could not wait to come back for more.

At the end of our class, he gave us our first assignment: to draw a wine bottle from "the perspective."

"Tiziano, I'm going to be completely honest. My drawing skills are shit. If I try hard, will I get a good grade?" I asked him half-jokingly.

"Hahahaha, no, I do not want you to draw shit. Draw the wine bottle from the perspective. You are great," he said.

Every day Tiziano and I would prank each other and always take it to new heights. One day I asked him what his favorite European clothing store was. He told me, so I went there after class and purchased the most ridiculous outfit I could find. A gray fedora, a shirt that had every color and pattern under the rainbow, and skin-tight dress pants that had a diamond pattern across them.

The next day I came in wearing them and he did not even recognize me at first. Once he finally did, he nearly burst into tears laughing and started running around in my fedora impersonating me. It's funny how a drawing class ended up being one of my favorite college classes all because of the experience he was able to provide.

There was so much going on with classes, traveling, and making sure we went out to enjoy the Italian nightlife scene, but something else amazing happened. My Network Marketing business was blowing up even more. I could not even put any work into it, but my paychecks were increasing drastically.

I would receive notifications on paydays and be blown away at what I was seeing. The amount of money I was making weekly would have taken me over two months to earn at my job in the restaurant where I used to work. What was even crazier is that I was not even actively working on my business. This was the residual income I had dreamed of when the business was first introduced to me three years earlier.

I started to realize that there was much more to the income I was earning than acting like a big shot. Income, and especially residual income, equated to freedom. The freedom to enjoy, to experience, to spend your time how you choose, to decide.

I purchased all of my weekend trips without even thinking twice about it. I did not cook once in our apartment. Instead, I ate at the most delicious Italian restaurants for every meal (other than my company's meal replacement shakes I was able to bring in my suitcase). I was able to go out every night and enjoy the experience to the absolute maximum with no restrictions. That is true freedom.

The experience was also grounding me. I was immersed in a culture where businesses would shut down in the middle of the day for hours to simply relax and enjoy life. I encountered people who barely made any money and could not be happier as individuals. I realized there was so much more to life than material possessions and balling out. I grew a fond appreciation for experiences and all of the different people I was encountering and building relationships with.

I also realized that no matter what, especially as an entrepreneur, there will always be people who simply cannot understand you. I came to know that this did not mean people wanted to see me fail; we just saw the world from two different angles. I used to get agitated and spill all the facts in people's faces as to why their logic was flawed when they did not agree with me.

One night when I brought a girl I met there out on a date, I noticed I had made progress in letting go of my ego and this bad habit.

I almost never went out on formal dates and kept a barrier the size of the Great Wall of China built around me. I had been crushed by three different girls in high school that made me nearly emotionless. I made the decision that I would never let my guard down or let anyone in unless I was positive it was the right person. I guess being constantly surrounded by beautiful ladies and the Italian vibes got the best of me this night.

I met this girl through my program and remember being particularly interested in her as soon as we met. She was exactly my type, looks-wise at least. Gorgeous with tan skin, dark features, and a phenomenal body from cheerleading. We hung out a couple of different times in a group setting, and I decided to ask her if she would like to get dinner together.

We went to an upscale restaurant right around the block from my apartment. The outdoor seating was adjacent to a beautiful park and with a view of the Arno running through the city. The scenery and perfect midsummer evening temperature combined with the sounds of an older Italian gentleman playing an accordion created the perfect ambiance. This was our first time one-on-one with each other, so we started off with wine to eliminate the nerves of being on a first date.

We began with some small talk about our program, how we were enjoying our study-abroad experience, and a few laughs about how we first remembered meeting one another. Then, we started to get a little bit deeper. Typically, I prefer to ask questions and let other people talk about themselves, so she was telling me all about her background, her plans in school, and what her plan for the future was. All of it involved finishing undergrad, going to graduate school, getting a solid job, and working for someone else.

Her answers bored me to death, but I still responded in a supportive manner. What is most important is that people are chasing their passion and doing what will make them happy. Different paths make different people happy, and if that is what would genuinely fulfill her, then that was fine. The issue is most people do it out of fear and because that is what they have been told to do. I find that path to be painstaking and miserable.

Shortly thereafter, the conversation turned to me.

"So what do you plan on doing? You said you're studying math? I hate math, haha," she said. "What do you even want to do with that? Have you gotten any internships yet? You're like twenty-one already, aren't you freaking out?"

I took a deep breath to compose myself because I knew the conversation could easily spiral out of control.

"Yeah, I'm studying math, but I don't really plan on using my degree. I've found that I'm very entrepreneurial, and multiple of my mentors have math degrees and are extremely successful businessmen. Also, I don't really care about internships. I don't see the point in working for free so I can get a job that I don't want. That path doesn't really interest me," I told her.

"I currently have a Network Marketing business. I plan on building this and using it as a platform to invest and start other businesses. It has been going well and really took off the past year."

She looked at me, mortified.

"No internships? You graduate next year, what are you going to do? Business is so risky. What are you going to do when that fails? You need to figure it out."

This is where the situation normally would have gone south. I was thinking of snapping back about how over 50 percent of people who graduate college do not get a job in their desired field. How they walk out with hundreds of thousands of dollars in debt and only earn $40k a year. That the very path she was pursuing was riskier than ever, that she would be depending on someone else for a paycheck her entire life. She could get fired at any moment, for any reason, and be replaced in seconds.

I could have dropped all of this logic on her, but I knew it would fall on deaf ears. I decided it was best to bite my tongue. I understood that I thought differently than most people, and no matter what you say, some people will just not understand. I knew she was one of those people.

Finally, our food came out and we returned to the small talk until the meal was over. It's crazy to me how some people love to talk about bullshit TV shows, their roommates, drama, and matters of zero importance, but as soon as you start talking about vision, goals, and ambition, they treat you like you are the crazy one.

The dinner ended and we got the check: 120 euro. She insisted that she cover her portion, but I knew she was just saying it to be polite. Besides, she had just told me about her limited budget since she was studying abroad and could only work at her internship half the summer.

At that point, I was completely over the entire date and realized this was no time to try and transform into Romeo. I slapped down the 120 in cash. Ironically, I had just made more than that over the course of us sitting at dinner and being told I need to get my life together. Funny how it works.

The following six-week period was one of the most action-packed times of my life. Every day my roommates and I would wander the streets of Florence, exploring random shops, markets, and hole-in-the-wall restaurants that would end up having some of the most exquisite food I've ever eaten. We explored all of the iconic landmarks in the city and absorbed the magnificent artwork and sculptures. None of us had cell service, so everywhere we went would be a pure adventure full of deep conversation since we were all present and completely in the moment.

On the weekends, we would travel to new destinations and absorb even more new culture and amazing scenery. So much was happening at such a fast pace that I could not process the speed at which it was changing me. I stood in the Colosseum in Rome trying to comprehend that some 400,000 people died right where I was standing for entertainment purposes.

I explored Pompeii and tried to imagine the feeling that every citizen of the city had as they watched Mt. Vesuvius erupt, fully knowing they were doomed. I laid out on the beaches of the Amalfi Coast absorbing some of the most astonishing views I had ever seen in my life. I island-hopped across the crystal-clear waters in Croatia, which before I came to Italy, I did not even know was a country. Every single day the lens that I viewed the world through was changing.

I experienced a tremendous shift in perspective. I came from a remote farm town where the farthest most people went was to the grocery store in the town over. Now, here I was, exploring the depths of foreign lands and completely immersed in cultures most people will never have the chance to experience.

I started to grasp how big the world actually is. I thought about how humans get so caught up in small-town problems, individual relationships, and what is happening in our immediate vicinity. When you understand that there are billions of people in the world, that devastating breakup you endured over leaving your girlfriend's Snapchat on open becomes much less serious. We place an unreasonable weight of importance on minor occurrences and lose sight of how insignificant they really are.

The education I received from this experience alone could not compare to what I received from any class, book, or seminar. From every interaction with a foreign individual, every new place I saw with my own eyes, every deep reflection forced upon me from visiting some of the most iconic sites in history, and every time I simply stepped onto the street to walk, I learned something new.

Julius Caesar once said, "Experience is the teacher of all things." I began to realize that my firsthand experiences were always what had the most profound impact on me.

Another revelation that grew inside me during this experience was my appreciation for the United States. The best way to gain an appreciation for something is to be deprived of it. I grew extremely grateful for all of our modern advances, our business efficiency, convenience, and of course peanut butter. Sometimes we can lose sight of how good we have it, and the best way to understand is to experience a different way of living.

As the six weeks came to a close, I was grateful beyond belief, but I was also bummed. The time flew by so quickly, and just as I was getting into the swing of the lifestyle, it was time to go home. On the last night, our entire friend group got together at our favorite bar to celebrate the experience. We drank, we laughed, we reminisced, and we fully enjoyed our last night together.

As I looked around at what was the end of my study-abroad experience, I knew this could not be it. I had gotten a taste, now I wanted the entire entree. The experience was so transformative, and I felt I just scratched the surface. At that moment, I decided that someway, somehow, I would be back for more.

13

AN EDUCATION WITH NO STAMP OF APPROVAL

When I returned from my summer in Italy, I could not have been more academically checked out for my senior year. I had to dig deep to get through my last few required math classes knowing full well I would never look at the information again in my life. For some reason, I just could not envision a scenario where I would need to write out a page-long proof that conclusively proved that 1+1 in fact equaled 2.

Even though the school portion did not do much for me, I still loved the social aspect of the college environment. I believe that the ability to properly socialize has a profound impact on your levels of success. Although there are many negatives that go along with going out and partying, it can serve as a great way to develop your social acuity. I attribute my ability to have meaningful conversations, pick up on social cues, and thrive in social environments due to the amount of "practice" I had in college.

One of the main outlets that allowed me to develop my social abilities was through my fraternity. However, during our junior year, the school cracked down on Greek life. They began to find any reason they could to suspend or expel organizations from campus. Some of the reasons were legitimate while some were a complete stretch.

At the end of the day, the reasons hardly mattered because the campus was in control and the decision was theirs. Unfortunately, during this time, they decided that our fraternity would be kicked off for four years.

When this happened, Brent and I had a conversation. Both of us grew very close while living together in the house from how well we could feed off each other's energy. For our senior year, we got our own apartment and started to formulate plans to move to California shortly after graduation.

He had the idea that we should just form our own little fraternity. We would lock arms with the most ambitious, driven, and social people we met at school. We noticed throughout college how some of the people who came before us did this, but every single group lacked the ambition and drive. They were solely in it for the girls and to look cool.

While we wanted to take over the social scene, it was equally as important to us to surround ourselves with people who were hungry for success. At that point, we understood the power of having an influential network and what it could do in the long run.

We promptly began to identify the people who fit the criteria. We kept the organization low key and only shared the vision with people that we 100 percent wanted in. Not one person declined our invitation. We started off with five of us, and over time it grew to about twenty people—all of whom were future doctors, lawyers, engineers, finance gurus, and entrepreneurs. In addition to their lofty ambition, all of them thrived in social environments.

The idea of this group may sound shallow, but one of the most important factors in success is who you surround yourself with. If you only hang out with the kids running around naked at parties with no goals in life, you are going to end up sitting on a couch together reminiscing about the glory days and what life could have been. The idea of that made me nauseous. I wanted the people I associated with to desire everything they could get out of life.

To go along with our group's strong presence, we had the hookup everywhere. The nightlife scene revolved around two bars on campus, and we would get taken care of at both. A lot of the guys in our squad bounced or worked at the bars at one point or another throughout college, which worked tremendously in our favor.

We also became close to the influential people in other fraternities that were kicked off campus. We would bring them to our events and parties, and, in turn, they would bring us to theirs. There were definitely people who hated our presence or who were jealous, but it attracted a lot of people to us who recognized what was going on.

Our goal was never the exclusion of others, but rather to be a magnet of great energy that attracted people with a similar mindset. Our influence grew to be huge, and all twenty of us had a blast enjoying the benefits of being in the upper echelon of the social hierarchy.

My favorite part about this unofficial social group was every person's balance. We were able to maintain a strong social life while staying focused on working toward our individual visions. Even though all of our goals and beliefs varied, one outcome was consistent among us. We all wanted to become the best possible version of ourselves.

It is absolutely imperative to be a part of a circle where everyone is obsessed with growth and high-level success if you yourself want to be successful. Today, almost all of these guys have begun to accomplish what they set out to do.

Throughout the year, I enjoyed every moment to the fullest. I was not trying to cling on for dear life, and I also was not trying to speed the experience up. Although I was excited about the future, I made sure that I was intentionally present. I had a feeling that life would only get better after school ended, but in the meantime, I wanted to enjoy what was left of the environment college provided.

One of our favorite environments to enjoy was the dining hall. Every now and then, a couple of us would go to the dining hall, wait until the lady working the counter had a group of students to swipe in, and then stealthily slip between the cracks straight into the food court without being detected and fill our plates.

The dining hall, however, was more than just a place where we went to avoid putting on our chef aprons. The food we consumed was great, but that was only half of the purpose. It was a place for deep discussion where we would sit for hours on end. Sometimes it was after a night out, recapping the crazy shit our friends did or our different female shenanigans.

Other times we got deep and talked about life, the bigger picture, and what life would be like after school. We engaged in many debates, laughed nonstop, and took advantage of the fact we could all get together at the drop of a hat. After school, this would not be nearly as feasible.

Many of the funniest moments I experienced in college spawned at the dining hall table. One time we were sitting there about three months before our trip to Cabo, discussing our excitement for our last spring break.

"I'm trying to have diamond shoulders. Ten pack. Leanest I've ever been in my life. This is the last hoorah. After Cabo, it's all over. Don't blow it, Stank," my friend Max proclaimed.

I rolled my eyes as I shook my head laughing. When school ended, life would begin. It was far from over. However, I was down with the mission to get as shredded as possible.

"Look, Max, I'll be ready to go come Cabo time. You're going to be the one hiding in a palm tree because you won't be able to put down the Ben & Jerry's." I laughed.

"Yeah, we'll see who's hiding in the sand when I'm in the best shape of my life, lying poolside, and sucking down a pina colada with a fat pineapple floater," Max said as he looked at Brent who was eating a slice of pepperoni pizza.

"I'm just not even going to acknowledge you fools. Just wait, once we are sailing in the open ocean, we'll know who put the work in."

And so it began. We recruited all of our friends who were going on the trip and officially started "The C16 Grind." For the next three months, we trained and ate like we were Floyd Mayweather preparing to take on Oscar De La Hoya. I'm not kidding. If anything other than chicken breasts and vegetables touched our plates, the whole peanut gallery would move in swiftly to give you an earful. Fortunately, I had my company's nutrition products to keep me in the game; otherwise, I would have been toast.

The challenge got so out of hand that we began going to the gym for a weight-lifting session during the day, then back at night for an hour of cardio. One night I was walking in the middle of campus, returning home after a late study session, when I felt a slap on my shoulder. It was my boy Trey.

I had just seen him a few hours earlier when we finished up our two-a-day. He blew by me dressed in winter gear like he was preparing to explore Antarctica. I realized he was on a midnight run and on his third workout of the day. He kept it moving and all I heard was, "Catch you in the coconut trees, Stank!" as he turned his pace up a gear. The sick bastard pulled off a three-peat.

I've heard many people say that the anticipation for an event can be just as exciting as the event itself. When I think back to that Cabo trip, I recall how the grind leading up to it was just as much fun as I think about the trip itself. We all showed up in tip-top shape and had an absolute ball.

With all the fun we were having, the year flew by and reached the point where people had to figure out what was next. I noticed many of my peers were experiencing monstrous levels of stress. They were frantically searching for employment while at the same time trying to live the rest of their glory days to the fullest. I watched as people refined their resumes and put on suits and ties to go impress employers who would not even give them an interview if their grades were less than perfect.

Other than the few who achieved a perfect 4.0 or had inside connections, most people were settling for jobs that required forty hours a week in a cube and paid $40k a year. From my perspective, they were settling for a life of survival. I refused to let that be me.

I wanted the most I could get out of life. I evaluated what was going on and realized that I was in a unique position. I was already earning more than all the people I knew who were heading to the cubes. The residual portion of my income was only growing as our base of product users and distributors continued to grow.

My income was also entirely location independent. I had some serious leverage and freedom to work with—more specifically, time freedom and the freedom to design how I wanted my life to look. So, instead of joining the masses, I followed my heart. I decided that after graduation, I would travel the world.

When I thought about the best ways to make this happen, one option appealed to me above all of the others. I had a conversation with a friend I made while studying abroad who worked for one of the travel companies we used for all of our weekend trips. She explained to me how it was the perfect opportunity for someone who wanted to see the world. The company provided a free apartment, paid you to travel on the weekends, paid you commission for trips sold, gave you a free gym membership, and much more.

To top it off, I would be based in Florence. She said the only downfall was that most people did not make much money. With my income and confidence that I would make sales, this did not bother me one bit. I decided that this was the perfect platform for me to see the world.

She set me up with a Skype interview, and I was hired on the spot. As soon as it was a lock, I decided that I would return to Italy prepared this time. I purchased Rosetta Stone and practiced Italian for at least an hour per day. I wanted to be able to experience the city on a deeper level than I was as a study-abroad student. Knowing the native language would give me a huge advantage.

For the remainder of the school year, I diligently practiced my Italian and prioritized the gym. I also spent a lot of time reading personal development books, which had become an obsession of mine. I barely went to any of my classes and would cram information for exams. I was so out of touch with classes that I even accidentally missed one of my midterms for a cultural nutrition class.

I missed the exam because I skipped school for a week to fly to Arizona for an exclusive event my company put on. They provided us with high-level leadership training, a tour of our brand new state-of-the-art world headquarters, and a tour of the ranch of one of the founders. I played with his pet giraffe and was brought inside his personal laboratory where he formulated our entire nutrition line. The walls were lined with jars full of herbs, roots, and some of the best ingredients on the planet. I found this to be a much more effective way to learn about nutrition.

During the final days before graduation, we were at one of the biggest outdoor parties of the year. One of the fraternities had an off-campus house in a relatively set-back location. The house itself was so run-down that it realistically should have been condemned.

At the party, I ran into a girl I studied abroad with. She came up to me with a smile and told me she heard that I was moving back to Italy to work with one of the travel companies.

"Yeah! I'm pumped. I think it will be a really cool way to meet a lot of people and see the world," I said.

She laughed in my face.

"Guess you really don't care about making something out of yourself in life. Have fun postponing being successful."

As she walked away, I smiled and shook my head. If she only knew the half of it.

Graduation day was filled with an entire slew of emotions. I was the first person on my mom's side of the family to get a college degree. I earned my bachelor of science degree in applied mathematics with a minor in economics. I officially and successfully finished my undergraduate studies at what was becoming one of the most prestigious schools in the nation. One of the biggest accomplishments of my life. Yet, something felt off.

Sure, I worked hard throughout my time there. I sacrificed a lot of time studying so that I could put the right answers down on a piece of paper that was supposed to judge my levels of intelligence. I completed some of the most difficult courses that the university had to offer. But for what? I had no intention of using my degree, and all of this information I learned was mostly just to get a good exam grade.

My levels of success so far had nothing to do with what I learned in the classroom. As I sat there looking at my cap and gown laid out on my bed on graduation morning, that's the moment I had the realization.

Every single important skill that I knew would be imperative to my success moving forward came from experiences and lessons I learned beyond the scope of the classroom. It felt sort of cynical to think that the past five years of studying my ass off was for nothing, but I knew that was not true.

Without taking this path, none of my experiences would have been the same. No fraternity and extensive network of irreplaceable relationships, no WeBusU, no textbook business, no study abroad, and probably no Network Marketing business. All of this happened because I chose this path and it was not a waste at all. In actuality, I received the most extensive and meaningful education that would serve me for the rest of my life. This education just did not have the stamp of approval from the university.

I thought to myself about the magnitude of the realization I had. What if I could show it to the world? I thought about how much more fulfilled and happy people would be if they knew the most important places to put their focus. How much more exciting their life could be if they received permission to pursue their wildest dreams. If instead of focusing on meaningless quizzes and exams, they put the most importance on living a life rich in experience.

How could I get the message out to the world? Maybe a book? The idea felt right, but the enormous task felt daunting. I free flowed all of the ideas I had into a Word document and saved it as "Beyond the Classroom." I closed my laptop with an inspired feeling as I headed to my graduation ceremony.

About twenty of my college friends and I were seated together in Gampel Pavilion, the arena where we watched our basketball team dominate throughout our time at UCONN, as we awaited our turn to walk the floor as college graduates. Behind me was Christian who waved down a vendor and proceeded to purchase a pile of hotdogs and popcorn for the squad. Not exactly how I had envisioned graduation would be, but what other way would we realistically go out?

For the next hour, we had our laughs, joked around, and took Snapchats of our last time together as students. The time finally came when we had to walk across the floor and receive our diplomas. There must have been thousands of us there, and I felt like they were just herding farm animals in one side and out the other. They were rapidly announcing the names, handing out generic diploma holders with no paper in them, and sending people on their way.

"John Stankiewicz!" I heard the professor dressed in a Harry Potter costume announce. I walked across the stage to grab my six-figure slip of paper, heard a few shouts from my family, and that was it. I waited at the other end because Christian was right behind me. We took a picture together on the UCONN backdrop, and just like that, college was over.

As I watched the stampede of students with generic degrees exit just as quickly as their names were called, my mind began to discern the reality of the situation.

You are a graduate now. You have earned our accreditation. Now you are free to work the rest of your life so you can pay back Sallie Mae at variable interest rates. Thank you for your money!

"Well, on to the real world!" I heard some guy say laughing as he nudged his friend. He returned a chuckle as he nervously scratched his arm. I could tell they were actually terrified and truly thought that their prime and lives of fun were over.

I never understood that. The real world? What does that even mean? This is the real world. I feel bad because most of the people graduating that day did not know it, but we are fully in control of the decisions we make to design our lives. We decide on everything, from the food we eat, the people we surround ourselves with, and, yes, the way we make a living.

People fold under the pressure from society, and mostly from their own families. They do not want to disappoint Mom or Dad, so they get that secure job working forty hours a week with two weeks of vacation per year. Even if deep down they want to be a musician, an actor, a painter, to travel the world, or whatever their true passion is. They are afraid of judgment and of disappointing others, so they conform. They sacrifice their goals, dreams, and passions to fit the mold of what someone else created for them.

They make the excuse "this is the real world," but the simple truth is the real world is whatever you want it to be. You just need to have the balls to go after it.

As for me, I could not have had a more opposite stance from most of my peers. Graduating college meant that a ball and chain was being released from my ankle. Now I was able to travel the world. Now I was able to pursue my passions with no limitations of a numerical analysis exam. I was fired the fuck up. Most people could not understand why I was so excited to leave the good ol' days behind. I knew those days were just beginning.

It felt like I had just moved onto campus for the first time yesterday, and now it was time to make the next huge leap in my life. This time, the leap was one that I knew aligned with my deepest desires. I was not doing what society suggested. I was doing what my heart told me was right. It was time to move back to Italy for round two.

14

PROMO CODE "STANK"

JUST LIKE THAT, I was on a flight back to the place where I had unfinished business. This time was different though. This would not be just a six-week getaway. I would have no diabolical Italian language teacher. There was also no obligation for me to return to the states. All I had was a one-way ticket. The whole idea was both exciting and nerve-racking.

For the excruciatingly long flight, I attempted to sleep as much as possible, but the flight attendants had a different plan for me. I was seated in an aisle seat, and every fifteen minutes they would zoom down the aisle like Ricky Bobby with their refreshment cart and smack me in the knee or elbow.

Thankfully, the second leg of the flight from Zurich to Florence was much more peaceful. Soaring over the Swiss Alps had me reminisce about being in the exact same position a year earlier for my first overseas experience.

We touched down in Florence, and I mentally prepared myself for what would be the experience of a lifetime.

"*Via Ghibellina centodue per favore,*" I said to the taxi driver. I was excited to start using the Italian language I had been practicing incessantly for months now. He simply nodded and brought me on my way. This time the tight streets, aggressive screaming, and erratic driving did not bother me. I knew it was just how the city was.

We arrived at our apartment and I was extremely puzzled. He dropped me off in front of a twelve-foot double wooden door that looked like a castle entrance. Above the door was an elegant emblem that represented the illustrious Medici family. *Am I going to be living in a palace?*

While trying to figure out my way in, a short, overweight Italian man with a button-down shirt that was way too small, slicked back reddish brown hair, and sunglasses that looked like they came from a 2 Chainz music video came flying up on a Vespa. He ran over to me out of breath, drenched in sweat from the intense Florence summer humidity, and stuck out his hand.

"John, it is great to meet you. I am Ivan. The manager. You must be tired. Let me show you the apart-a-ments," he said to me in his Italian accent. I shook his hand and he opened up the castle door.

A cool draft greeted me as the door opened and we walked down a cobblestone entrance into a garage constructed out of stone. At the far end was an exquisite iron fence that separated the enclosed courtyard that was covered in gardens in full bloom. At that point, I fully expected a maid to show up and start hand feeding me grapes.

I followed Ivan up three large sets of stairs until we reached the second floor. I looked around at hand-painted palace ceilings, artwork covering the walls, and a few perfectly carved wooden doors that I assumed led to private rooms. *Holy shit. It is a palace!* I could hardly contain my excitement anymore.

We walked down another hallway, then up three more sets of very tight stairs. By the time I reached the top I was profusely sweating due to lugging my suitcases in the infamous summer heat. He reached into his pocket and pulled out a skeleton key, swung the door open, and gave me a tour.

He led me into a scorching hot living room with an assortment of rotating fans making a miserable attempt to cool the place down. The dated couch had a tear in it, and the dining room table was surrounded by plastic chairs; half of which seemed to be broken. There was not room for much more than that.

I noticed a musty scent as he led me to my room, which was crammed with five cot-sized beds. He pointed to the bed right next to the entrance of the room and said, "You will be sleeping here. Take a rest. The students are coming. Tomorrow you must be handing out the flyers at eight a.m. It is great to meet you."

He took off and I started unpacking and evaluating the situation at hand.

Yes, the apartment was free; however, they made sure that not one square inch would be put to waste. Yes, we were in a palace, but I quickly realized that we were stuffed in the attic. The space we were living in was more likely the quarters where the Medici family stored their peasants and serfs.

I gave myself a tour of the apartment and found a tiny kitchen, a small bathroom, another small bedroom with three beds, and a makeshift wooden staircase that led to a hallway with another bed in it and a slightly larger bathroom on the far side. This "apartment" was probably intended to house three people tops. There would be nine of us sharing this space for the foreseeable future: six guys and three girls. I decided not to think about it for the moment and headed to my bed to get some actual sleep.

After waking up early in the evening, I felt fully refreshed and was finally ready to socialize with the crew I would be sharing this brothel with for my tenure there. There were a few roommates who were there from previous semesters, a few new ones, and about half who had not yet arrived. By the grace of God, we all got along phenomenally and spent the night getting to know each other.

In hindsight, it's obvious how we all got along. We all were young, decided to move to Italy on a whim with no promise of anything, and were just looking to explore the world. It takes a special type of person to do that, and for that reason we all had common ground that we could meet on.

The rest of the night I spent preparing my promotional flyers to hand out on the streets the next day. In terms of making sales, I had done nothing to prepare prior to my move. Furthermore, the company had strict sales quotas, and if you did not meet them, you risked being fired.

From what I understood, people made sales in two ways. They would add all of the people who would be studying abroad on Facebook and send them messages, and they would hand out booklets with travel deals and their promo code on the streets when they saw students.

I strategically picked "STANK" as my promo code. At first, my manager questioned my choice and suggested I pick something else. I stood firm with my decision. I knew it would stand out, make people laugh, and help me brand myself.

I was no stranger to this flyer game, and I figured I would thrive with this tactic. The veterans told me it was a breeze and that if you get your flyers out there, the sales will come. I mentally prepared myself to paint Florence orange.

At 8:00 a.m. sharp, it was time to hit the streets. There was a strict policy for us to be out of the apartment and promoting from 8:00 a.m. to 4:00 p.m. Ivan paired us newbies with a person who was a company veteran to go out and flyer with. I suppose this was to teach us the ways, but also make sure we got out of the apartment. My partner that I got assigned to was a kid named J-Bone.

At the time, J-Bone was twenty-five. He had a job in computer programming and made a large amount of money before he moved to Italy. He reached a point where he was no longer happy and wanted a change so he could experience more of what the world had to offer.

Everyone seemed to love J-Bone, and for the life of me I could not figure out why. The kid's teeth were stained dark red from drinking wine and refusing to brush them. Apparently he did not shower either. His corner of the room was an absolute disaster. The image of some sort of splattered foreign fluid all over the wall next to his bed will forever be burned into my memory. I had a terrible first impression and was pretty bummed that this was my assignment, but I tried to make the best of it.

We emerged from the apartment to the serene streets below, and J-Bone started lecturing me.

"Dude. We gotta go to this street. There are so many students there. Nobody knows about it. I'm only telling you because we are partnered up."

"Dope," I replied. "Let's head there, I appreciate you letting me in on this," I said to him thinking maybe I had been wrong.

We took a few steps in that direction and abruptly stopped.

"Wait," J-Bone said. "I'll be right back."

He headed into a restaurant and came back with a full glass of dark, sparkling liquid.

"What's that?" I asked him.

"Jager and Coke. Really helps me be more social with the students."

I looked at my watch. It was 8:10. *What the fuck have I gotten myself into?*

We made it about a block further

"Hold up one second. Hey, dude," he called out to some random guy standing outside a coffee shop. "Do you have a cigarette?"

The guy looked at him funny. He handed over one from his pack.

"Uh, do you have a lighter?" J-Bone asked. The guy looked at me. I shrugged and looked in the other direction.

He lit up the cigarette and we were on the way. On our walk to J-Bone's sought-after location, we saw two students walking toward us. J-Bone was still smoking his cigarette and sipping his Jager drink. I decided to approach them and see if I could get them my flyer.

"Good morning, guys. I don't want to bother you, but we work for a travel company here in Florence. We have a big sale going on. Here take one of our flyers so you can take a look later," I said.

They looked at each other.

"We are late for class. I have another one of those, sorry man."

"All good. Catch you guys around," I replied knowing that this would be part of the game.

They began walking away.

"Wait, wait, wait," J-Bone called out.

They turned around and looked at him,

J-Bone paused for ten seconds. He looked at me, looked back to them, and said, "Take one anyway. Do you guys want to party here? We can tell you all the good locations. Just hit us up."

J-Bone took a drag of his cig and sip of his drink. They looked at him like he was a freak, took a flyer, and got the hell out of there. They threw it away at the nearest trash can. He smiled at me with his wine-stained teeth, and we kept it moving.

At that point, I was almost positive that I absolutely blew it. Did I make a huge mistake? I moved to this foreign country knowing nobody, was essentially living in a crammed hostel, and now I was stuck with this kid who is getting fucked up at 8:00 in the morning. I started regretting my decision to move there. I should have just stayed home, chilled with my actual friends who were all parting ways, and lived with them. Now I was stuck. I had no idea what the hell I was going to do.

We got to his secret location, and it was a ghost town. We paced around the piazza in front of a church and only found locals who were relaxing in the quiet neighborhood where they knew they would not have to worry about seeing tourists. They certainly did not want to go on a trip with a bunch of college students. My regret was at an all-time high, and I needed to get out of there.

That night I had a conversation with my mom who assured me that the situation would turn around. She reminded me how many times I've gone into situations like those, and although sometimes it took time, I always figured out how to make the best out of them. I knew she was right, so I tried my best to keep my head in the game.

Fortunately, my regret only lasted a few days. As I spent more time with J-Bone, I realized he was an extremely genuine and nice person. His sense of humor grew on me, and I began to understand how everyone liked him so much.

When he was drinking a bottle of vino at 8:00 a.m., smoking a cigarette, and chatting up a random Italian girl, it was just J-Bone being J-Bone. He was harmless and despite his lack of hygiene, he was genuinely a good guy. On top of that, a few more of the guys flew in and we all hit it off immediately.

The first one was Andrew. A super humble and down-to-earth dude. He came in depending on the opportunity as his job and needed the income to make it through the summer. He struggled at first with his flyering attempts and had extreme doubt set in. I offered to go out flyering with him, taking turns to hand out our promo codes, to show him what I learned about soliciting people over the years.

I knew we did not benefit from helping other people succeed, but I was here to make friends. My income was solid, and any income that I earned here would be a bonus. I knew the money would come for me, and it always feels great to be able to help other people.

We hit the streets and found our groove. Andrew was getting his flyers out there, and we shared a ton of laughs and talked deeply about our bigger goals in life. I noticed that even though he was an attractive guy, he was rather reserved and quiet. Partnered together with my shamelessness, we made a perfect duo. We approached the groups of study-abroad sorority girls on the streets with extreme success.

All the girls in our company complained we had an unfair advantage. There was a minimal number of men who studied abroad, and when they approached other girls, they would just get looked at up and down. We would approach and get googly eyes, and they would take our flyer whether they wanted to travel or not. Supply and demand working at its finest, my friends.

Then there was Tyler. You know when you enter a social situation and you subconsciously gravitate toward someone else and immediately know they are best-friend caliber? Tyler was nineteen, only two years through college, and the absolute man. He rocked a full beard and a man bun that made him resemble no one other than Jesus himself. Tyler was a complete stud and all the ladies loved him. Thank god we had opposite tastes or else I'm sure our friendship would have been short-lived.

Being nineteen, he obviously could not drink back in the states. Here in Florence, it was an absolute free-for-all. He was ready for the time of his life. Since I had no financial stress and life was going smoothly, I was looking for the exact same experience. We could not have been more on the same page, and I knew that we were about to have an extraordinary experience.

The new lifestyle was coming together. Just a couple of days prior I thought I had made the biggest mistake of my life. Now I could not have better feelings about the situation. With all of the momentum of positive energy, our experience was poised to only get better. Just one week into my time there, I attracted a person into my life who falls into a small group of individuals that have single-handedly shaped me into who I am today.

15

YOU WORK WITH ME NOW

A BIG FACTOR that separated us from the other travel companies was that we were able to go out and enjoy the nightlife scene. The other companies restricted it, but ours understood the importance of camaraderie for building relationships with the students. The students wanted to travel with people they considered to be friends and knew they would have fun with.

When we went out and had a great night with them, they ended up wanting to spend more time with us and, in turn, bought our trips. For me, this was the area I would flourish in and needed to take advantage of the most.

Our first night out on the city was one that changed my entire experience there. Everyone went to the local Conad to purchase their wine and cheap vodka. They were all dependent upon the unpromised commissions from selling trips and needed to save money wherever possible. I grabbed a bottle of my favorite: Bombay Sapphire.

We began the pregame in the sauna that we called our apartment. The guys were shirtless, sitting around fans with a cup full of their drink of choice. We took turns playing our favorite music while opening up about our backgrounds and where we came from. The conversation went deep as we began to develop our relationships with one another.

When 11:30 p.m. hit, we went to the bar directly across the street from our apartment: Green Street. All of the veterans said that we had a fantastic relationship with the owners and that this was the spot they always promoted to go before the club. We collected the squad and headed on down.

At first glance, I was unimpressed. The narrow front entrance was completely open to the street, where people poured out and flooded the sidewalk. I noticed the neon green sign above the door that said "Green" within a circle as I walked inside. The crammed area contained a small bar on the right, and a little bit of space to get by on the left when it was not crowded with people. There was also a small loft upstairs with a few tables and chairs. At first, I questioned why we would limit ourselves to a bar that small, but for that first night, I decided to just go with the flow.

We were having a great time sending around shots, meeting students, and preparing for the real party at the club after. During this, the inner businessman inside me could not help but look around and evaluate the situation at hand.

I looked behind the bar and saw a shorter white guy appearing to be in his early thirties pointing in different directions trying to keep up with the orders flying in. Next to him was a taller African dude, with his headphones in, taking a pull off a hookah. He had a pair of designer shades resting on the back of his head atop well-groomed twist curls and was dressed in a full Armani jump suit.

I could tell by his presence and demeanor alone that he was the guy who ran the show. I watched as he quickly ran through the crowd outside and started shouting on his phone in a language I had never heard before. My roommate Hannah pointed to them.

"That's Bryan and Poggi. They own this bar together. They are both people you need to know. I'll introduce you," she said as she pulled me toward them.

First, she introduced me to the guy behind the cash register, Poggi. He had just finished yelling in Italian to one of the bartenders. He looked over to me.

"This is John. He just started working with Smart Trip," Hannah said.

"S'up dude?" he said as he shook my hand while barely making eye contact. He quickly returned to the chaos he was a part of.

"Seems like a dick," I said to Hannah.

"No, no, he's awesome, he's just busy. You'll have to come around a couple of times so that he starts to recognize you."

As we turned around, Bryan was passing by.

"Bryan. This is John. He just started working here," she said as she stopped him.

"Hey!" he said as he took a moment to stop, smile large, and shake my hand. He then quickly ran off to the other side of the room and began talking on his phone in yet another language.

"He is always running around like a crazy person," Hannah said.

"He will remember you, though, and he's a very important person to know. He runs the entire club scene in Florence. I do some work with him on the side promoting the different clubs. I get free entry and drinks pretty much everywhere. It's awesome," she bragged.

I looked around and noticed the people who had worked for the company for a while getting special treatment. They were handed drinks for free, standing behind the bar, and essentially doing whatever they pleased. It seemed like the hookup I had in college, and I wanted the same, but I knew it would take some time.

You cannot expect to just show up somewhere and have the red carpets unrolled. You need to earn respect and prove your value. Also, relationships don't form overnight. I was not offended by Poggi and Bryan being short with me. I knew the game and knew that they would see me as an asset soon enough.

We wrapped it up at the bar and walked to the Monday night club, Yab. On our journey over, I could hardly comprehend the beauty of the marvels we passed. Every turn featured hand-carved statues and ancient architectural masterpieces that far defeated the test of time. The city radiated a magic similar to that of Disneyland, and I was so grateful to call it my new home.

When we arrived, the front entrance was roped off and a line extended from the entrance all the way down the block. I went to get in line, but Hannah motioned for me to come with her. She went to the front of the line where the bouncers ran over and hugged her.

They unhooked the red rope and let her in, then went to shut me and a couple of others out. She said something to them, they looked at me displeased, then let us in. We got handed bracelets to access the VIP portion of the club and made our way down the swanky hallway inside.

There was hardly any room to move with people chatting and dancing everywhere. The entire place was illuminated in blue and pink flashing lights, and I could see why the line to enter was so long. The venue radiated elegance and prestige as I felt as if I had just entered a party full of celebrities and the wealthy. To top it off, it was hip-hop night, and the music catered perfectly to my taste. The energy of the club took ahold of me.

We walked as a group up to the VIP section and were escorted right in. Hannah brought us over to the biggest table right next to the DJ booth. Sitting at it was an African dude decked out in a Gucci jumpsuit. At first glance, I was convinced that Biggie Smalls had been reincarnated. He was wearing a large pair of shades, and a magnum-sized bottle of Grey Goose was sitting in front of him in a bucket of ice.

I shook his hand and he motioned toward the bottle and told us all to help ourselves. This was my first interaction with Abraham, Bryan's partner in the nightlife business.

Our entire group took full advantage of the hospitality received. We were drinking from the bottle, dancing, and having the time of our lives together. As I looked down from the elevated platform at the sea of people swaying to the music, I could not believe it was my first time going out in the city and I was able to skip the entire line, get escorted right into VIP, and drink as much as I wanted for free. We partied away next to the DJ booth until the lights came on and left the club feeling like we just walked out of a music video.

As I walked outside, the bouncers were everywhere trying to facilitate the drunken herd going home. Out of the corner of my eye, I saw Bryan standing there, no longer with his headphones in. He was also dressed like a rock star, with his outfit highlighting the two Gs of his Gucci belt sticking out. I walked up and said what's up to him, and, sure enough, he remembered me.

"Love the belt, dude!" I said to him as I flashed the Gucci belt I had gotten in Italy a year earlier.

He put on a huge grin.

"You like Gucci? You come with me tomorrow. We go to the Gucci store. I get 50 percent off anything you want," he fired out in his choppy accent.

The next day Bryan and his Gucci connect brought me to the outlet and their private stash where they let me buy any item I wanted for a huge discount. The entire trip he treated me with cordiality like we had known each other for years. I was blown away that I had just met him twenty-four hours earlier and he already took me under his wing like a brother. I was also so fascinated by the influence and power Bryan had.

That's why when he dropped me off after the shopping spree and patted me on the shoulder with a huge smile and said, "You work with me now," I asked no questions.

I was not positive what this entailed, but I really did not need to know. There are certain times in life where you do not need to ask any questions. You just take the opportunity in front of you and run with it. That was one of those moments.

I returned to the apartment to find my roommates who also worked for Bryan to figure out what working with him entailed. They explained to me how Bryan and Abraham ran the largest nightlife promotion agency in the city—Florence First Class Promotions. Their group had partnerships with all of the best venues in the city and promoted a different party each night of the week. Our job was to bring as many students as possible to the clubs. Additionally, it was even better if they bought bottle service.

Our whole job with Smart Trip involved meeting students and showing them a good time. Some trips we hosted would have over 150 students on them. Bryan and Abraham understood how many people we interacted with and the influence we had over where they would go out and party while in Florence. They also understood if they provided us with VIP treatment at the nightclubs, it would help with our influence levels and in turn help sell more trips. It was a win-win for everyone.

I knew I could kill it with club promoting, but I wanted someone I could partner with. I told Tyler about my new work with Bryan and that we had to get him into the same position. We knew we could crush it together, and it would also be cool to have a venture we could work on together. Over the course of the next week, we finagled him into the same position, and we were eager to get the show started.

16

FROM SELLING UMBRELLAS TO RUNNING THE CITY

THE NEW NIGHTLIFE gig kicked off with a bang. We began going to all of the best nightclubs in Florence and were treated with the utmost importance. We were escorted straight to VIP and given either a handful of drink tickets or bottle service upon entrance, all for free.

We loved the treatment, but I knew that we would need to produce in order to keep it up. It was also important to remember what we were truly there for—selling trips. If we were not selling, we would be fired.

The flyering had gotten me a decent amount of sales, but where I hit it big the first semester was with social media. I had never used social media as a platform to monetize up until that point. I was also behind the game. Most of the people I worked with did prep work to connect with the incoming students on Facebook before they got to Florence. I had not made a single effort until I arrived in the city. I decided I would give it a shot one afternoon because social media would be a much better option than sweating my ass off in the streets.

I started off with what I thought would be the most efficient strategy: connect with the people who had the highest probability of responding to me. That meant the study-abroad population that came from UCONN. I was easily able to get into their Facebook group and had immediate access to their entire list of students. I noticed that I had a ton of mutual friends with them from back home and that most of my coworkers were not on that list.

I went down the list adding them all and the requests were being accepted immediately. Next, I would send a generic message. It would be along the lines of this:

"Hey, Jack. I'm reaching out to you because I noticed you will be studying abroad in Florence this summer. I live here and work for a student travel company that offers the best-priced trips to destinations all over Italy and Europe. Additionally, I work with all of the night clubs in the city. If you ever have questions about traveling, nightlife, good places to eat, or anything about the city in general, feel free to reach out, and I'll definitely be able to help you. Hope to see you in Florence."

For this particular group of UCONN students, mostly everyone replied to my message. I had a genuine conversation with them and helped answer all their questions. This would then typically result in their using my discount code and sharing it with their friends. It also had them reserving tables at the different clubs I told them about. This was the first time I experienced the power of what we are able to do with social media from a business stance.

After the success I had with this group, I started connecting with other students I could find studying abroad in the city. This did not work as well. Most of my coworkers had already friend requested them and sent their spiel. Most people did not respond to my friend request, ignored my message, or told me to go die. I took no offense to it though. That's just how the numbers work in the game of sales.

I now felt comfortable with the level of sales I brought in. I was in the top tier and knew that I had surpassed the possibility of getting fired. The next stage for us was to actually start conducting the trips we had sold. This was the part of the experience I looked forward to the most. We were literally getting paid to travel to the best destinations in Italy and Europe. How does it get better than that?

The office assigned the trips based on people's experience, the number of sales they had overall, and the number of sales they had for a particular destination. Overall, the more sales you had, the more trips you went on.

The leadership roles for the trip were Tour Manager, Tour Leader, and Tour Guide. We only had Tour Managers for our trips of over 100 students, which was not too often. The Tour Leader was in charge of the whole trip. Mostly that involved making sure every piece of the trip was executed properly and smoothly (which never happened).

The Tour Guide was simply there to help the Leader. Normally that person would go around interacting with the students, make sure that no one was left behind, and take pictures. This is the position where you learned the trip so eventually you could lead it yourself.

For the entire summer, I went on every single trip as a Guide. I started off with simple day-trips to Venice, Cinque Terre, and local vineyards, but as more sales came in, they sent me on the bigger trips like Croatia, Budapest, Vienna, Salzburg, and the Amalfi Coast. I was fortunate enough to experience most of these amazing destinations multiple times, and I made sure to take advantage to the fullest extent.

I would always eat the traditional food, partake in all of the local activities, and fully immerse myself in the culture. Further, I made sure to build relationships with every student on the trip. Typically, we would get along great and they would want to hang out after the trip. This would result in their using my code to purchase more trips and in their coming to party with us at the clubs.

It only took a few weeks as club promoters before Tyler and I had the scene on lock. We cut no corners and did whatever was necessary in order to earn respect. One of my great friends, a Haitian guy we called Pretty Face, was also a club promoter and set me up for ultimate success. He moved there by himself a year prior, and I remember being blown away as soon as I met him.

He was twenty-one at the time and had just recovered from a meningitis scare that left him in a coma and nearly took his life. This resulted in him having black splotches all over his body, except for his face. Hence, Pretty Face. He spoke four different languages, was completely self-sufficient, and had one of the most profound mindsets and outlooks on life that I have ever encountered.

In one of our early conversations he told me that when he first moved to the city, he saw Bryan and Abraham and wanted to be like them. The issue for him was that he had zero influence, and they did not see where he could provide value. So he started using his food money to pay for club entry and began to make a name for himself.

Every night he would shake the hand of every single worker, from the big shots all the way down to the bathroom workers, until people began to recognize him and started giving him free entry. From there, he began to immerse himself in the study-abroad population and brought them to the club. Once they saw that he was generating business, they gave him a spot as a promoter.

His advice to me was just that. Shake every hand of every person and greet them with a huge smile, every single night. At first, the people may be cold, but after a while, they will remember you and grow to like you from the consistent outgoing gestures alone. I saw the results that he had, so I made sure to follow his advice every single night.

After doing it for just one month, every single person working at the club would go out of their way to give me a warm greeting and make sure I was taken care of.

The Summer '16 Smart Trip squad outside of Green Street promoting a club event on the Fourth of July. I am crouched in the front and center.

*A scene from the VIP section in Space Club Florence where I promoted
with Bryan Sow (center of picture with dashiki and sunglasses)
and Tyler Chimarusti (between Bryan and John).*

As we built more and more relationships throughout the summer,
our influence skyrocketed. Our pregames at Green Street would be
packed to capacity with an overflow of people partying out on the
streets. I earned my spot behind the bar and would even throw on
a playlist of my preferred music. When it was time for the club, we
would gather the entire crowd and lead them to the venue.

I specifically remember one night where Tyler and I were marching
through the narrow cobblestone streets, and as we approached the
club, we looked back and could not even see the end of the crowd
following us. There must have been over one hundred people, with a
good portion of them purchasing VIP tables and bottles. I shot Tyler
a huge grin as the bouncers let down the red rope and escorted us
directly to the VIP section. My life was beginning to feel like a movie.

Almost every single night extended until 4:00 a.m. The 8:00 a.m.
rule still applied, so we would have to be out of the apartment early
the next morning. I would get out most of the time, but I stopped
flyering during the day. I found it to be inefficient and a waste of time.

Instead, we would typically get breakfast at our favorite spot while the rest of the crew would normally go flyer, and I would complete my routine. This consisted of heading to the gym, having my protein shake and showering, then heading over to Green to practice my Italian.

Every day I spent about an hour on Rosetta Stone, getting better and better at the language.

Bryan's boy whom we called Ba was normally at Green around this time. He only spoke Italian. I would always practice talking with him. Mainly I worked on my humor, or what I at least thought was funny, and he would always laugh every time he saw me because he knew something ridiculous was soon to be said. The majority of our relationship was fueled by body language and energy. It's fascinating how unimportant actual words can be to building a great relationship.

When evening came around, we always had a variety of options. Our Monday night routine was dinner at a restaurant on our street called Rubaconte. They had a fantastic deal where they offered unlimited appetizers, bottomless wine, and either four kinds of pasta or steak and potatoes. If we brought three students to dinner with us, our meal was free. We normally packed the dining room out and never had to pay for a meal.

One of my favorite places to go during the evenings was the Piazzale Di Michelangelo. This giant platform overlooked the entire city of Florence and the surrounding Tuscan hills. We would walk up there and simply sit on the staircase overlooking the screen saver–esque view. To this day, this spot is my favorite in the entire world.

No matter how many times I went there, it always felt like the first. I could sit up there forever and admire the rolling Tuscan mountains surrounding the city tucked away in the valley. The architectural marvels, like the Duomo and Santa Croce Church, towered over the low-rise building line covered in orange clay shingles. The curving Arno River that swept beneath the iconic Ponte Vecchio. The music that someone was always playing on an accordion.

Then the eventual sunset that would fall right into the Arno river and set the whole city on fire. There is truly not a sight like it.

When we were up there, it was like an escape. All of the fast-paced club life and chaos from our prior weekend trip was forgotten. Living in a brothel with nine people. The bullshit anyone was dealing with from the office for not having enough sales. None of it mattered. When we were up there, it was pure gratitude. We remembered why we were there and could not be more thankful for the experience we were having at such a young age. It was the times that I was sitting there that I looked around, reflected on my life so far, and realized this is what it was all about.

When Thursday night rolled around, it was time to roll out for our weekend trips. We always met at the same spot, where we would load up the buses and account for all of the students. Then, depending on our destination, the bus ride would be anywhere from six to twelve hours.

I remember absolutely dreading the rides, but they eventually grew on me. It was a great time to relax, enjoy the beauty of the European countryside, and, of course, watch *Mean Girls* for the fiftieth time.

Then there was my relationship with Bryan. We thoroughly exceeded his expectations of what we were capable of when it came to club promotion, and he began to treat me like royalty. He would go above and beyond to make sure I was taken care of and truly felt like an older brother to me. Our conversations were typically brief, and the running around yelling on the phone never stopped, but I knew it was just part of the hustle.

Every now and then, Bryan would randomly find me and take me along on what would always be a crazy adventure. I learned quickly that when Bryan said, "Come with me," you didn't ask questions. You stopped whatever you were doing, and you went. He took me along to dinner at his family's house, to the jewelry store, to restock the bar, to the best seafood place in the city, and much more.

One day, however, I seriously began to believe there was nothing the man was not capable of.

The biggest event of the year was going down in Florence. This is called Calcio Storico. Each of the four major neighborhoods would assemble a team to compete in this sport that is a cross of rugby, soccer, and MMA. Highly regarded as the most violent sport on the planet, this shit is no joke.

The men competing were mostly ex-convicts who would train all year to literally kick ass. The huge piazza in front of the Santa Croce church would be turned into a modern-day gladiator stadium. The entire city of Florence would let loose for this event whose roots run deep in the history of their city, with origins dating back nearly 600 years.

I remember the event happening when I studied abroad the year before but was unable to secure tickets and attend. Since the event is only two matches played one weekend with the final match the following weekend, it was difficult to secure a seat even if you were willing to pay the price.

For the weekend of the championship, I desperately wanted to go, but I had given up. Tickets were sold out, and there were three layers of security that left no chance of me finagling my way in. I decided to chill at Green Street, practice my Italian, and watch it on the big screen there. I was up in the loft, and I remember as the games were about to begin you could hear the roar in the streets.

Packs of Italians were stomping down the road, wearing their neighborhood color, and screaming at the tops of their lungs in anticipation of what was sure to be a spectacle. I was bummed out, but it would still be cool to catch it on TV. Minutes later, Bryan came running in from god knows what he was doing before. He looked up at the TV.

"Ohhhh shit. You see this, John?"

"Yeah, bro. I wanted to go but it's impossible to get in."

Bryan looked at the TV then back to me.

"Come with me," he said.

No questions asked. I left my belongings at the bar and started following him down the street.

Out of all the time I spent in Italy, I never saw a sight like this. The Italians hated how Americans came and were shit faced all the time. They rarely lost their composure and were disgusted when they saw the sometimes belligerent Americans storming the streets. The tables had turned completely.

Mobs of people were chanting and screaming. It looked like a rebellion was about to occur as police and security were making their best effort to maintain order on the streets. People were shoving, pushing, and fighting to get closer to the action. I had no idea what the plan was, but I continued to follow Bryan.

We approached the first line of security. The sawhorses could barely hold people back as they were waving their tickets, angry they had not been let in yet. Bryan walked up to the first security guard he saw.

"Bryan, *Come Va!*"

Bryan smiled and shook his hand. He pointed back to me and the security guard moved the sawhorse to the side and let us both through, no questions asked. As I passed by, he shook my hand and gave me a huge smile.

We approached the next line of security. At this point, everybody was holding their ticket for the event. We were empty handed. Again, Bryan went to the first guard he saw. He immediately gave Bryan a hug and let him past, but then stepped in front of me.

"No, no, no. He comes with me," Bryan told the guard as he waved his hand signaling me to keep moving forward. The guard gave me a look as if he were trying to figure out who I was and then let me through.

We were now inside the event. The ground was shaking and the entire place was roaring. The two final teams remaining were Santa Croce sporting blue, and Santa Maria Novella rocking red. As I looked at the layout of the stadium, I saw a wall of fans wearing red on the far end line with the enormous and intricate marble facade of the Santa Croce church behind them, mirrored by a wall of fans wearing blue on the opposite end. Bryan headed straight for the lower level seating at midfield.

Without any surprises, the next security guard knew Bryan as well. This one was a girl, and she greeted him and then let us by with a huge smile. We proceeded to walk in and took a seat at the front row of the arena just minutes before the teams were to be announced. With three handshakes, Bryan had gotten us into the best seats at the biggest city event of the year.

"You like that shit?" Bryan said with a smile as he dapped me up.

"Couldn't appreciate you more, man. Thank you."

The announcer came on and the chaos began. I could make out about every third word he was saying in his screaming, lightning-fast Italian mixed with the roar of the crowd. I realized that he was bringing out the blue team first as their section started chanting "Azzurri, Azzurri!" As soon as the chanting began, the fans began climbing up the fence separating them from the arena. There must have been twenty people, and they were all holding blue smoke bombs.

Before I knew it, the whole backdrop and half the arena were covered in a blue cloud. Streams of fireworks were launching in the air and exploding all over the place. From the sounds of it, people were also lighting off firecrackers in trash cans, which elevated the screaming even more.

Then it switched. The other side of the field started screaming and chanting. I had absolutely no idea what they were saying, but it sounded fierce. As their team came out to enter the arena, they began lighting off red smoke bombs and fireworks. The red smokescreen collided with the blue, and I could not see anything now. Nobody seemed concerned so I figured why should I be? I was fired up and ready to see this event go down.

The entire piazza of cobblestone was covered in a thick layer of dirt. On each end of the field was a wall, then a low net that rose a couple of feet above it. That was the goal and the teams were supposed to get the soccer ball in it by any means possible. That was how you won. Simple, right?

After a ceremony with hundreds of people marching around the arena in colorful jester-esque outfits, the players lined up with their teams. Their arms were over one another's shoulders in a line, staring down the opposing team just a few feet away. A long moment of silence occurred as both teams prepared for battle. The silence broke, everyone started clapping and going crazy, and the players went to take their positions in the arena. The whistle blew.

What happened next I did not expect at all. Instead of going for the ball, every single player matched up with someone on the opposing team and squared up. Fists began flying. People were running, launching their bodies, and kicking. Goliath men were grabbing their opponents and body-slamming them into the earth. Men were pouring blood and getting knocked out cold.

Paramedics with stretchers were running onto the field and collecting the bodies as they dropped. There was no exaggeration when people explained this sport as a competition of modern-day gladiators.

Throughout the match, the teams attempted to score, but often were thrown into the bleachers or beaten to oblivion. By the end, every man who had not left on a stretcher had either a broken nose or a limp as they left the field. Regardless if they needed facial reconstruction or a hip replacement, they all left the arena with the utmost respect from the entire city for their valor.

When it was over, Bryan and I resumed business as usual. Huge pregame at Green Street and then straight to the club. The club that night, Space, was about a thirty-minute walk. I had no desire to walk, so I went outside to hail a taxi. Bryan abruptly stopped me and offered to drive me.

As I said before, my conversations with Bryan never went crazily deep. We were both hustlers and had a mutual appreciation of each other's capabilities. We made shit happen, then made it happen again, and then again. However, I was starting to get curious about what exactly his true background entailed. I knew who he was currently, where he came from in Senegal, and even met parts of his family. But I wanted to know his story.

I knew he came from humble beginnings, and I wanted to know how he made all of this happen. We could not go anywhere without people praising him and rolling out the red carpet. So as he was driving me in his BMW to the best club in the city, I decided to ask.

"Bryan, how did you do all of this? How did you get into the position you are in now? You have this entire city and nightlife scene on lock, but where did you start?" I asked him.

"You see that, bro? It's crazy." He laughed. "I come here and I would do anything. We sold umbrellas on the street. I bag groceries at the store. Whatever. I don't care. I would take every opportunity."

I could sense some nostalgia as he was staring down the street ahead.

"Over time, I meet more and more people, do some work with the clubs, meet Abraham and we just make it happen. Then we start to know everybody in the city and decide to do our own thing. Now—" He motioned his arm in a circle toward the city that he had risen to the top of.

"You can do anything, bro. Anything. Just want it bad enough. Then, remember where you come from. Take care of your family. Your family is everything. I'm telling you."

We pulled onto the street where Space was and there was already a mob of people waiting to be let past the red ropes. He pulled up front and we hopped out of the car.

This small talk, although it may have been brief, had a tremendous impact that has stuck with me to this day. No classroom or teacher could possibly convey to me the lesson that had resonated with me at that moment. This was real.

Up until my short study-abroad experiences just a year earlier, I had spent my whole life in the United States. The true land of opportunity where there are no rules surrounding success. Where it could not be more possible to take control of your life with some determination and grit.

Constantly we see people rise to stardom, introduce a groundbreaking product, create a business that impacts the lives of millions. People who understand that we are so blessed to live in a place where you are able to risk it all to chase your passion.

Yet, the majority of our population settles for much less than they are capable of, are ungrateful, and show pure jealousy and envy toward the ones who make it big. All because they did not have the courage to go after their own dreams. Then, they sit there and shame the people who have made it because they are miserable with their current situation, even though they have access to the same resources to make their dreams happen if they are willing to dig deep enough. In the land that has the most abundance to offer, it is full of people with a mindset of pure scarcity.

Meanwhile, we have men like Bryan in the world. He was born in a place where his ancestors were kidnapped from their very homes and forcefully brought across the sea to be tormented as slaves. His outlook and opportunities for success were slim to none. Regardless of his efforts, it would be unlikely for him to make something of himself strictly based upon the circumstances he was born into. So what did he do?

He let none of this deter him. He got out of his country and came to Italy. He did quite literally anything he could to earn some money and make a name for himself. He learned six different languages to communicate with everyone around him. He knew he wanted more and what he wanted to make of himself, and he went for it. No excuses, no feeling bad for himself, and certainly no promises of success.

This made me think even deeper. What is everybody else's excuse? What is my excuse? People are bitching and complaining that they have to go to work so that they can pay for their apartment, car, cell phone, and clothes. They complain about how hard life is and how unfair it is. They do not even realize that people are waking up daily without even the most basic of necessities with no idea where their next meal is going to come from. Where they are going to get clean drinking water. If they will even survive to see another day. People who would be ecstatic to have a stable roof over their heads.

The majority of people do not even have the slightest idea of how lucky and fortunate we all are. They take life's gifts for granted and have zero gratitude. They play the victim and come from a place of scarcity, without even realizing how blessed they are to be born as who they are, in the place they live, at this specific time in history. It has never been more possible to do whatever it is you set your mind to.

So what is holding people back? They have created a story. A story they tell themselves of why it cannot possibly be them. Why everyone else is so lucky, but how they got the shit end of the stick. And what is the very reason they aren't getting what they want? It is because they actually believe these stories they are telling themselves.

At that moment so much gratitude rushed through my veins. I felt like I had already known how fortunate I was, but right then is when it really hit me. I felt terrible that I ever complained about situations that did not go my way or complained about my circumstances. If Bryan made it happen, there is absolutely no reason that anybody else on the planet cannot bring their dreams to fruition as well.

"Stank! You coming or what?" One of the students yelled to me from across the street as they were about to make their entrance into VIP.

I snapped back into the present. I looked over at the group of students eagerly waiting to enter the club to get their magnum Grey Goose bottles we had sold them.

"Let's get it!" I yelled back.

17

FINESSING WITH THE FLYER MONSTER

THE SUMMER BLEW by like a LaFerrari on the German autobahn. Tyler and I decided to cap it off with a two-week European adventure to Amsterdam, Dublin, Iceland, and Stockholm before he returned to the states for school. After one of the greatest adventures of my life, I returned to Florence ready to tackle one more semester.

Within our company, there was an abnormally high turnover rate due to the cutthroat nature of our job, and most of the people I worked with during the summer returned to the United States. They needed stable pay, stable hours, and a lifestyle that did not involve a 24/7 grind. For me, I knew this semester would be better than ever.

I had formed so many valuable connections, was fully supported financially with my growing Network Marketing business, and now had seniority in the travel company. It would have been foolish for me to return without first reaping the benefits of the groundwork I put in to get where I was.

The new workers began to arrive over the next few days, and we saw there would be a serious problem. Our apartment had an extra promoter staying with us; the downstairs apartment had two extra promoters; and the company leased a new apartment down the street for five more promoters.

By the end of the summer we added twelve promoters and now had twenty-three. They had drastically overstaffed and many red flags were raised. The rumor going around was that the new apartment was on a month-to-month lease, with the plan being to fire at least five or six people in order to consolidate. Everybody freaked out and prepared to do whatever was necessary to avoid the chopping block.

Toward the end of the summer, I diligently worked to add incoming students on social media, messaged them, and started to provide value. However, most of the other promoters prepared the same way. Countless hours of social media work landed me three trips sold. I knew the dynamics had changed, and I would need to get creative in order to compete in the new semester.

I figured I could make it up with traditional flyering; however, the first day out on the streets painted the picture for exactly how that method of promotion would go. About a week before students arrived, our manager posted a schedule with exact locations of where the study-abroad schools were, what day students arrived, and what time their orientation would be. Typically, this would be information you would have to uncover on your own, but they handed it right to everybody.

The first orientation was at 8:00 a.m. on a Tuesday. Every single alarm in the apartment went off at 7:00 a.m. Both the newbies and veterans packed their bags with promotional flyers and headed to what would become an absolute war zone. I foolishly joined in and was appalled at what I witnessed upon arrival at the battle scene.

All twenty-three of the promoters from our company were staggered around the street at all potential entry points of the school building. To top it off, at least fifty more promoters from the other three rival travel companies were present, locked and loaded with promotional materials of their own.

Moments before, the area was a peaceful piazza where one could relax on the San Lorenzo church steps, shop in the famous outdoor leather market, or take in the view of the Duomo's orange cap towering above the low-rise buildings. Now, it was a war zone littered with weekend trip slingers desperately attempting to meet their sales quotas.

Although everyone was technically competing with one another, our company did band together when it came to hatred for the other companies. It was a never-ending battle of sabotage among all of us. Immature? Maybe. But it was one hell of a way to stay on our toes and keep a competitive edge. Plus, there was an oddly enjoyable feeling that came from stealing their sales.

All four companies stood on the street, facing off against each other. I envisioned in my head the Calcio Storico event from the summer. I almost sprinted across the street and drop-kicked my archnemesis from our biggest rival company, but then I snapped back to reality and realized I was not a gladiator and I would just get charged for assault. I settled for a flyering battle.

At 7:45 a.m., a group of four girls dressed in jean shorts, spaghetti string tank tops, and backpacks approached with obnoxiously loud voices as they had their phones out to Snapchat their first morning in the city. All telltale signs of American study-abroad students. Another group appeared behind them. The gates were officially open, and it was every man for himself.

I saw my competitor going for the group of girls, so I dashed over, cut him off, and handed over a stack of my travel deals. He looked at me with disgust. I taunted him with a fat grin and a head nod.

By the time I turned to find my next target, every group of students was being bombarded by every single company. It was like sharks feeding on a school of bloody baitfish. The students were being flanked from every direction and began to run for cover in the safety of their institution. I tried to approach another group, and one girl screamed telling me to go fuck myself.

I looked around the street. There was simply no hope. The garbage cans were overflowing with our flyers. Even the best veteran flyer guy we had, Drapes, was striking out left and right. The teachers began coming out into the streets and shooing us away. After a short-lived battle, I saw no hope for victory. I retreated and knew that a new plan needed to be devised. After our embarrassing loss, all the promoters regrouped at Green Street.

"We are all fucked," said one of the new girls, Caitie.

"Maybe you are, but I went to a different section of the city and handed out twenty flyers," another kid said. Everyone looked at him with jealousy, but I knew he was lying.

"Face it, guys, we are all getting fired. Might as well enjoy our time in Florence while we are here," said one of the new guys. He approached the bar and ordered a tall beer. A few others joined him.

Everybody eventually dispersed to try and make some sales. I sat at Green on my computer and stared at the schedule that management had given us. All of a sudden, I noticed a key piece of information that changed the entire semester for me.

I looked over at Drapes, the promoter who had been with the company the longest, who was still at Green as well. Until that point, we had not talked much since he went home for the majority of the summer, but I heard stories about how well he did.

I have to admit, when I first heard that he led the company in sales, it surprised me. I would never have guessed that out of everyone, the short and pale guy who always carried a smug look on his face, was the top seller. Normally, he would have 700+ sales, while the average promoter would finish the semester with fewer than 100.

Everybody would try to validate why he had so many sales and they could not. They would say his promo code was easier to remember, that he's been here so long that sales fell into his lap, or that he stole other people's sales. I knew how people acted when someone outperformed them, so I took all of this with a grain of salt. I decided to ask him.

"Yo, Drapes. I heard you always trounce the rest of the company in sales. What do you normally do if you don't mind me asking? I know you probably don't want to share, but I feel like none of the traditional promotion methods are going to cut it this year."

"Dude, I'm just a flyer monster. I would normally go out on the street from eight in the morning until it's dark out and hand out flyers to everyone I came across. Last year my feet would be bleeding by the time I got back. There's really no secret. I just researched where the most students would be and would spend all day getting my flyers out to as many people as possible.

"That's it. But I'm not sure what I'm going to do now. The company gave away key information I normally would have to research on my own. Plus, nobody wants to take a flyer because there are way too many promoters."

I thought to myself for a minute. Should I share with him what I just found? I could easily take advantage of this myself, but it's always more fun to have a partner in crime. Plus, if I shared this, I was sure Drapes would have much more value he could provide to me in the future. I decided that it could be the start of a mutually beneficial relationship.

"I think I found something we can do. Come take a look at this," I said.

He perked up and came over to my computer.

"So look at this schedule. It has all of the orientation times and locations. All of the classroom building locations. All of the start dates for every program. The issue is, everyone has access to this information now and the buildings will be swarmed. It will be a repeat of this morning for every single one of the orientations," I explained.

"But look at this." I pointed to the next five days coming up on the schedule. "They also included the arrival dates for every single one of the schools coming into the city."

"So?" Drapes asked. "That just means the promoters are going to be all over their campuses harassing them with flyers."

"Exactly, which is perfect. Because here's the thing. There's only one place for them to arrive when they come into the city: the airport."

A light bulb went off in his head.

"Instead of dicking around, competing with all of these other promoters, and trying to get our promo code to these students who want nothing to do with us, we do this instead," I proposed.

"We leave the apartment before everyone wakes up, get a cab to the airport for the next five days, and stay there all day. Airplanes full of students are going to arrive, they are going to be pumped for the experience coming up, and we simply greet them: 'Welcome to Florence!' with a huge smile and hand them a flyer. They will have had no exposure to what they are about to deal with inside the city limits, and I'll bet they welcome it with open arms. Instead of battling for scraps, let's go straight to the honey hole."

"I am 100 percent in," he said. "Let's do this. I appreciate you sharing this with me."

Without any further conversation, we locked into the plan. We went back to the apartment that night and started to prepare hundreds of flyers. Everyone laughed at us.

"What are you going to do with all of those? I spent all day promoting and couldn't even get out ten," one girl said.

"Just trying to be prepared for the best possible outcome," I replied as Drapes shot me a grin.

The next morning, we began to execute the plan. Drapes had his own room, so he set his alarm for 6:30 so nobody else would hear it. He came down to our room and quietly woke me up so that we could sneak off undetected. Upon waking up, I realized two of the younger guys were already gone. I hoped they did not have the same idea that I did.

With our backpacks filled with hundreds of flyers, we snuck off into the streets. It was a beautiful morning, the air was crisp, and the street cleaners had all of the sidewalks squeaky clean. You could literally eat a serving of penne ala vodka off the curbs. I was always impressed with how spotless they kept the city.

We headed to the taxi stand, summoned a cab to the airport, and the mission was under way. As soon as we took off, the other promoters hit the group chat asking where we were. They knew we were up to something. We decided no response would be the best course of action.

The arrivals terminal was empty other than the guards who were holding assault rifles. I gave one a head nod as I passed through the glass doors into what would soon become the scene of the greatest promotional effort the Florence travel industry had ever seen.

We walked straight to the arrivals board to see what we were working with. Typically, the study-abroad flights came from Newark or JFK, connected in Zurich, Paris, or Dusseldorf, and then landed in Florence. We looked at the monitor and saw a flight coming in from Zurich in two hours. We took a seat and waited for the frenzy.

Two hours later on the dot, I looked over to the arrival gate. A group of five girls who had neck pillows on with their hair in sloppy buns and their school letters across the chest of their oversized hoodies came out into the waiting area with faces full of excitement. Two ladies in red shirts with the school name on the front were there to greet everyone and get them to their apartments safely—just like what had been done for me the previous year. Then a group of eight girls came out, then another ten. Before we knew it, the lobby was full. I looked at Drapes.

"Game time," I said with a grin. He nodded. We both picked a side of the room and worked our way in.

"Hey guys, hope you had a great flight, welcome to Florence," I said to the first group of girls.

"Oh my god. Thank you so much. I'm dying to travel to the Amalfi Coast while I'm here," said one girl as she gracefully accepted my flyer. I handed four more to her friends. I approached the next group.

"What's going on, girls? I hope you guys enjoy your stay here in Florence," I said with excitement as my plan was going flawlessly. They all accepted with a huge grin and thanked me.

"Hey? Can I get one of those?" a random girl came up to me and asked.

"Absolutely. Here you go," I said as I handed her a flyer.

She looked back. "Can I have some for my friends as well?"

"Absolutely!" I smiled and handed her a stack of flyers.

We continued until every single person in the lobby had an orange flyer. I saw Drapes on the other side of the room and now knew what he meant when he referred to himself as a flyer monster. All I saw was orange flashes as he handed out flyers faster than people could take them. It was a sheer numbers game. Meanwhile, the teachers noticed us but did not say a word. The guards stood there, assault rifles in hand, simply looking forward. It was an unbelievable success.

After the first wave of students cleared out, we regrouped. We each had gotten out over fifty of our flyers in a fifteen-minute period. Two full days of street flyering in the books and I would be surprised if anyone got out over twenty in total. Plus, they were running around the hot city streets sweating their asses off after people who avoided them like the plague. We were sitting in the airport AC letting the sales come to us and being thanked.

The next group of students arrived no more than an hour later. Same thing. We both started on opposite ends of the room and worked our way in. People thanked us, began asking more questions, and were distributing our flyers to their friends. The plan was going exactly according to the playbook, but, of course, you always hit some sort of turbulence no matter how great a plan you have.

I heard an angry yell that turned my attention to the far side of the airport lobby. I looked over to witness a teacher latch her hand onto Drapes's shoulder as she waved her finger at him and pointed to the door of the airport. I began handing out my flyers at a quicker pace. Within seconds my shoulder was being tapped.

"You stop this right now or I am getting security," the lady yelled angrily.

The students I had handed the flyers to looked at me confused.

"I apologize, ma'am, I will stop. Have a great day." I quickly went back to where Drapes was sitting.

"What the hell is their deal?" I asked him.

"These schools sell trips to their students and make tons of money off it. They can't compete with our prices, so they try to tell students it's a scam or unsafe, so they don't book trips with us. It's absolute bullshit. I'm not having it," Drapes replied. He was pissed.

"Yeah, well, the last thing we need is to get deported from Italy. I think we should just chill and wait for the next group of students. Besides, we already got half of the—" I stopped because Drapes was gone. I looked over at the sea of students and saw flashes of orange in every direction. I started laughing hysterically watching the flyer monster at work.

Moments later the teacher screamed at him and he retreated once again. This time, she went and grabbed the security guard with the gigantic machine gun in his hands for reinforcement.

She pointed at us and the security guard marched over like he meant business. Drapes did not so much as flinch and firmly held his ground. Drapes was fluent in Italian and started to explain the situation to the guard. For being a smaller, nonintimidating guy, he sure had some balls. He was unphased by the heater that was inches from his face and began spinning the situation on the teacher, saying how she was a crook, unfair, and so on.

The guard certainly did not get paid enough for his job, and he eventually just walked away, deeming the situation to be above his pay grade. After that, I realized it was a true free-for-all and went outside to flyer the rest of the students we had missed.

Around midafternoon, we had to leave the airport. Not because we were kicked out or ran out of people to promote to, but because we had run out of flyers. We collectively brought at least 300+ flyers and handed out every single one. We were a little frustrated that we hadn't brought more, but at the same time, we had reached full capacity in our bags and had no idea it would be this successful.

We got back that night and the collective morale was even lower. Apparently, day two of flyering was even worse. Everyone asked us how our day went.

"It was all right. Nothing to brag about," I replied still trying to keep our new outlet secretive. I felt terrible that I could not just help everyone out, but, unfortunately, that is how this game had to be played. I would love if everyone could benefit from each other and work as a team, but if I wanted to stay, I needed to take care of myself first.

Before bed, we started preparing hundreds of more flyers. Everyone knew something was up. The new guys watched but did not say a word. A few of the girls rolled their eyes and shook their head. Then, J-Bone approached both me and Drapes.

"Guys, what the hell. What are you doing? This is fucked up. I'm your boy. You really aren't going to let me in on this?" He wanted in.

"You're going to the airport, aren't you? I saw you guys take a cab this morning. There's no way you got that many flyers out otherwise. I'm coming tomorrow. If you don't bring me, I'm going to take my own cab."

"Dammit. Fine, J-Bone. But do not say a word to anyone. You really piss me off, dude," Drapes chirped back at him.

The next morning it was off to the races. Same deal, except this time we had a third person. So instead of splitting the sales fifty-fifty, it was now thirds. Still, I knew we would all make out much better than everyone else.

J-Bone had only brought fifty flyers with him and ran out quickly. He went back to the apartment after a few hours. Drapes and I had come overprepared and distributed about 200 each, going back with only a few remaining in our bags. We dealt with the same issues as the day before, yet we still prevailed. Well for the most part.

I was actually pretty sure one of the teachers was going to take the gun from the security guard and off Drapes herself. She told him three times to get away from the students or she would call the police. Since we now knew they were blank threats, nothing stopped us. She would yell at him on one side of the airport, then he would go to the other side and begin distributing.

She would yell at him on the other side, and then he would be flyering to the students outside. Once she caught him outside, he headed over to the bus they were getting on and started handing students flyers as they entered. After she saw that, she nearly blew a head gasket.

"GET OUT OF HERE! WHAT IS YOUR PROBLEM! STOP IT! STOP IT NOW! SECURITY!" the lady screamed as I saw Drapes running from her with a huge smile.

"Dude we have to go now. Right to the taxis," he said as he went sprinting by. I grabbed my bag and handed a few flyers to the remaining students outside who were clearly entertained by the show.

The next three days we went through the same process. Every day was a huge success. We must have handed out over a thousand flyers each in five days. Numbers like that were unheard of. At the end of the week, every one of the other promoters knew what we did because when they went to hand out a flyer on the street, if people would even talk to them, they would say they already got one at the airport.

Upon investigation, every single student told them the promo code was either STANK or DRAPES. A few were J-Bone's. Obviously, they thought it was unfair, but it's what we had to do. Overall the other promoters respected it and wished they had done it first.

Bookings started to pour in, and the office could not have been more pleased with us. Our promo codes were everywhere. Further promoting on our trips and through nightlife would be more than enough. We celebrated our victory together that night at the club, knowing that we were a lock for top salespeople the entire semester.

As important as it is to celebrate all major accomplishments, you need to be ready to get right back in action and start from ground zero all over again. I woke up the next morning and got hit with my next major challenge. The first tour assignments of the semester were posted, and there I was: STANK—TOUR MANAGER, AMALFI COAST.

18

MAMA MIA! NO NO NO!

WHEN I SAW the assignment, I knew I was screwed. There were multiple challenges that I would be facing. The first was that I had only been to the Amalfi Coast two times ever—once when I studied abroad, and once as a lower-in-command Tour Guide the past summer. The second issue was that I had never even led one of our trips, let alone managed one.

Now I was expected to oversee six other workers and more than 150 students on the most complex trip our company offered. It was my responsibility to make sure every part of the trip ran smoothly and that 150+ partying college students made it back to Florence in one piece. No more casual travel, mingling, and taking a few pictures. Now I seriously had my plate full.

"I am fucked, dude. I have no idea how I'm going to make this happen. I barely even remember all the parts of the Amalfi trip," I said to Drapes.

He laughed hysterically. "You'll be all right. Ivan has a lot of faith in you."

"Very reassuring. I'm going to talk to him," I replied as I began counting down the days to my impending doom.

I made my way to our office. I always made a scene when I entered that involved over-the-top jokes to the office staff, trying to marry the intern, or attempting to get the entire company to take a horse-drawn carriage to our favorite night club. Today it was strictly business. I walked into Ivan's office, and he peeked up from behind the computer screen.

"Tour Manager, Stank. How are you?" He immediately burst out into laughter. Ivan loved to mess with me and got great joy out of it.

"Well, Ivan, I was great until I learned that you guys are sending me down to Pompeii as a human sacrifice," I replied.

"Hahaha, Stank, you will be fine. The students love you. The trip will be mostly girls. Use your charm," he said in complete hysterics.

"My charm can only get me so far when I don't even know how to execute the trip. You realize I have only been to the Amalfi Coast two times ever, right?" I asked him.

"Two times is plenty. You have my number, if you need anything just call. I have faith in you."

"All right, Ivan," I said as I acknowledged the other manager, Andrea, in the opposite corner of the office. "But let it be known that I did warn you."

They both laughed, made a few more jokes, and I walked back to our apartment to prepare myself for the weekend ahead. If it was all laughs and jokes, then I was not going to let it stress me out. I would do my best and more than likely everything would work out fine. Besides, I had finessed so many situations in the past, what would be different about this one?

Thursday rolled around and it was time for action. I spent the morning studying the itinerary. So many moving parts and room for error.

Then I asked the few people who had been there longer than I had for any advice. Fortunately, the girls who were coming on the trip as leaders and guides had at least been to the Amalfi Coast before. I figured collectively we would be able to piece this together.

Alas, it was time to head to the meeting point. I put on my orange Smart Trip shirt, said a few prayers, and hailed a cab. It was time for all of my collective years of finessing to be put to the test. I mentally made the decision that I was ready for the task at hand.

I arrived at the meeting spot where three buses awaited. Scattered about the piazza were sorority girls as far as the eye could see. Normally this would not be a scene to complain about. In this case, I knew I was doomed.

For some reason, they never knew our trips involved bus rides and hostels. I don't know what they expected for an entire weekend trip priced under 200 euro, but it seemed to me like a first-class flight with a stay at the Four Seasons clearly did not fit the budget. When I had to break the news to them, they would look at me with a glare that pierced through to my soul.

We began the check-in process and loading up the buses. This just involved making sure everyone received a wristband, had their passport, and had paid. This was always the easiest part of the trip, except at least one person always forgot their passport and had to sprint back to their apartment in a panic.

A huge factor was always the bus driver that you got for the trip. I had great relationships with most of them. They all only spoke Italian, so it was a good outlet to practice, and they usually got a kick out of what I tried to say to them. Those guys always made the trip more pleasant and helped make our job easier.

Then there were a few drivers who sucked. They would never stop for the bathroom, refused to adjust the temperature, and would smoke cigarettes the whole ride. The students would complain about them, but there was simply nothing you could do. I prayed that I got one of my favorites.

All the buses were loaded, and Ivan came over to me. I was expecting to get more shit from him.

"Stank, two of the buses are Smart Trip. But we ran out of buses this weekend because of all the trips. So the third bus we rented from another company. The driver is one from the other company too." He waited for my reaction.

"Let me guess, it's that one?" I said as I pointed to the third bus in line that looked like it came straight from an episode of the Flintstones.

"Hahaha, yes. You will be fine. I talked with the driver, he is very nice."

"Really breaking my balls, Ivan. Hopefully we make it there in one piece." At that point, I truly expected nothing less.

I'll give Ivan this. The guy never slept. He truly would answer the phone at any hour I called him, so I did have faith in him on that end. The issue is I would be six hours away. If shit really hit the fan, what could he actually do?

I got together with the guides. All of them were brand new to the job, except for Jacqueline. She was my biggest hope of surviving the trip. She and I had gotten really close over the summer, so it was a relief for her to be there. We had a deal worked out. She had a boyfriend back home so I would politely get rid of any guys hitting on her, and she would do the same for girls I was not into. It was a win-win.

We split up the guides onto the three buses. The next responsibility would be collecting cash for activities while we were on the six-hour ride. I explained to everyone what they needed to collect and how to account for it. Then we were off.

The first order of business would be to introduce myself and announce the plan for the weekend. From observing other Tour Leaders make announcements in the past, I learned an important lesson. The more specifics you revealed, the higher the expectations and the more disappointment when things inevitably went wrong. The other leaders would always layout every little detail of the trip and all of the extras that we may or may not actually get to. This would raise the students' expectations.

Then, when we had to skip an activity, they would be pissed off at the leader and feel like they were getting ripped off. I decided I would only announce the parts of the trip that I knew were a lock, then the extras would come as a surprise. When we did the extras, they would think I'm the man for going above and beyond. When we did not, they would not even know the difference. I grabbed the microphone as we started to approach the outskirts of Florence and made my introduction.

"What's going on everyone? Thank you so much for deciding to come to the Amalfi Coast with us this weekend. This is one of the best trips we offer, and we are going to make sure you have the time of your lives. My name is John, and I will be here to make sure everything goes smoothly and to help you guys with anything you may need," I began.

"Are you Stank?" a bro with long curly hair yelled from the back of the bus.

"Yessir!"

"Hell yeah. We all used your promo code. You're the man." The bus began to cheer.

"Appreciate you guys. Wait until I get you back to Florence safely before you decide if you like me or not though."

I went through my announcements and began the endless process of collecting cash for the weekend's extra activities. Everyone was always indecisive, never had the proper amount of change, bitched that it was not included and so on. After two hours, I had finally finished collecting everyone's money. Shortly after, we decided to make our first bathroom stop. I was about to be put to my first test of the weekend.

We pulled off into an AutoGrille. These were all over Italy and were basic truck stops with low-quality food. The only advantage was that I was always able to negotiate free food with the workers by showing the group of students I had brought with me. Other than that, the offerings were a disgrace to the Italian people.

I got together with the guides from the other buses and compiled all of the money they had collected. Over 10,000 euros in cash. I would have to carry this around with me the entire weekend until I safely returned it to the office on Monday. If the cash went missing, I would be held responsible to pay it back. I made sure it was in my bag in clear sight at all times.

We corraled all the students back onto the bus and did a head count. We double-checked to make sure everyone was there, and we were back on the road. Only three more hours until we would arrive at the hostel. I sat down, finally, began to relax a little, and was just about to attempt to get some sleep. The Amalfi trip was so jam-packed that you would be lucky to get ten total hours of sleep the entire weekend as a Tour Manager, so every hour counted. About an hour after we left the rest stop, I started to close my eyes. It lasted less than five seconds.

The bus suddenly veered into the other lane of the highway. I opened my eyes and looked up. The bus then jerked back to the right side of the road. I stood up and looked down at the driver. He had no hands on the wheel and no eyes on the road. Instead, he was wildly scouring the floor surrounding his seat.

"ARTURO!" I yelled to him. The students began to wake from their slumber and peeked over their seats to try to figure out what was going on.

"Ahhhhhh. No no no no no NO NO," Arturo said frantically as he began to fully lose his composure.

"*Che cosa?*" I shot back to him. The bus was now zinging all over the highway like a pinball. He spoke zero English, and it was time for my Italian skills to be put to the test.

"MAMA MIA! NO NO NO!" His voice had now elevated to a scream. The students were now fully freaked out and looking to me for answers.

"Just a second, guys, I got this. ARTURO! *BASTA! TRANQUILLO! CHE COS'È?*" I shouted at him.

"*HO DIMENTICATO LA MIA BUSTA!*" Arturo yelled back at me.

He was in a full-blown panic because he forgot his bag at the rest stop. The front window of the bus had now steamed up, and we could no longer see the road. To top it off, he began to fart, and the entire bus smelled like a dead raccoon. Pure pandemonium ensued as the panic spread to the students who began to scream because they had no idea what was happening.

I hopped down next to the driver and began wiping down the window so that we could see where the hell we were going. I looked back and all the cars behind us were pulled over to steer clear of this maniac who was about to kill us all. All over a forgotten bag. I decided that this would be the best time to call Ivan and let him deal with it.

"Arturo. *Sto chiamando il mio capo. Hai bisogno di rilassarti. Troveremo la tua busta,*" I said to him. I grabbed his hands and put them on the steering wheel. Then I wiped down the windshield one last time as I called up Ivan. He answered and I shoved the phone to the driver's ear.

They talked for a few minutes, and Arturo seemed to calm down enough to at least keep the bus in one lane. He handed the phone back to me, and Ivan assured me the situation was taken care of. They called the rest stop, the bag was there, and they would get it to the driver. I stood up at the front of the bus to take care of the second part of the issue: the fifty students who were holding onto each other for dear life.

"Everything is cool. This guy is batshit crazy. He forgot his bag and decided the best course of action would be to completely disregard the fact that he was operating a motor vehicle, and instead scream at the sky until it reappeared." I joked to ease the tension.

Everyone let out a laugh and sigh of relief. I got back to my seat, sat down, and knew that there was not a snowball's chance in hell that I would get a minute of sleep the rest of that ride.

Two hours later, after I watched the road ahead like a hawk, we arrived in Sorrento. This is the town our hostel was located in. It was 2:00 a.m., and I already began to dread the morning and weekend I had ahead of me.

For one final kick in the pants, Arturo had no idea where our hostel was actually located. In an attempt to locate it, he pulled down a one-way road that curved into a dead end. On our way down, the road got so narrow between the buildings alongside it that there could not have been more than a foot of clearance on either side of the bus. Once Arturo realized he royally screwed us all, he began cursing and throwing his arms around like a mad man.

A group of Italian men came up to his window. I was so checked out at this point that I could not make out exactly what they said, however, they saved the day. They took it upon themselves to help guide Arturo out of the rabbit hole he had gotten us into by running up and down the street like they were air traffic control. After thirty minutes of finagling the bus back to the proper road, the men gave Arturo directions to the hostel.

Around 3:00 a.m. we finally arrived at the Bleu Village. I have to say, this place was incredible for a hostel. The entire mountain side that the village was built into was covered in peach-colored bungalows tucked between lush trees and vegetation. Every morning the sun would rise over the jagged cliffs and turn the ocean the bungalows overlooked into a boundless sheet of glimmering diamonds. The one frustrating part was the never-ending staircase to get around, especially if you stayed at the top of the village, but it was a small price to pay.

We were greeted at the entrance by the workers who gave me the keys to all of our rooms. I had all the assignments ready and tried to get everyone situated as quickly as possible. At this point, all the students were drained, cranky, and ready to never see Arturo again in their life. I could hardly blame them.

We got everyone settled into their rooms, then the other guides and I made our way to ours. We all sat down and could not help but laugh at everything that had gone wrong already. Getting frustrated and worked up over stuff you have no control over serves no purpose. It's better to laugh and embrace the shit show when you are knee-deep in one.

Finally, it was time to get some sleep. I would get about two and a half hours if I slept straight through until my alarm, and I needed every second. I hopped in bed and closed my eyes.

Moments later, I heard a faint shriek. I sat up. After a moment, I decided that I must have been delirious and just hearing things. I laid back down, and as soon as my head hit the pillow, I heard two more screams, this time much more clearly. My eyes shot wide open. I could only imagine what this was all about.

Before I could process what was going on, I heard a noise at the door that sounded like a SWAT team was trying to forcefully enter with a battering ram. I jumped up, only in my boxers, and opened it up.

"ANTS! OH MY GOD. THEY ARE EVERYWHERE." A girl screamed as she pointed down to her bungalow.

"Hold on," I said as I wiped my eyes. I remember hearing how ants sometimes ended up in the rooms in the Bleu Village. For that reason, I had come prepared.

I grabbed a bottle of Raid out of my suitcase. "Bring me to your room. I'll take care of this," I said as I began to follow her down the stairs. At that point it could have been a room full of grizzlies, I would not have cared. Whatever was in there stood a minimal chance of surviving the wrath of cranky Stank.

As we approached her room, the screams got louder and louder. I clenched the bottle of Raid prepared to do whatever had to be done. She opened the door to let me in. No man could be prepared for what I saw next.

The door swung open, and, by the sounds of it, you would think that I had just entered a scene from the *Texas Chainsaw Massacre*. Ear-piercing screams were coming from all six girls in the room. One girl was jumping up and down on her bed and pointing at the ceiling where a parade of little black ants was marching across. She grabbed a towel from her bedside and began to swat at them. She made contact and a black cloud fell to the floor, directly into her friend's purse.

"OH MY GOD, MY LOUIS VUITTON," her friend screamed as her bag was now full of ant corpses.

Another girl was in the bathroom with her head wrapped in a towel because she was afraid the ants would get into her hair. She was holding her hand over her mouth trying to contain her shrieks as she pointed to the ants that covered the bathroom sink. I ran over to the rescue.

With one quick, swift spray I eliminated all ant life forms from the sink area. This cycle continued. The girls would run around the room screaming and pointing anywhere there were ants. I would eliminate them and move on to the next target. Finally, I dealt with the ceiling. I climbed up onto the dresser and sprayed down the parade of ants. They began to fall all over the room like an ant rainstorm. The girls had now run outside of the room to their porch.

I gazed around the room. All ants had been eliminated in a matter of minutes. The issue now was that hundreds, if not thousands, of ant corpses covered their entire room. They were all over the bathroom, in one girl's purse, and covering the floor surrounding their beds. The girls refused to go back in.

I had no choice other than to find the hostel workers and get their room relocated. The girls were absolutely livid; however, they thanked me for my valiant effort for risking my life to put an end to the insect infestation.

After one hour of sleep, it was time to execute the most complex day of the trip. The day would be spent exploring the Island of Capri, then later that night we would go out to a local bar. We started at 6:00 a.m., and I probably would not be going to bed until 2:00 a.m. at the earliest. I slugged back the first of many espresso shots, got everyone accounted for, and loaded up the bus to the ferry terminal.

To the dismay of many, we were back in the hands of Arturo. I prayed that we would have a much better experience than the day before.

The roads all over the Amalfi Coast are narrow, winding, and hard to access, especially when you are on a bus. For this reason, we had to park a considerable distance from the ferry. The only way to get down was a gigantic staircase cut into the mountainside. More complaints and moans came from the students, but I kept them going with hopes of it all being worth it once we got to the island.

After a twenty-minute climb down, we were at the ferry terminal. There, I was supposed to meet the lady who had all of our tickets for the day. Ferry tickets, boat tickets, and gondola tickets to get to the top of the island. She was nowhere to be found. The ferry was taking off in ten minutes and we had nothing. I stayed calm, knowing that getting aroused would only cause mass panic among the students and make matters much worse. I dialed up Ivan.

"*Ciao*, John! I am hoping today is better for you?" he said as he answered the phone.

"Well, everything is great except we have to get on this ferry in ten minutes and the ticket lady is nowhere to be found," I replied.

"Oh, Marika. She is always late hahaha. Just make your way to the departure area. She will arrive," he said.

I rallied up the troops and got everyone to the departure site. Five minutes before the ferry was ready to take off, Marika came running up to me with a folder in hand.

"John, here you are. Have a great time," she said as she handed over the tickets. I split them up among all of the guides so that we could rapidly distribute them. We got all the tickets out and everyone loaded up on the ferry with about thirty seconds to spare.

After about forty minutes we started to approach the island. This was the moment in the trip that people started to decide that all the bullshit we had been dealing with so far was worth it.

On a Smart Trip tour around the island of Capri in the Amalfi Coast when I was a student. This is the same trip that I managed one year later.

Looking out the window, you could see the breathtaking landscape of Capri. Gigantic rugged cliffs that extended straight up, hundreds of feet above the water capped in green vegetation. The pristine water that surrounded the coastline was a color blue that I only thought existed in the movies. Crisp and warm sea air blew between the yachts scattered around the harbor. The energy of the group was rejuvenated as the ferry docked and we got ready for our boating adventure around the island.

Fortunately, the boats were ready for us upon arrival. They were much smaller and could only fit about twenty-five people on each one, so all of the guides split up with a group of students. The ringleader bro from the bus and his friends who used my promo code insisted that I go with them, so I hopped onto their boat without hesitation.

One of the kids proceeded to grab the aux cord and the party escalated quickly. Fetty Wap was banging through the speakers as the group started pulling out enough booze to immobilize the entire Island of Capri. Bottles were passed around; everyone was dancing, singing, and having the time of their lives. I was sitting there laughing, thinking about being in their exact same position a year earlier when I was on this trip.

With the energy levels at peak heights, I looked around and was instantly reminded why this was all so worth it. While most of my friends were at a job they hated back home, I was on a boat in the Amalfi Coast with a group of people having the time of their lives. People were counting down the days for their two weeks of vacation time per year. I was getting paid to go to some of the most sought-after vacation spots in the world.

The party continued as we approached the first major landmark of our boat tour. Right in front of us was the Faraglioni: three goliath rock formations protruding from the Mediterranean just off the coast. The girls started pulling out their phones and diving toward the front of the boat to get in formation for Instagram pics with this iconic landmark.

I just soaked in the moment as I had seen it a few times before. I made it a priority to live in the moment. I watched so many people have a miserable time on trips yet get the pics to show off to people back home. That is what was most important to them: other people's perceptions and opinions. It did not matter if they actually had fun, as long as all of the people they knew thought they were having a blast. Social media is such an amazing and powerful tool, but so many people horribly misuse it.

After the photoshoot, the boat stopped to let everyone hop out and swim. There were also no bathrooms on the boat, and this group was doing damage to their alcohol stores. Everyone hopped into the water together, and I made sure to jump in the other side. I backflipped into the ocean and came to the surface.

The water of the Mediterranean was always the perfect temperature. The salt content was also so high that you can stay completely still and float there with no effort. It was absolutely incredible to float and look up at the monstrous cliffs of the island, simply thinking about how grateful I was for this insane life I was living.

After a fifteen-minute swim, we loaded up the boat and headed to our next stop: the Blue Grotto. This is by far the most famous attraction on the island. The Blue Grotto is a sea cave whose miniscule entrance is only accessible by a small canoe and ducking your head. Inside the entire cave is illuminated by sunlight passing through an underwater cavity through the seawater. The water has the same color as blue Gatorade and is one of the most incredible sights I have ever seen.

That day the line to get in was ridiculous, so I decided to sit it out since I had already been in a couple times. The students took turns hopping into the canoes and experiencing the marvel. Everyone returned to the boat mind blown after seeing the UNESCO World Heritage Site with their own eyes.

The boat tour came to an end and we all unloaded on the island. We gathered the entire group and I made a few announcements.

"You guys have the rest of the day to roam the island. We have a great lunch spot, so if anybody would like to come with us, you are more than welcome. The ferry will be leaving at 4:30 p.m. sharp. If you are not at the terminal, you will be left on the island," I instructed.

The ferry actually left at 5:00 p.m., but I knew how this game needed to be played for the highest probability of getting the most amount of people on the ferry. The kids on my boat were already bombed, and I knew that they would more than likely be left behind as it was.

About fifty students followed us to the restaurant, which was typically always the case. On every trip, we had certain restaurants that we would promote to the students. The Italians were extremely generous, especially when you brought them business, and this always resulted in free meals.

I am a huge seafood fan, and the fresh seafood from the coast of Italy was some of the best to ever grace my taste buds. I took down an entire plate of crispy calamari followed by an entree of pasta covered in shrimp, shellfish, and assorted sea creatures. The other guides ate like kings as well. The servers came over, comped the meal, and gave us an envelope of money as a thank you for how much business we provided them that day.

After our lunch, the guides and I escaped the group to get a few moments to ourselves. We decided to take the chairlift up to Anacapri, the highest point of the island. We spent the next few hours up there, entranced by the various shades of blue making up the ocean below and appreciating the moment of relaxation. We talked about how this entire experience was so crazy, yet so worth it. We discussed what our plans were when we would eventually return to the states. Our conversation got so deep that we lost track of time. One of the guides, Alex, looked down at his watch.

"Guys, we need to be back to the bottom of the island in forty-five minutes! We have to go now!" He stood up in a panic.

I looked at the line to the chairlift to get down from Anacapri. The line was at least 200 people long. If we waited in it, we would surely miss the ferry. I gathered the group and walked right to the front of the line. I pointed to our orange shirts, explained that we were group leaders, and needed to get down ASAP. The people were kind enough to let us in line, and we hopped on the chairlift to make our way down.

Once we got to the bottom of the lift, we still had a walk that would take at least forty minutes to get to the harbor. We had fifteen. Waiting next to the chair lift was a convertible with no top that was offering to bring people to the harbor. We hopped right in and explained that we needed to get to the ferry terminal as soon as possible. Our driver understood and put the pedal to the metal.

We pulled up to the terminal with a few minutes to spare. Most of the group was already gathered and ready to head back. Surprisingly, even the group that I had been on the boat with was all there, physically at least. I sent out a few messages and the entire group was present as the ferry docked in the harbor. I took full advantage of the forty-minute trip and passed out the entire ride.

When we got back to the shore, we got everyone off the ferry, did another quick head count, and headed back to the buses. Everyone complained as we approached the staircase carved into the mountainside, and even more sighs were released as I tried to pitch it as an opportunity to burn gelato calories off.

We finally got up to the road and were back in the hands of Arturo. Now it was time for me to decide how to deal with the next piece of the night. A key piece that I left out of the itinerary was a night out to the bars after Capri. I thought that I would be able to get away with skipping it and sleeping, but there were other plans in store for me.

I received a text from one of the girls in the office that read, "John, we have not yet received confirmation for how many students will be attending the bar tonight. Can you give us a number?" On top of that, the drivers began pressing me for times of departure from the hostel and what time we would return. I knew there was no way I would be able to skip it. I mentally accepted another near sleepless night and began to collect the numbers and prepare for the night out.

I made the announcement to the students about the bar and asked who was interested in going. Every single hand went up. I was hoping everyone would be exhausted from the entire day of activities, but they were all ready to rally and keep the show going. They were also all ecstatic because they did not expect this to be part of the trip. I really couldn't even blame them.

When I was in their position, I made sure to take advantage of every single experience that came my way. I updated the office, informed the bus driver of our departure times, and we all got ready for a night on the town.

A few hours later, we gathered at our meeting spot outside of the hostel cafeteria. I led everyone down the stairs and to the road where our buses were awaiting us. At this point, it was 10:00 p.m. and I was running on fumes, but I still attempted to keep my energy levels high. We loaded up the buses and were off to the town for a night of debauchery.

About halfway to the bars, I noticed a few drops of water on the windshield of the bus. Seconds later the floodgates opened, thunder began to boom, and lightning illuminated the entire night sky. Nobody thought to check the weather before we left. I looked on my phone at the weather app, which told me that there was a severe thunderstorm warning in the area for the next few hours. Exactly what I needed.

We got to the parking lot for the buses, and it was raining so hard that we could not even see outside the windows. The bus could not physically bring us to the front of the bar, so we had a fifteen-minute walk ahead of us. At that moment it seemed like the only way we were getting there is if we hired the boat company that gave us the tour around the island earlier.

The roads were flooding, and most of the students with us were girls who had just done their hair and makeup to look nice for the night out. There was not a chance they were about to step out into this monsoon.

We waited it out for an hour, and the rain continued to pour. Everyone was sick of sitting on the bus, so they decided to make their way to the parking lot building overhang to wait out the storm. Another fifteen minutes passed, and the students were beginning to lose their buzz. The rain had slowed a little bit but was still coming down with no end in sight. The bro who had been dictating the energy of the group decided to take the floor.

"That's it. I don't care if I get wet. I'm going to the bar. Who's with me?"

Before I knew it, half the group was ready to man the storm. The bro was now beating on his chest, yelling at the sky to bring it. Nothing would be able to stop him.

Half of the group was still hesitant and looked at the group of people going like they were a pack of looney toons. I did not want to leave these people at the overhang all night, so it was decision time. We had two buses, so I decided that anyone who did not want to go out could take one of the buses back to the hostel. The second would wait for any of the brave souls who were taking on the elements to return to bring them back safely. Everyone agreed, most people were happy, and we got the show on the road.

A few of the guides went back with the group going home, but I had to stick around to make sure the situation was under control. We began to walk down the road with about sixty kids who were drunk, soaked, and had nothing to lose. Everybody was singing, yelling, and fully embracing the storm. I knew that things could get very dangerous once everybody adopted the mentality that they were in for a shit show. I had to be on my toes to deal with the inevitable situation of something going wrong.

As we approached the bar, I decided to announce the plan of return once again. I had already told everybody on the bus ride to the bar, but I needed to drill it into their head once again. We set our phone alarms for 1:25 a.m. (even though I knew our departure time was 1:45).

The bar was one that I had been to in the past and that our company always brought students to. It was a cool setup, including an outdoor area with seating and decorations that made you feel like you were in a jungle. For that night, they had closed the canopy over it due to the rain. Adjacent to that was a bar area with the same jungle-esque theme with seating and more standing area that people would often dance in. Even though the rain had been in full force, the place was still pretty full as always.

I was lost in deep conversation with the other guides about how crazy the weekend had been so far when the phone alarms started to go off around the bar. We wrapped up our conversation and made our way outside. The students already began to gather, even though they could barely stand, and I could tell by their eyes that nobody was mentally present. The 1:30 a.m. meeting time came, and I had the guides do a quick head count. A few were missing.

I had the guides go into the bar and do a quick search to see if they could find everyone. They came back out with a few stragglers, but we still were missing two people. It was 1:45 and everybody was growing impatient. I called the girls who were missing three times each and got no answer. They had gotten the instructions, and I had no choice but to leave them behind.

After four whole hours of sleep, I woke up, felt somewhat human, and got prepared to deal with the wrath of the girls from the night before. I got dressed and headed down to get breakfast at the cafeteria. I descended six flights of stairs, took the corner to enter the cafeteria, and there stood one of the girls. She looked like Samara from *The Ring*, ready to devour my soul.

She threw a fit of rage and berated me for "leaving her to die in a foreign country." I tried to reason that we had set a clear meeting time and I could not punish a group of sixty people because she failed to follow instructions. She was having none of it. She continued yelling at all of the guides while I prepared the rest of the group for the day ahead. I figured if only one person out of over 150 disliked me, I was doing a pretty good job.

We got down to the meeting spot, and every person was miraculously on time after an entire day and night of partying. The good news was that this day was the most relaxed of the trip. We would be going to the beaches of Positano for the day where everyone was on their own. I could finally kick back and relax, which I planned to take full advantage of. We loaded up the buses and were on our way to one of the most beautiful beaches in the entire world.

This particular bus ride was not for the weak. It took about an hour to get into Positano. Half of that ride was on winding roads through mountain passes that were literally on the edge of a cliff hundreds of feet above the ocean. The views were absolutely breathtaking and remarkable if you could get past the fact that we continually came within a few feet of plummeting off the cliff into the ocean. Heights do not bother me, and I do not suffer from motion sickness, so for me, it was an incredible experience. For others, the experience was a bit different.

About ten minutes into the perpetual winding, I sensed some unease toward the back of the bus. The entire bus was full of people who had been slamming back drinks all night, so most were definitely at a disadvantage to begin with. When that mixes with a fear of heights and motion sickness, things can get ugly quickly.

I noticed that my friend who had just freaked out on me for leaving her behind the night prior was not looking too hot. She had a blank expression while staring down at her lap as the bus swayed side to side from turning the corners. At that point, I knew it wasn't a matter of if chunks would fly, it was a matter of when.

I kept my eyes on her from the moment I knew a disaster was on the horizon. Sure enough, just minutes later, the ticking time bomb was ready to detonate. She raised her head, looked left, looked right, and placed her hand over her mouth as she attempted to conceal the projectile vomit. Needless to say, it did not work. Puke began to spray between her fingers. Within moments she was like an unmanned fire hose with vomit flying freely in all directions around her.

"EWWWWWWWW OH MY GOD!" The girl next to her screamed as she dove for cover toward the back of the bus. This was followed by a series of screams from the rest of the girls around her who all began gagging, screaming, and scattering.

I waited until she fully drained the tank and grabbed a roll of paper towels and a plastic shopping bag from the bus driver. It took extreme self-control to hold back from bursting into laughter. This was karma at its absolute finest. I walked back to her seat, which was painted in last night's vodka cranberries with a mix of hostel food. The look on her face was one of pure defeat as vomit particles dripped out of the corner of her mouth down onto her jean shorts. I stuck out the bag and paper towels.

"Here's a bag in case you get sick!" I said with the utmost amount of sarcasm. She shot me a look of death, tore the bags and paper towels from my hands, and began to clean her explosion. Her friend came to assist her, and I went straight back to the front of the bus. This whole event gave me a sickening sense of pleasure after dealing with her attitude for the previous twelve hours.

The winding finally ended as we arrived in Positano. The bus could only take us so far, so the group had to descend on foot through the narrow alleys of shops selling trinkets and garments until we made it to the beach. I announced what time we would be meeting to go back, gave people recommendations for the day, and then sent everyone on their way.

Some people went on another boat tour, rented paddle boards, or just took the opportunity to relax. The guides and I went straight to the cabanas on the beach and spent the next six hours lounging, taking occasional swims, and absorbing the beauty of where we were.

To this day, out of everywhere I have been, Positano has remained at the top of my list of favorite places. When you are down on the beach, it feels like you have entered an entirely new world. The mountainous surroundings look like they could have been filmed to depict part of Pandora from the movie *Avatar*.

The vertical town consists of pastel-colored Mediterranean houses carved into the mountainside that defy all rules of architecture. The turquoise blue water rolling onto the beaches of perfectly rounded pebbles and sea glass is the ideal temperature to refresh and rejuvenate from the hot sun. Multi-million-dollar yachts drift along the entire coastline, enhancing the allure of the magical scene.

When I envision paradise, Positano is the scene created in my head. Lounging on that beach was just another reminder of how fortunate I was for the lifestyle I was leading. All worries and stress were put on the back burner. Even the worry about the 10,000 euro in cash I was carrying in my backpack, sitting there nonchalantly on the beach.

The day flew by, and before I knew it, it was time to return to our hostel. Only one more day left before I could return to Florence having conquered this seemingly impossible task at hand. Everybody returned to the meeting point from their days of various activities absolutely ecstatic and full of gratitude that they had the opportunity to experience that utopia.

We hit the road and this time everyone was ready for the curvy ride ahead. The hurl queen came prepared this time, bag in hand, in hopes she would not repeat her act from the morning. I low key wanted an encore.

I instructed everyone that we would be leaving at 8:00 the next morning to head to Pompeii and Mt. Vesuvius. Some people kept their party going and some went to explore the town. I went straight to my room and right to sleep. I was running on fumes and needed to get some actual rest. At this point, however, I was no longer concerned with my ability to keep order and knew that the rest of the trip was going to work out just fine.

I slept like a rock straight through to my alarm clock. We all woke up, packed our bags, and went to the meeting spot to make sure no one was left behind at the hostel. A few people came scrambling last minute, but we managed to scrape everyone together. As we walked down to load the buses, I looked down at my phone.

"Severe Thunderstorm Alert: Napoli Region" read the banner across the top of my iPhone. I laughed. As far as I was concerned, unless there was a tsunami heading toward us, nothing could interfere with my completing this trip.

About halfway to Pompeii, it began to pour. At this point, the students were no longer phased at all either. I sat there with a smile, with the full intent of sitting the tour out in the hotel just outside the gates. I had been to Pompeii multiple times, and we had hired professional tour guides for this part of the experience. You know, ones that actually were trained and knew what they were talking about. All we had to do was send in a couple of our guides to keep track of everyone.

Upon arrival, everyone was dropped off at the entrance gates. The wind was whipping, the rain was pouring, and the gypsies appeared in flocks attempting to sell everyone umbrellas and useless trinkets. The professional guides were there waiting for us, and two of our tour guides offered themselves as tribute to watch after our group. Everybody went in, and I headed straight to the hotel with the remaining guides.

If it had not been raining, I would have absolutely taken the tour again. Pompeii is a must-visit place for everybody. In 49 AD, Mt. Vesuvius erupted and buried the entire city in thirteen to twenty feet of volcanic ash. That ash preserved the entire city and those who were unfortunate enough to be in it when the volcano erupted.

Today, you can visit the site and get a glimpse into exactly that period of time in history. The world is a crazy place and having the opportunity to visit a site like that helps keep you grounded and fortunate for everything you have, because it can all be taken away in a matter of seconds.

After lunch, the rain cleared, and the sun peeked back out. We loaded the buses once again to head to our final stop before returning, Mt. Vesuvius—the goliath volcano that caused all of this destruction. A lot of people felt daunted by the task of climbing this monster, but they soon found out that was hardly the case. The buses would drive up the majority of the mountain roads that weaved back and forth for another stomach-churning experience.

When we finally reached the point we would hike from, it took only about forty minutes to reach the peak. However, the hike was still a challenge. It was extremely steep, and the ground was composed of volcanic ash. For every step you took forward, your foot would slide back half a step. This combined with the strong Naples sun had people drenched in sweat by the time they reached the peak.

I decided to join the group for this hike. I had done it a few times before, but I've always enjoyed the challenge of hikes and even more the views when you reach the peak. There's something so fulfilling about looking at a mountain from the bottom, then looking down at the earth around you from the top. It's always so funny to me how challenge oriented we are as humans and how we view everything as an obstacle that must be conquered. Part of me thinks we are all crazy, but, on the other hand, once you complete a sizable challenge, the feeling of fulfillment is paralleled by none.

I feel like everything worth pursuing in life can be compared to climbing a mountain. Most people will stand at the bottom, staring at the top without ever beginning the journey because the whole task seems way too daunting. Some will start the journey, but after realizing that each step is barely getting them anywhere, they retreat to the bottom where they can tell people "they tried but it doesn't work."

Then there are the few who decide in their head they will make it to the top. They make the decision, then they go. Inch by inch, step by step, foot by foot. They simply continue going because they know the pain and struggle will all be worth it in the end. They ignore the excuses going through their heads that they should just turn around and go back to the bottom with everyone else.

They don't view each step as barely any progress; they view it as the necessary motion to see the task at hand through. With each step, they know they are getting closer and closer to accomplishing their mission. When they make it to the top, they are able to enjoy the fruits of consistently doing the small actions enough times to manifest the biggest rewards. Everything worth it in life comes as a result of taking one more step up the mountain.

Back at the bottom of the mountain, we did one last head count, loaded up the buses, and headed back to Florence. As I took a seat, I let out a smile and sigh of relief. I had successfully carried out this trip that I thought would be impossible. I knew that Arturo still played a factor in whether or not we got back, but for now, I considered it mission accomplished.

The next six hours on the bus were mine. I had no responsibilities left other than to make sure everyone got back to Florence, which there was not an awful lot I could do about. I put my headphones in and threw on my favorite album to listen to while engaged in my deepest thinking—*Nothing Was the Same*. I started from the top with "Tuscan Leather," my favorite song by Drake.

I have never found a tool that motivates me more than music. I also have never found an outlet that does a better job of getting you through your toughest moments in life than music. When you feel like every person in the world is doubting you, music is there for you. When you feel like there is no one who can relate to you, there's a musician out there who is able to articulate feelings that you've had that you never knew there were words for.

Music has a supernatural ability to unlock mental places that are otherwise unreachable. For myself, and hundreds of millions of other people, Drake has the ability to do all of the above the best. As a result, his level of earnings reflects this. In my opinion, an iconic artist deserves every single penny they make. They have an uncanny ability to play our emotions like Beethoven played the piano. That skill, to manipulate emotion, is one of the most powerful talents that an individual could possess.

As I gazed out the window, the first place my mind went to was the most important place to be. A place of gratitude. I thought about how fortunate I was, at the age of twenty-three, to be living this lifestyle. None of it even seemed real. Five years ago, I could not afford to go to a real college. I was working long hours behind a grill in a steaming hot kitchen for basically minimum wage. I dreamed of being able to travel to a foreign country.

Now I was living in one. I was traveling to places regularly that most people would only ever dream of going to. I had a successful Network Marketing business that was continuing to grow as I lived overseas and providing me with a level of residual income that allowed me to not have to worry about finances at all. I was meeting thousands of people from all over the world and forming friendships that would last a lifetime.

I was gaining such an appreciation for simple living. When I first started succeeding financially, I thought designer clothes, lavish living, and balling out were the rewards that would make me happy. While these luxuries were cool, I realized that is not what drove me. Here I was, living in a shitty apartment with nine people, traveling Europe in buses built during Julius Caesar's rule, staying in hostels with ant infestations, and I was the happiest I had ever been.

I realized that the most important things to me were the journey and people I was on it with. There will always be a next level, and if you don't find fulfillment in the journey, you will never be happy. Also, think about some of the best moments you've had in your life. I can guarantee you that these moments are heavily influenced by the people you were with at the time.

You can be traveling in private jets, staying in five-star hotels, wearing all the diamonds and jewelry that your body can sustain, but if the people around you aren't right, the experience won't mean shit. People you can laugh and converse with at the deepest level and purely feed off each other's energy will define your experiences.

The next level I slipped into after gratitude was where I was headed in the future. While it is so important to always be in a place of gratitude, the most dangerous place you can be is in one of satisfaction. When you are satisfied, you no longer possess that internal flame to pursue becoming the best version of yourself. You become content, and you become stagnant. In my opinion, every single one of us has unlimited potential. Success is all about the fulfillment we find in the journey of pursuing that unlimited potential.

The moment you stop pursuing your unlimited potential is the moment the output of value you are creating in the world comes to a halt. You are either growing, or you are dying. It is our responsibility to stay on a journey of growth for ourselves and the people around us. Always stay grateful, but never be satisfied.

This applied to me big-time. Nothing gives me more anxiety than the thought of staying the same. I knew how much this chapter of my life was changing me, especially my perspective and on a spiritual level. I had not reached the point of stagnation, but I knew if I stayed in Italy too long, I would get there. I was starting to realize there was only so much that could be accomplished there. I saw some of my peers who got so sucked into the lifestyle that they had become completely out of touch with reality. It was easy to fall into a place of satisfaction over there, but once the growth stopped, I knew I would have to be out. I started thinking about what the next step would be for me.

I thought about my business. While we were making a huge impact on the finances and health of thousands of people, I knew I could take that impact to the next level. I was not putting forth the effort that I was capable of. On a more macro level, I knew that I had an even bigger purpose to serve.

I kept thinking about my realization I had on graduation day. All of my success and useful skills I developed so far had nothing to do with actual school. I was living this insane life that was so far off the conventional path, yet one that was so attainable with the resources we have available today.

All of this growth was because of my experiences and lessons I learned outside of traditional schooling. I thought about how much I learned from getting expelled, all my past business ventures, my failures, from living in another country, from taking chances on opportunities where there was no guarantee of success.

The ventures I had done so far could literally be made into a movie, but they would always stay concealed in my mind if I did not take any action. I thought about the impact I could make on the younger generation if I could just show them that there is another way.

I made a few attempts to break ground on my book idea during my time in Europe, but every attempt resulted in frustration and me being way too overwhelmed with the magnitude of the task at hand. The idea of it all seemed so daunting at the moment, but I knew if this mission was still on my mind, there was a reason it was there.

While thinking about everything I was fortunate enough to experience, I thought about why people would ever settle. I never thought that people wanted to live an average life, but I knew the reasons they stayed the course. One of the biggest reasons was to keep the people around them happy. Their family, friends, and loved ones wanted them to get a good degree, get a good job, get a house with family and kids, and eventually retire with a pension and benefits.

Deep down, most people have desires for much more. They want to be entertainers, to start a business, to travel the world, and to pursue the dreams that keep them up at night. However, if they were to tell their family they were going for this, it would be received with disappointment and a lack of support. They would remind them how risky it is. They would try to protect them from failure. They would tell them that type of life is only possible for a certain type of person. This often results in people never even attempting to go after their passions in the first place.

In terms of what is possible, I truly believe that when someone sets their mind to something, there is nothing that cannot be accomplished. Look at this trip I had just executed, for example. I had no idea what I was doing going into it, yet I successfully finessed the entire weekend just because I knew there was no other choice. People get so hung up on the how. In fact, they get paralyzed and never even take action. When you focus on the end goal, the resources that you need to accomplish it will start falling into place.

If you look at every single success story, no one knew what the exact route would be. Even if they had a plan, the actual execution looked 99 percent different by the time they accomplished their goal. When you believe in your capability to accomplish anything, shit starts to fall into place.

I snapped back into it as we were entering Florence and the trip was officially coming to an end. I picked up the microphone to thank everyone for coming on the trip. I let everyone know about our weekly dinner at Rubaconte, about our nightlife schedule, and our upcoming trips. Everyone applauded and cheered as I hung up the mic.

As we unloaded the bus, everyone got off and thanked me for the whole weekend. They told me they would definitely be going out to the club with us and attending our future trips. Some people went as far to even say that it was the best weekend of their lives. I felt accomplished and so grateful that I was able to make this type of impact on people.

As everyone disappeared, Ivan came from around the corner.

"John! You made it back as one." He laughed as he patted me on the back.

"Yessir! We did it, Ivan!" I said.

"I knew you would be just fine. You are a boss. There was only one problem, right? With the angry girl who got too drunk and was left behind?"

"Well I'd say we faced much more than one problem, but yes she was acting very irresponsible and was thirty minutes late to the meeting point. She said she was going to complain to you so be prepared."

"Sounds to me like she deserved to be left. Do not worry about her. You did great."

Technically the next day would be my day off, but there were never really days off. I would get up, hit the gym, practice my Italian, and get right back to promoting at the club the next day. However, at this point, the circumstances were different. My trip-leading confidence was through the roof. I had secured a position as a top salesperson in the company.

On top of that, Ivan was thrilled with me and I could do no wrong in his eyes. Every shit show I entered ended up working out terrifically, and I knew the next few months would contain some of the most memorable experiences of my life.

The semester rolled by, and I did not take a single moment for granted. Every night I dined at different restaurants and enjoyed some of the best food on the planet. During the week we partied like rock stars. Every single weekend would be a new adventure with new crazy challenges, just like the Amalfi Coast had been.

Riding camelback through the deserts of Marrakech, Morocco, with authentic attire acquired at a local market.

I was traveling to so many new places and broadening my perspective day by day. Throughout that fall, I traveled to Croatia, Spain, Hungary, Austria, Czech Republic, Switzerland, Germany, Portugal, Morocco, Netherlands, Ireland, Iceland, Sweden, and all over Italy. Many of these places I was fortunate enough to travel to multiple times. I experienced so many different cultures in such a short period of time that forever changed the way I viewed life.

I was able to paraglide over Interlaken, Switzerland. I attended Oktoberfest in Munich, Germany. I also went to the Dachau concentration camp where one of the worst genocides in history occurred. I partied all day on a luxury yacht in Ibiza, Spain. I rode camels through the desert in Marrakech and attended a dinner afterward with traditional dancing, music, and food.

Paragliding over Interlaken, Switzerland.

I experienced hallucinogenic mushrooms while strolling through one of the largest parks in Amsterdam. I climbed castles in Budapest. In Iceland, we rented a car and drove, sometimes with no destination, just absorbing the spectacular waterfalls, mountains, and scenery surrounding us. In Croatia we spent a full day island hopping, drinking champagne, and eating seafood that looked like the restaurant dipped a net into the ocean and cooked up whatever they caught.

I rode on the famous gondolas in Venice multiple times. We rented bikes in Dublin and spent a full day exploring the city and the surrounding parks. I was able to relax and let my mind wander on some of the most beautiful beaches in Europe. I had deep conversations with local people and formed relationships that will last a lifetime. I laughed, I grew, and I experienced an adventure that changed me forever.

With Willie Fair of The Lost Breed (left)
on the steps of a castle in Budapest, Hungary.

In many ways, it felt like I was at the pinnacle in life. I had a great stream of residual income. I was experiencing some of the most amazing places this world has to offer. The relationships I formed were some of the strongest bonds I ever built. The energy was always perfect, and I was always in a fantastic mood. In fact, I could say that I was the happiest I had ever been in my entire life. I was living my dream and a lifestyle that most could only ever dream of. There was only one real issue, and I was not even experiencing it yet, but I knew it was right around the corner waiting for me.

The issue was that the lifestyle was not sustainable, and I started to feel the same type of content that I saw so many people fall into who lived over there. As I said before, if you aren't growing, you are dying. Although this experience helped me grow drastically as an individual, I started to see stagnation on the horizon. I knew that if I stayed too much longer, the growth would come to a halt and I would be trapped in that crazy lifestyle. Instinctively, I knew that was not an option.

As soon as I had that feeling, I made the decision that at the end of that fall, I would return home and focus on taking my business and career to the next level.

19

KING OF CLUBS

ONCE I BOUGHT my return flight, I made sure that I fully enjoyed and appreciated every remaining moment I spent in Italy. The food, the people, the travel, the parties, all of it. By the time I was set to go home, I felt ready. I was exhausted from minimal sleep, constant travel, partying, and the toxic parts that come with living that type of lifestyle. When the final night rolled around, we made sure it would be one that would never be forgotten.

A few of my coworkers who had not returned home yet decided we would go all out. We started the night at our favorite restaurant, La Giostra. The Michelin-star-rated food is to die for and the authentic atmosphere featuring a ceiling of tiny white lights that sparkle like stars in the night's sky with walls covered in fine wine and photographs of celebrities who dined in the establishment is unparalleled. I ordered their famous pear ravioli coupled with an entree of sea bass and a glass of my favorite Chianti.

After we finished up dinner, we headed to Green Street for one final pregame. I got into my position behind the bar and reached into the refrigerator. This time there was a bottle of Moët champagne waiting for me to celebrate. I popped the cork, took over the aux cord, and started playing all of my favorite songs. The vibe was perfect, and I mentally entered one of those zones where you know you are going to have one of the best nights of your life.

I started to make my rounds in the bar and went up to the loft to take a seat. I was at a table with six of the girls I worked with, feeling nostalgic that this would be the last of the nights that we had grown accustomed to having together.

After our pregame, we made the walk down to our Monday night club, Yab. This was the same club I went to on the night that marked the beginning of my relationship with Bryan. The same club that Hannah had to vouch for me as the security guards hesitantly let me in. Boy, had we come a long way.

As I approached the red ropes, the security guards turned around and were shouting my name with huge smiles. They immediately escorted our squad inside and gave me hugs because they knew it was my last night. We were escorted into VIP, and for that night, the table next to the DJ booth was all ours.

As soon as we got into our section, Bryan had bottles of Grey Goose sent over and handed out sparklers to all the girls we were with. They started waving them around with no care in the world that they were coming within centimeters of turning their besties' hair into a crisp. We all got on top of the couches and entered full-blown celebration mode.

I zoned out for a moment and looked around the club. Different colored lights were flashing and illuminating a sea of beautiful European women dancing to my favorite music. Around our table were all of the best friends I made during my stay in Italy putting on a show with their dance moves.

I thought about how I did this Italian experience to perfection. The hype had me feeling like the fourth member of Migos and I started doing my signature dance move, The Hurricane, to celebrate. As I rotated my body in a storm-like motion, the energy of our group elevated even higher.

Midway through my performance, I heard a voice on the microphone as the music and crowd of people dancing momentarily froze.

"John!"

I looked over to see the owner of the club standing behind the DJ booth pointing at me.

"You are my brother, man. Enjoy your final night and thank you for everything, big guy."

He shot me a smile as the music picked back up and the attention of the club turned to me.

Seconds later, Bryan appeared at our table with another bottle of champagne and started spraying it all over the place. To this day, the way that I felt at that moment in time has never been matched. I felt euphoric and almost invincible. I was so grateful that I attracted all of this into my life.

What I accomplished there in such a short period of time blew my mind away. I felt like there was nothing I could not do, no goal I could not accomplish. I went to this country not knowing a single person and made all of this happen.

For a moment, I started to wonder to myself if I made the right decision by leaving this all behind. I absolutely loved every moment. I felt like I was on top of the world. I knew that going forward I would probably never have another experience like the one I had in Italy. I hustled hard to get in that position, and I was going to walk away from it.

On the contrary, I thought about the bigger picture. Being prominent in the Florence nightlife scene was awesome, but it was a dead-end street. There was no future for me there. There was no career for me in it, and I had reached the pinnacle of what was possible. If I stayed, I would get sucked into this lifestyle that simply was not sustainable and would not get me any closer to my long-term goals.

I knew going home to pursue building my business was the right choice. I saw what it was producing for me while I was basically unplugged traveling the world, I could only imagine what it would do with my focus and attention. I knew if I set my mind on any goal, I would make it happen.

My biggest problem was that I had a few mental hang-ups with my business. The failure of my first Network Marketing business lingered in my head. It prevented me from diving back into the industry and giving it 100 percent effort. Sure, I had been sharing with people here and there, but I was not treating it like a business. I would have to do some serious mental reconditioning to get back in the game.

What confused me was that I did not have any of these issues in any other category of my life. The fear of judgment and social rejection did not bother me in any other business or area of my life, only there. I knew it was an obstacle I would have to overcome.

We partied until the club closed. I said my bittersweet goodbyes to all of the people who had become family to me during this period of my life and returned to our shit hole apartment for the final time. I felt like I had just closed my eyes when the sound of my alarm pierced my ears.

The cab pulled into the airport and dropped me off. I surveyed the scene where Drapes and I pulled off our historic flyering stunt. I could not help but burst out in a huge smile at the thought of him sprinting for the taxis with an angry teacher trying to chase him down.

I checked my bags, went through security and sat down with my headphones in waiting to board. This time, "The Best Is Yet to Come" by the legendary Frank Sinatra circulated through my head. This chapter of life had been one that could never be replicated. However, I also knew that the next one would be just as great in a way of its own.

20

I'M GOING TO BE ON
THAT STAGE NEXT YEAR

My FIRST FEW weeks back were full of spending time with family and catching up with friends I had not seen since graduation. In catching up with all my friends, I noticed some trends.

People treat you like a superstar once you've returned from living outside of the country for a period of time. All my friends followed my Instagram and Snapchats. They saw me in a different country every weekend, a different club every weeknight, and the amazing selection of food I ate on a daily basis. All while most of them were transitioning into their full-time jobs or still in school.

Some people think posting stuff like that is arrogant, but I knew it was just advertising. Every time I saw someone in person, they would rant and rave about how surreal my life looked. They would confess how jealous they were and how badly they wanted to live a life like that.

The truth was, I did not want people to be jealous of me or envy me. I wanted to help people live the same life I was designing. What's awesome about my business is that I had the platform to offer them that could allow them to live the same life. I was gearing up for the next big wave in my Network Marketing business, and showing everyone the experience I had in Italy via social media was a key element.

My friends could tell I was in a different zone and that I was looking to make serious moves. I was ready for more. I estimated in Europe that I probably received $200,000+ worth of free bottle service, VIP, alcohol, and food. Not that I would never party again, but I had gotten so much out of my system. My business was now the focus, and the timing was perfect.

My Network Marketing company has a huge event at the start of every year to gear everyone up to crush the year ahead. It is normally a three-day conference where the top producers in our company coach, inspire, and teach us how to take full advantage of the opportunity. I had been to a couple of these events before, but there was normally conflict with school, so it was difficult for me to attend. This one I had had no distractions and no excuses. I would absorb all of the coaching and get myself into massive action.

After Christmas and New Year's passed, it was time to get on a plane to head to San Antonio for the New Year's kickoff event.

The whole weekend was exactly what I needed and put me exactly in the place that I needed to be mentally. I saw that my mom and Cyndi had over one hundred of their team members there, most of whom were around their age. All of them came up to me to express how impressed they were with the life I was leading. They all asked if I could talk to their kids to share with them what I had been able to accomplish so far with the business and how they could do it themselves.

I saw Cyndi announced on stage as one of the company's newest millionaires. I listened to story after story of how people were able to take control of their lives with this vehicle. But there was one segment in particular that launched me into tunnel vision mode.

As I was sitting in the crowd of about 5,000 of our associates, they began to do a recognition segment. Six-figure annual earners. Seven-figure annual earners. Top-ten income earners in the entire company. Then, the group that made everything relatable to me came out.

"And now, I would like to take a moment to recognize a very special movement within our community," announced the company owner's son. "The START group. In START, our vision is to ignite all young people to own their lives physically and financially and, through our contributions, create freedom and a lasting legacy. Every single person you are about to see has made a significant impact on the lives of thousands of other people, and that's the reason they are as successful as they are today. This group is special and the future of our company. So, without any further ado, I would like to announce the top-ten income earners for ages twenty-five and under!"

The upbeat dance music started playing and everyone stood up cheering. Starting from number ten, they began to announce the ten young leaders who were leading the charge in the START movement. As they walked across the stage, I noticed something.

There was no difference between them and myself. They were all normal people who simply yearned for more out of life. Normal people who were committed to making a substantial impact. Normal people who refused to settle for a normal life and the status quo. Seeing them walk the stage inspired me beyond belief. If they could do it, so could I. I leaned over to my mom who was sitting next to me.

"Mom. I'm going to be on that stage next year," I said to her with an unshakable level of confidence.

She looked at me with wide eyes, smiled, and nodded her head. "You belong up there. I already see it happening."

A fire lit inside of me. Some people get jealous when they see other people succeeding at a higher level. Not me. It could not motivate me more. For me, it instills the belief that what you are going after is possible. Those ten people up there, whether they knew it or not, instilled a resolute belief in me. I decided that the following year I would be up there with them.

I came home and wasted no time. I had the same levels of excitement and conviction as I did when I was first introduced to this industry. The first person I went to was Brent, my roommate from my last two years of college and the most well-rounded person I knew who was now like a brother to me. He had been watching me use and share these products for almost three years now, two of which while he was living with me.

For some reason, he always was hesitant to try them and share them, even though I knew he could absolutely crush the opportunity that went along with it. He was the most knowledgeable person I knew when it came to exercise, and on top of that, he had a vast network. Years of bouncing at the bar, being the president of our fraternity, combined with being an extremely outgoing person led to him having an abundance of connections and influence. This time, the conversation went much differently.

During my seven months in Italy, he had been working at a supplement store. There, he was forced to sell products based on what the store would make the most money from, not based on what was best for the customer. Being as passionate as he was about the health and wellness field, he found this upsetting and wrong. He decided to quit because he felt scummy by going along with this.

In addition, he had been working sixty-plus-hour weeks the entire time I was away. He was managing a bar, which included bouncing, cleaning, and cooking in the kitchen. He worked at the supplement store and was also working with a physical therapist. With all of these hours he was putting in, he was making just about as much as I was while I was having the time of my life traveling the world. This caught his attention.

Brent agreed to hear me out and told me he was way more open to the business this time around. We met up at his house, and I brought a wide variety of products for him to take a look at along with materials to show our compensation plan. After an hour of considering with a refreshed, open mind, he could not deny the quality of our products and how lucrative our compensation plan was. To go along with the opportunity I showed him, he had ideas of how to take the business to a whole different level.

Back in college, he made a substantial amount of money selling meal and workout plans. In fact, he almost jeopardized his entire career by doing so. Brent was notorious for his infrequent, however impactful, social media posts. They were insightful, hysterical, and extremely offensive to some.

When he decided to launch his workout/meal plan business, he made it public on the UCONN Buy or Sell page—the same page we used to flip tickets and salvage our bus business. In his long post, he absolutely shit all over our subpar recreation facility and staff. Everyone found it hysterical, except for the rec center, of course. They sat him down and threatened his degree and future for the slander. Ultimately, they couldn't do anything about it, but it certainly pissed people off.

Anyway, hundreds of people reached out to Brent to purchase one of his programs. They were top of the line and designed with his extensive kinesiology background. Everyone loved them and he made a lot of money providing people with a plan of unparalleled value. Toward the end of the semester, as we approached graduation, he had stopped making them and the whole operation died off.

Now, he wanted to get back in the game. He saw our business as an opportunity to provide people with top-of-the-line nutrition, but we could take it even a step further by adding in the workout expertise that he could provide. He had been thinking about the idea for a while and thought this was the perfect storm to execute it.

Myself, Brent, and our friend Robinson made the decision during senior year that we would move to California sometime after college. Now that I was back from Italy, we planned on making the move in a few months, and if we did it right, we could get a team on the East Coast and one on the West Coast to spread our movement. We would call it Coast2Coast Fitness. The whole movement bred even more excitement and excellent grounds to present our opportunity to people. We were fired up and got the ball rolling right away.

I knew exactly what we had to do. The beautiful part about Network Marketing is that the road map is laid out for any individual who wants to succeed with the business. The support is there, and so is the coaching and mentorship. The reason why people fail is because they take no action, or they quit. If you simply do what is proven to work and stick with the course, success is inevitable in the long run.

We sat down and started listing off our friends whom we thought would be a good fit for this. From a product perspective, almost everyone was a candidate. All our friends worked out, were in great shape, and used supplements, so from that side, it would be a simple matter of switching them over to our far more superior products.

From a business standpoint, most of our friends were ambitious and wanted to live life to the fullest. If we could paint the picture properly, we could show them how this is a vehicle that we could all do together.

The next step? We jumped into action. There is never a perfect time to contact someone or perfect words to say. Without jumping into action, you will paralyze yourself and ultimately end up doing nothing at all. From the island in my mom's kitchen, we picked up our phones and started messaging our friends to set up meetings. We messaged them with excitement and confidence. We told everyone we were launching something huge and wanted them to hear us out and potentially be a part of it.

Nobody could ignore the synergy Brent and I had. Before we even officially set up meetings, people were already telling us that they wanted in.

One after another, everyone was hopping on board with our vision. We would not even be able to finish explaining what we were doing and people would want in. They did not ask for the price, small details, or any other information. They understood the bigger picture and wanted to team up with us. After we talked to the core group of people we originally wanted to partner with, most of them joined us.

The next step was to have an event. When you have a room full of people and you are speaking to them, the vision feels much more real. People can feel your energy, passion, and excitement. They conceptualize your words in a tangible way. That is the way to build this business. So we scheduled an event for the following week at no other place than UCONN. A few of the people we enrolled still went to school there, so it made sense logistically to host the event there.

Leading up to the event, more and more people were getting on board. We told everybody about the event and to simply show up with a couple of their friends. With the momentum we had going, my excitement and passion were fully back. Every phone call and every conversation lit a fire inside me.

When the calls were over, I would be pacing around with an adrenaline rush. I felt unstoppable and I could not wait for the event. I always thrived in front of the room, and I knew this was going to be the catalyst for the snowball effect.

The weekend came and it was time for the event. We met up at a friend's off-campus house. He had joined our team, was full of excitement, and offered to host the event. The only issue was that the night before he had a huge party. The house was littered with beer cans and empty liquor bottles.

On top of that, there was about a half-inch of "aftermath fluid" on the floor from spilled drinks, tracked-in dirt, and whatever other nastiness goes on in a fraternity house. Everyone was set to come in the next thirty minutes, so we got to work making the place look presentable.

People started to show up, and the turnout was much larger than we expected. We did not have ample seating, and people were even pouring into the side rooms surrounding the living room. A lot of them we knew from school; some we were acquaintances with; and some we did not know at all. We walked around greeting everyone as they entered. There was a huge buzz of excitement from those who had already joined us and a lot of curiosity from those who had not.

We waited ten minutes past the official start time to get the event started to make sure everyone was there and settled. About forty people in total showed up and formed a large circle around the room. I looked over to Brent who was wearing the purple polo of the new chiropractic school he would begin attending in a few months. He was set to kick off the event, my mom would share, I would close it out, and then we would have a few testimonials and answer any questions.

I nudged Brent to get it started. He stepped in front of the crowd and all of the girls turned their attention to him with starstruck eyes as he was essentially a campus celebrity. He started to speak and took control.

"All right, guys, we are going to get started here. First of all, thank you all for coming. For those of you who do not know me, my name is Brent Young. I graduated from UCONN last year with my degree in exercise science and will be attending Palmer Chiropractic next year, the best chiro school in the country. I am very passionate about fitness and nutrition, and that's why we invited you all here today. We have an opportunity for you to experience the best possible nutrition and even create a business opportunity out of it," he said. The crowd was already dying to hear more.

I could not have been more impressed. This whole time I knew how great he would be at this. To see it actually happen in person was so fulfilling.

He went on to describe his background in more depth, his passion for the field, his experience at the supplement store, his reluctance to join me at first, and ultimately our vision moving forward. By the time he passed it off to my mom, I could tell everyone wanted in.

My mom stepped up to speak her piece. She has a special type of energy when she gets in front of a room that I have never experienced from anyone else. She is funny, genuine, inspirational, and captivating.

Everyone always is teetering between laughter and tears from how motivational her story is.

She described how she grew up and never even went to college. She talked about her different hustles, which included cleaning houses, owning a bakery, and working for other direct sales companies. She talked about the devastating injuries she overcame. She shared how she decided to become a marathon runner in her forties. She described how hard she worked and how she never was able to earn a six-figure income.

She shared how this nutrition had completely changed her life in all facets. She showed everyone what Network Marketing has done for her and why she is so passionate about it. Ultimately, she brought an abundance of legitimacy to the audience. After fully showing the room of people what's possible, she passed it off to me.

I had nothing prepared. I did not need anything prepared. I had grown so passionate about this industry that my presentation came straight from the heart when I spoke. I stood up to talk and looked around at forty faces of twenty-somethings like me who desperately needed what we had to offer. I told them all they needed to hear. My story.

From not being able to afford school. To attending a branch school from home. My first experience with Network Marketing. All of the ventures I tried in between. How I graduated with an income that allowed me to move to a different country and live there for seven months, getting paid every week. The pain and suffering all the way to the greatest gifts we can get out of life. The vision of what we could build together. The impact we could have on world health and finances.

After about fifteen minutes I wrapped it up. I thanked every single person for taking their time to come and hear us out. I informed them that we would be hanging around after and if anyone had questions, we could answer them. If anyone wanted in, we could get them started. I let them know to simply talk with the person who brought them there, and they could give them the next steps.

After one last thank you, I walked back to my seat to have a sip of water. There were a few seconds of silence, then the room erupted in chatter.

The girls stormed my mom asking her all about her journey and told her how amazing she was. The guys came up to Brent and me, seriously impressed with what we were doing and where we were about to go. People were taking out their computers and enrolling with us on the spot.

Of course, there were the few people who had stale faces and did not like what we were doing one bit. You will have that with anything you do. However, for the most part, the first event was a big win in my eyes. After we set up all the new people with accounts, set up times to follow up with people who expressed a lot of interest, and answered everyone's questions, we had a short meeting with all of the emerging leaders.

We knew we would be moving to California soon, but until then we would have these events weekly to show new people our movement. Everyone was fired up and extremely excited to build this business. We created a large group message for everyone to stay in touch, support, and help one another. I made sure everyone knew how to follow up with their prospects and that they knew I was here to help them with whatever they needed.

I left the house with a huge smile on my face. I had been envisioning this exact scenario for two years, and it was finally coming to fruition. There is no feeling that comes close to the one when you are experiencing manifestation. On top of that, I knew that these products would be life-changing for everyone, as they had been for me and hundreds of thousands of other people.

True fulfillment comes when you know you are positively impacting the lives of others and bringing them serious value. I knew we were on to something huge, and it made it even better that I was doing it with some of my closest friends.

Not even a half hour went by after I left and I was already receiving text messages from new teammates who had prospects who wanted in. My phone was blowing up. We had successfully launched this exactly the way we wanted to and had created momentum.

Once you enter momentum, you need to keep your foot on the gas. I offered my assistance with phone calls, video chats, and meetings to every person on our team. On top of that, we planned our next event. There were always open classrooms at UCONN, so we scheduled one for the next weekend in one of the newer buildings. We figured that it would be a lot more professional and classier than the fraternity house. Plus, it probably would not require cleaning up beer sludge either.

The next week was filled with calls and excitement. I was at my parents' house running between my bedroom and my mom's office, where we would sit, strategize, and envision. We would be up at midnight, her at her desk, me on the couch, strategizing and talking bigger picture.

We talked much deeper than business alone. We would talk about what motivated us. About what we wanted out of life. About our beliefs and values. We would have the type of conversations that actually had meaning behind them and lit a fire inside of you to kick ass. After our long talks, we would get right back into action.

Our event the following week was just as big a success. We filled up the lecture hall and gave our presentation again. We went with the same format as last time; however, it went a bit differently this time around. We all were a little better. We had a better flow, better confidence, and better conviction.

The best part is that when we were done, the presentation continued in the form of testimonials. People began to get their products and had earned some money. Person after person, they raved about their product experience and how blown away they were by their energy levels after just a few days. They talked about how they had already earned a few hundred dollars, which would take them an entire week at the jobs they had alongside school.

What started off as our vision was starting to become real. The new prospects were seeing real people who were having real results. This helped tremendously. I personally had a phenomenal transformation with the products over the years and also had reaped extreme financial benefits. This was valuable to share, but it did not hit home with everybody.

Some people looked at the situation like it was fine for me, but their vision was not yet big enough to see themselves in my position. They figured I could do it because I was me, but they never could because they were them. If they only knew.

On top of that, some people did not want a life where they were living in another country and traveling all over the place. Some people thought they might need to adopt that sort of lifestyle in order to succeed, which was certainly not the case. They would be inspired but, in the end, think that it could never be them. However, for the others who were similar to me, they were fired up to know this lifestyle was possible. They were excited to change their life, to take control, and for the permission to dream much larger than they had previously allowed themselves to.

We had it all in the room from multiple six-figure-income earners to people who made $100 on the side. People who were gaining energy from the products, who lost a few pounds, or even had life-changing transformations. We were building a community of different experiences that made us relatable to a much wider range of individuals. This was instrumental for relating to those who only wanted a little more energy or to lose a few pounds. This showed them that they did not have to build some massive business in order to have a positive experience with the opportunity.

At the end of our presentation, we had the same results as our first. People stayed around for an hour after we ended, chatting and asking questions about our opportunity. More people signed up on the spot. One of my friends, in particular, came up to me right after we finished.

"I should have joined you when you told me about this years ago. Watching you do whatever the hell you want and use the world as your playground has made me a bit jealous, but more inspired than ever. I want in," he told me.

After that last night at the club in Italy, I had been worried I might have made the wrong decision. I now knew that this was exactly how my story was meant to play out.

The next month we kept up the same routine. All week I would be assisting new team members with calls for coaching and new prospects. On the weekend we would have an event. It got to the point where one night I was sitting at home, and I got a Facetime from my future roommate in California, Robinson. As his fully bearded face and eyes full of mystery appeared on my phone, he turned the camera to show he was at the bar with three of our friends surrounding him. He had been talking to them at the bar for the past hour, and all three wanted to join. He literally pulled out his laptop and began to sign them all up in the middle of the chaos as I helped him over the phone.

Since I returned from Italy, we kept pushing back the moving date for California. Brent wanted to earn as much money as he could from the bar, and Robinson wanted to do the same at the restaurant where he worked. The beginning of Brent's semester at chiro school in California was starting in a couple of months, so we knew we had to decide on a date soon.

Considering these factors, the momentum with our business, and leaving behind everything we built the past five years, it was a tough move, but we were all excited for the new adventure and growth it would bring. We finally all sat down one day and locked into a beautiful apartment in San Jose, California. We had exactly one month before we would head west with nothing but a pickaxe and pan in search of gold. People told us we missed the gold rush wave, but we told them it was better late than never.

A few days before our moving date, I was scrolling through Facebook. A live video popped up on our company's group page from the founder's son. It was titled January Top Income Earners. I tuned in.

The first few minutes he talked about the company, how much of an impact we were making, and how proud he was to be part of such a fantastic group of young professionals impacting the health of the world. Then he got into announcing the top earners for the month, starting with ages eighteen to twenty-five. He announced number ten, then nine, then eight.

"And our number seven income earner for the month of January is John Stankiewicz from Goshen, Connecticut. John has had a ton of action going on in his organization this month, keep up the hard work, bud," he announced.

I yelled to my mom to replay her the video.

"Oh my gosh. Congratulations," she screamed as she gave me a huge hug. I was on track for my goal of being a top earner for the year, but I needed to keep up the hard work. I knew it would not come easy. Still, I could already see and feel it happening.

This little video provided so much encouragement and belief that I would make it happen. Even though it hardly felt like work because I enjoyed it so much, I had been grinding ever since I came back, and it was fulfilling to see my goals coming together.

Moving day came and the all-too-familiar feeling of leaving everything behind for the unknown set in again. As many times as you do it, I do not think you ever feel comfortable about it. This is a good sign because when you get uncomfortable, you know you are going to experience growth, but, at the same time, you cannot help that little voice inside your head that questions your every move. All you can do is stay optimistic and positive that the experience ahead will be an amazing adventure.

I loaded up what was left of my belongings into my mom's car to head to the airport. The rest of them were in my car, which was being shipped out to California. All of my furniture was with Robinson, who had rented a trailer to drive out. In fact, I had just gotten off a Facetime with him.

He was in Colorado where he got hit with a huge snowstorm in the mountain passes. He had to pull off and get a hotel. There, he was experiencing altitude sickness and had tacked on another day to his adventure. And he wondered why I did not want to ride shotgun with him on that adventure.

"Now boarding for flight 8044 to San Jose, California," the flight attendant said over the intercom. We got up and boarded the plane. I found my seat, next to the window, and threw my headphones on. This time I went with Kanye's album *Graduation*. "Good Morning" began to play, and I slumped back into my seat and stared out the window onto the runway.

I always loved how unconventional and against the grain Kanye is. His music helped me through so much, especially in times of transition and immense change. It also served as a reminder and permission to stay true to myself, especially when I was making moves where no one else understood my perspective. It helped me realize it doesn't matter as long as it feels right to me.

Next stop, California.

21

THE ROLLER COASTER OF LIFE

THIS IS WHERE I wish I could tell you that we moved out to California, flourished in success, bought a mansion in the hills, became the real-life *Entourage*, and lived happily ever after with wives of Sommer Ray caliber. Unfortunately, that was hardly the case.

If life was a roller coaster, I was at the peak height of Kingda Ka when I moved to California. I had just come off the time of my life in Italy, and as soon as I got home, my business began to explode.

My happiness, relationships, fulfillment, energy, attitude, confidence, career, and outlook on life were all at record highs. Just like when we were making a killing in the stock market, you never expect a sudden downturn when all you see is green and everything is trending upward. The undesirable truth is that all markets correct themselves. Life's highs are so marvelous because of how dark the lows can be.

It's important to remember that life is just that—a roller coaster. However, unlike a traditional roller coaster, this one is not a loop. This roller coaster is a line, from start to finish, where there are peaks, drops, twists, flips, and unexpected turns. You have no idea what exactly the course will be in front of you, and you can always reach new record highs and lows. Additionally, you can never get off the roller coaster, so you must embrace the ride until it is over.

One month into California, I rounded my record-high peak and was sent into a free fall.

The first month was fantastic. We had a gorgeous three-story apartment with a roof deck overlooking the rolling golden mountains that was nicer than any place I had ever lived. We settled in and the three of us explored California like we had just discovered the New World.

We wandered aimlessly through the famous Redwood Forest. We spent a couple of days on the beaches of Santa Cruz. We crossed the Golden Gate Bridge and sipped champagne while overlooking San Francisco from one of the most high-end rooftops.

We frequently went on hikes and got completely lost within the beauty of the state. We found a gym that felt like a Cancun resort where we spent multiple hours a day at working out, playing basketball, and lounging by the pool. At night, we ate at great restaurants and enjoyed the nightlife scene.

The new experience was a blast. However, as the first month was coming to an end, I was ready to get back on the grind and into a good routine. Brent was close to starting school and knew that most of his time would be consumed with class and studying. Robinson was running out of money and needed to get a job. As for business, we were facing some problems, and it was no wonder why.

We had just uprooted ourselves and moved across the country. When you are in a mode of growth and momentum like we were, taking your foot off the gas pedal is the worst thing you can do. We had cast a big vision and created a movement back home, and then all of a sudden left. Our support, leadership, and culture of events were driving the growth.

With all of us gone, our team back East was beginning to lack direction. Throughout our first month, I was still getting on phone calls, but I noticed that as more time passed, more people started to quit. They stopped ordering, made excuses about the products and business, or just stopped answering my calls altogether. I was getting discouraged by it and, as a result, so were Robinson and Brent.

Before we knew it, Brent started school and Robinson found a job selling designer jewelry. Both were completely unplugged from the business, and most of the team we had built just a month earlier had unraveled.

I started having negative thoughts and beliefs surrounding my business. I started to feel like I did after I failed my first business. I started to blame the business model. I blamed other people for being quitters and lazy. The craziest part? I was still making great money. I was just so beat up from losing all of the people we had just brought on board.

One of the strangest parts for me was that for almost my entire life, I lived places where I had a huge network or had an abundance of resources to build one. Here, I felt completely alone. I spent the majority of the day alone while my roommates were at school or work. I noticed that the majority of the population here in Silicon Valley was foreign, working high-end tech jobs, and not the most outgoing. I also didn't have a platform like school, the travel company, or club promotion to meet people through.

I thought of the different ways that I could meet people, earn extra money, and ideally still be on my own schedule. Regardless of the funk I had fallen into, I still wanted to keep my business the main focus. Only a few options fit the criteria of what I was looking for, but I soon found what I thought would be the perfect platform. The ultimate side hustle of our generation: Uber.

My thought process was that I could drive for a few hours a day when it was convenient for me and make some extra money. More importantly, I saw it as an opportunity to have conversations with anyone who entered my car. I thought this would be a creative way to bring new people into my network and, ideally, my business. It all made sense and I had nothing to lose, so I quickly took action and got everything I needed in line to begin driving.

On my first day on the road, I began around noon. I thought that the app must have been broken because it took forty-five minutes until I received my first ride request. I jumped to accept it and was directed to a grocery store within a strip mall. An Indian man with a few bags of groceries hopped into my car, and I drove him ten minutes down the road to his apartment. I dropped him off and immediately was compensated for the ride.

Easy enough, I thought to myself as I pulled away. I drove for two more hours before I went back to work on my business at our apartment.

Through trial and error, I realized that the afternoon was the worst possible time to drive. After a couple of weeks, I noticed that 7:00 to 10:00 a.m. was the best window to be on the road. This is when everyone was commuting to work. Mostly, I would deal with professionals. Uber also offers surge rates in times of high demand, and almost all the rides during this time frame would be higher than normal.

Another bonus was that there were no drunken fools who could potentially puke all over your car at this hour. I got into the routine of driving in this window during the weekdays. Then I would go to the gym and work on my business throughout the remainder of the day. This was working out well, and I was certainly bringing in decent money on the side, but as time went on, I began to doubt my original thought process.

You really never knew exactly what you would get when a passenger got into your car. Sometimes the person was silent; sometimes they were extremely outgoing and chatty; sometimes they were complete dicks; and sometimes they were psychotic and boldly stated their controversial thoughts.

I had a ton of great conversations, yet for many, I could not wait to get the person the fuck out of my car. I learned a lot from the interactions themselves, but my plan to promote my business was simply not going the way I planned.

Everyone who was talkative would always ask what else I did along with Uber, which would be a great segue to explaining my story and my business. A lot of times people would just say "that's awesome" and then talk about themselves. Sometimes people would inquire further and ask a lot of questions. Some would seem seriously interested in the business opportunity or even in losing some weight. We would have a long discussion, but the trend was always the same in the end. After we connected at the end of the ride and they got out of my car, I would not hear from them again. It seemed to me as if there were a few reasons why.

The first was that I was their Uber driver. I already had a disadvantage from the beginning of the conversation. I was working a not-so-desirable job in a 2008 Nissan Altima trying to preach about a business where they could have financial freedom. From their perspective, they were probably thinking, "If this kid is really crushing this business, then why the hell is he driving for Uber?" It did not matter what my true intentions were, because that is the way they viewed the interaction.

Another issue was that I only had so much time with them. People entertained the conversation, but almost as soon as they left my car, they forgot about me and moved on with their life. It is not a reasonable amount of time to form a real relationship and, more importantly, trust. A lot of people will entertain the conversation for the sake of it but have no intention of taking any action.

I am a very optimistic person who gives every idea I try a fighting chance. After a few months of this strategy and gaining zero customers or business partners from it, I started to fall into a funk. The entire team we formed earlier in the year had fallen off, and even though I was still making good money, I began to second guess myself. I was spending most of my time alone; my business was not exploding the way I thought it would; and I started to doubt my future with Network Marketing.

I sat down after Ubering one morning with no prospecting calls booked, no training calls booked, and an empty schedule for the day. I was frustrated and was in a position where I had no idea what to do moving forward. Negative thoughts started to run through my head, and I began to question everything. I wondered if moving out to California was an awful decision.

I talked to my mom on the phone daily to stay motivated to kick my business up a notch, and even she could tell I was mentally off. I would not say I was depressed, but I felt like I was completely lacking direction.

I decided to start looking for other opportunities.

I was scrolling through different sales opportunities in the area, and I stumbled upon one that caught my attention. I found a company in search of a representative to sell solar panels. I contacted them, went to a group interview, got the position, and went through a week of training.

The company provided leads, which was appealing to me since I did not know anyone out there. The commission for a sale could range anywhere from $2,000 to $6,000, depending on the number of panels sold. This sounded awesome and I was ready to make some sales.

During the training, I did not learn much about solar. Just their elevator pitch and sly tactics to use to get the potential customer to sign the paperwork. The quintessential slimy salesman training us frequently ran his hand through his slicked back black hair and talked about how much money he made selling panels.

At the end of the week of training, we took a test, and if we passed, we would be ready to go on house calls. I passed the test with ease, and the next week I would start to put my training to the test.

Here's how their leads worked: The company paid a call center to get people on the phone, ask them a series of questions, and then ideally set up a meeting at their home to learn more about solar. From there, the call center would notify the company that the person agreed to a meeting, then the company would reach out and confirm a time. Once they confirmed a time, they would call one of the sales reps to go and make the sale.

Basically, they could call me at any time of day, and I was expected to make it happen. They additionally were adamant about making the sale at the first meeting.

I received my first call for an appointment that was thirty minutes from my apartment. I showed up to the house with my notebook and computer to hopefully close on the spot. Even though the house was modest, I knew that we were in the Bay Area where homes typically cost no less than a million dollars.

I knocked on the door and was greeted by a stressed-out middle-aged woman who brought me to their kitchen table. There were at least five kids running around the living room screaming, multiple dogs barking, and a full family in the kitchen cooking food for a party they were hosting in an hour.

The disgruntled woman and her husband sat down at the table with me. I started to make small talk, which they completely breezed over because they only had ten minutes to talk. I thought back to my training where they told me I should be in the house for absolutely no less than two hours. What the hell was I supposed to do here?

I jumped right into our pitch without building rapport. I started firing through the preliminary questions that helped us get an idea of the potential customer's situation to see if solar would be a good fit. I asked what they currently pay for electricity. If their home is mortgaged or paid for. If they have ever looked into solar in the past. Have they ever had any home improvements done, and if so did they pay in cash or with a loan?

"That's pretty personal. Why do you need to know that?" the lady snapped.

"Yeah seriously. What does that have to do with solar?" the guy wanted to know.

It was a tactic to figure out how they would pay for the solar panels if we were to get them to agree to buy.

"They are just a few questions we ask everybody before we can decide if solar is the right fit for you!" I replied. They looked at each other with unease.

I started to break down their electricity bill to show them how much money they were already spending monthly.

"We really don't have time for this. How much is solar going to cost us?" the guy asked.

I could tell they were getting ready to kick me out of the house. I rushed into the estimate and showed them the numbers.

"This is outrageous. How the hell does this make any sense?" the guy yelled at me with disgust.

I tried to explain to them how, when you broke it down monthly, they would be paying less than they do to the electric company currently and after a period of time it would lead to free electricity.

"We just can't afford this. Sorry."

I thought back to my training. They said when you need reinforcement, call our sales hub and a top salesperson will answer to support the process.

"I am going to call my boss quick. He will definitely be able to explain how this is going to help you stop wasting money," I said as I was already dialing the phone. They told us to never ask before calling.

A man with a thick Australian accent answered. I briefly explained to him where we were and put him on speakerphone. He introduced himself, then rapidly tried to close the sale. This made the couple even more uncomfortable. They pulled every excuse out of the book until, finally, the guy gave up and got off the phone.

Now the family wanted me out of there immediately. I got their information to contact them to further the discussion, but I knew there was no shot they would answer me back. I left the house to go back to my apartment.

On the ride home, I was thinking about what I could have done better. To be honest, I was not discouraged for some reason. I just figured I got unlucky with the awful circumstances. The next time would surely be better.

This pattern continued for the next six meetings. Every single house I went into contained an extremely underqualified lead like these: People who had horrible credit and could not get access to financing even if they wanted to. Old people who asked me why they should care about the money they would be saving in twenty-five years when they did not think they would live another five. People who did not care about solar at all, they just wanted someone to come to their house to vent to about their horrible life.

After a few tries, I was much better at our pitch, but it did not matter if the people weren't eligible to buy.

The eighth meeting was with a couple in a relatively nice home and who seemed pretty normal. I hit it off with the wife right away, but the husband was insistent that this was not going to happen from the start. The wife kept telling me I reminded her of her son, which is why she liked me so much. They were skeptical because they had been ripped off in the past and lost a ton of money, but they felt that they could trust me. They told me they only had one hour tops, but I managed to stretch it into three.

I strategically weaved through the sales process, building rapport when they started feeling uncomfortable. Whenever the husband sensed I was pushing to the next step of the process, he would show resistance. The wife and I turned it into a joke, and, eventually, he caved and said it was her decision. It got to be late at night, and we decided to schedule a meeting in a few days. I was going to return with a more accurate estimate, and from there we would make it happen.

I felt great about the meeting. I talked to my boss to ask for any tips. He just assured me that he had faith in me. I returned two nights later and was able to close the deal. They decided on redoing their roof and putting panels on it. The cost of this project would be $45,000, which they would use a special type of loan with specialized tax benefits.

The commission I would receive would be about $4,000, which felt incredible after all the failed interactions. We signed all of the paperwork, and I left the house with a feeling of accomplishment.

Two days later I received a voice-mail from the wife.

"Hi, John. I am very disappointed. You told me that the cost of this project was $45,000, and I trusted you. The finance company just called me and told me that the loan is actually $55,000 after all their fees and will be $85,000 once I pay the entire balance back. I cannot believe you kept this from me. I canceled the loan and will not be working with your company. Click."

I was just as shocked as she was. I had no idea about all these additional fees or the total repayment amount. No one ever told me about them. I went straight to my office to get to the bottom of the whole situation.

When I got there, I was greeted with the news that the main guy who was in charge of us had left the company. A new guy was appointed to be in charge. He was an absolute greaseball and called the lady with a barrage of lies to try and fix the situation. It obviously did not work at all. I felt let down, betrayed, and completely out of integrity.

I decided to leave the company at that moment. There was no part of it that I could stand behind. The operation was underhanded, slimy, and strictly conducted in order to profit via deception. I keep a positive attitude, so I was reframing all of the negative situations that had happened, but the truth of it all was staring me right in the eyes.

Even though I still believed in solar, I did not believe in how the company conducted business. They ate by taking advantage of customers who did not know the full extent of what they were signing up for. Most of the people who were working there when I started had quit in just one month's time. When I quit, it was received with anger and bitterness. I took this as a sign that I made the right decision.

Through a very negative experience, I was able to search and find some positives. I learned a few key findings about myself. I am fantastic at sales; however, if it's an offering I cannot put my passion and belief behind, I am awful. I refuse to compromise my integrity and to fuck people over for the sake of putting money in my pocket.

You can have all the scripts and pitches in the world, but if you do not believe in what you are doing, no one else will either. It is not until you come from a place where you are genuinely looking to provide value in the lives of others that you will start seeing success.

More importantly, you will actually feel good about yourself and find fulfillment in what you are doing. You can certainly make some money by being a sleazeball, but trust me when I say that it will come full circle to bite you in the ass.

After this experience, I was even more lost than before in California. I had a hard time taking any action with my business. I was still driving for Uber for some extra money, but I was hardly even trying to discuss my business. I was thinking of anything I could do to get out of the funk I was in, but I had no answers. I needed a major change to happen and I needed it quick.

22

WHAT HAPPENS IN VEGAS CHANGES LIVES

A FEW DAYS after I quit selling solar, I was on the phone with my mom. I was telling her how I did not know what I should do. She always stayed positive and reminded me of how great I am in our current business. She reminded me of when I said that I would be a top income earner for the year. We talked about how much momentum I had going earlier in the year.

I logically knew what she was saying, but emotionally was so out of tune. We discussed the upcoming event our company was having in Las Vegas. The event would be huge. We would have an action-packed weekend of training and team parties. And Tony Robbins was set to be our keynote speaker. She told me it is exactly what I needed to get out of the lull I was in. I knew I had nothing to lose, so I agreed to go.

The weekend of the event came, and it could not have been better timing. I needed a change, and I needed a change quickly. At the last minute, I convinced Brent to skip a few days of class to come along with me. This got me even more excited for the trip. I knew we would both learn a ton and on top of that have a fantastic time experiencing Vegas.

Our schedule for the weekend was jam-packed, and as soon as we got off the plane, we had to rush to the hotel, then hop on a shuttle with our team for a yacht party on Lake Las Vegas. Cyndi had organized this whole party and all of the top performers on our team would be there.

Our shuttle was waiting at the front of the Venetian hotel. I could feel the Vegas magic in the air as I looked up at the towering hotel illuminated in gold lights. Men and women dressed in their finest tuxedos and gowns hopped out of limousines in hopes of earning their fortune at the roulette table.

We made it in the nick of time to join about fifty people on our team. I had at the very least met each individual at one point or another, and all of them were making a substantial impact with our business. I greeted them all as I went down the aisle with tons of hugs, cheek kisses, and handshakes. Everyone in this community was awesome and had such phenomenal energy.

Many of them were congratulating me on the success I'd been having. They told me how much of an inspiration I was and how it has been so amazing to watch my journey. I thanked everyone with the utmost gratitude. It felt incredible, and I questioned myself why I had been so down. The showering of praise had me feeling better inside for the first time in a few months.

During the forty-five-minute ride over to Lake Las Vegas, I chatted with my teammates about all my adventures in Italy and now California. Everyone was so impressed with how mature of a mindset I had at such a young age. Just like the previous event, everyone kept asking me if I would speak to their kids and younger people on their teams. It made me feel a little uneasy. They had no idea about the internal struggle I was facing regarding my business and overall career.

I kept my composure and offered to set up phone calls to speak with every single one of them. I knew it was my responsibility. Even though I was feeling inauthentic, the reality was that very few people my age were living this type of lifestyle. I had to do whatever I could to pay it back.

During the shuttle ride, my mom introduced me to a man sitting toward the front. His name was Rod Hairston. I had heard him speak in Phoenix a few years back when I cut out of class to attend a prestigious trip my mom earned for her hard work in the company.

From growing up without much in an African American home to serving in the Navy and eventually going on to coach star athletes and business leaders to the Forbes 400 list, his remarkable storytelling abilities kept me on the edge of my seat for the entire hour he held the stage. It takes a special type of person to step on a stage and have the entire room feel like you are speaking to them at an individual level. Rod was that guy.

He was the creator of an online program our company used to instill lasting change in its customers and distributors. The program lasted sixty days, and every single day you would log in to watch short videos and complete various entries. The entries consisted of affirmations, goal setting, vision setting, rewiring your belief systems, and gratitude. This program was a huge hit in the company and was conducive to retention and helping people become a person with a new, healthy identity. My interaction with Rod was brief.

"Rod," my mom said, always capitalizing on any chance she got to brag about me. "This is my son John. He has been building this business with me for a few years now. He was able to graduate and move to Italy because of the income this has provided him. He's now living in California and living the dream."

Rod shook my hand and gave me a warm smile as he made direct eye contact.

"Great to meet you, John. You are a lucky man. Your mother is an amazing woman. There are not many people who are fortunate enough to have this kind of support in their life." He transitioned from a welcoming smile to a wide-eyed head nod that had me physically feel the confidence in what he had just said to me.

"Great to meet you as well," I said. "I really appreciate that, Rod. I know, I feel so fortunate that I've been able to live the life I have so far. My mom has been instrumental in all of this."

I continued: "By the way, this was a few years back, but I was blown away by your piece in Phoenix for the Welcome Home event. You have such an inspiring story and an incredible amount of wisdom to share. It is truly an honor to meet you in person."

"Thank you, John, that really means a lot to me. I wish you continued success. You have so much ahead of you, man. This is just the start," Rod said.

I thanked him, and as our short conversation wrapped up, we pulled into the entrance to Lake Las Vegas. Everybody started cheering as we pulled up to the docks of this gorgeous man-made oasis and saw our gigantic yacht waiting.

I relinked with Brent, who had been having conversations of his own the entire trip over. This was another reason we got along so well. He was one of those people I could bring anywhere, and I never felt like I would have to entertain or babysit him. By the time the ride was over, he had a fan club of his own.

We hopped aboard the yacht and were immediately greeted by servers with trays of hors d'oeuvres and glasses of champagne. Brent and I headed straight for the bar at the front of the boat where we began chatting with the bartender. The situation escalated into us ending up behind the bar helping her serve drinks to everyone on the boat.

At one moment we looked at each other with huge grins as we were handing drinks out while collecting money and asked ourselves the recurring question that came up in nearly every situation we were ever in: What the hell is going on?

After our bartending stint, we headed to the top of the boat where we took a moment to take in the scenery. We were so perplexed by where we were and talked about how crazy humans are. In the middle of the desert, someone decided to dig a 320-acre lake and build luxury resorts surrounding the entire perimeter.

The vision that human beings possess is miraculous. We absorbed all of it and expressed to each other our gratitude at that moment. Gratitude for the moment and all of the life events that had led up to it. Gratitude that this was just the beginning.

We were fully in the moment and entertaining everybody that came up to us on the ship. Somewhere during all of this, we noticed the wheelhouse where the captain was. We climbed a staircase up to it and knocked on the door. The captain greeted us with open arms. Before we knew it, Brent and I had full control of the ship.

Somehow, we convinced the captain that it was a good idea to leave the fate of a boatload of people in our hands, and he was in fact very entertained by it. We both had captains' hats on and a firm grasp of the helm. The entertainment spread to everyone on the ship, especially my mom. Everyone started taking pictures and laughing in hysterics. After about ten minutes, we decided to resign from our new positions strictly to prevent a remake of the *Titanic*.

We returned to the main area of the ship just as Cyndi got on the microphone. She congratulated everyone for their success so far and thanked them for their contributions to the team. She talked about how none of this would be possible without the hard work of each individual who was there. She went on to talk about the upcoming event and how excited she was about our future together. She then passed the microphone to Rod.

Rod gave an insightful speech about how who we are comes down to our beliefs and habits. When we make a conscious decision to change our beliefs surrounding something, we change our thoughts and then we can begin to take action daily toward making that new belief part of our identity.

Once we consciously take action daily to form that new habit, it becomes an unconscious action and part of our identity. He related it to our business and how once you believe you can make it happen, it is as simple as taking the proven action steps until it becomes second nature. At that point, you will have an identity that is in alignment with success in our industry.

I looked around as everyone listened to every word he said with the utmost focus. The best way to describe the crowd was that they were mesmerized. I listened to his message, but the whole time I was fascinated by his influence. This power he had was rare and unique.

Once the boat docked and we shuttled back to the hotel, most everyone went to bed, but since it was Brent's first experience in Vegas, this was not an option. We decided to hit the casinos for some blackjack parlayed with a little exploring of the Strip. By some blackjack and a little exploring, I mean we gambled for hours and explored every square inch that the Strip had to offer. This adventure lasted until 4:00 a.m., which gave us only four hours of sleep before the conference began. Absolutely worth it.

In the morning, we headed down to the conference center that was attached to our hotel. When we got there, it was hard to tell if we were entering a business conference or the Electric Jungle. There was a DJ playing dance music, green lights flashing, and people dancing all over the conference room. The energy had me feeling like I was at a hip-hop concert rather than a business conference. I was getting accustomed to this and knew it was the culture of our company. Brent, on the other hand, could not believe it. He expected us to be in a formal setting, seated, quiet, and serious all day. Our company could not be more opposite to those expectations.

The conference was similar to the ones I had been to in the past. The company owners opened by welcoming all the existing and new distributors. Their genuine levels of excitement and confidence in the vision of the company could turn the biggest skeptic into a believer surrounding what we were doing.

Throughout the day they brought out top performers, scientists, and the corporate team to educate and excite us. They even brought out Flo-Rida for some midday entertainment. They did a fantastic job of creating an environment that was both educational and exciting. By the end of the day, everyone was ready to get to work building their businesses.

Unfortunately, the second day Brent had to go back to California because there was only so much class he could miss. I used this as an opportunity to spend more time with my mom and our team who were all absorbing the immense value that was being poured into us. I diligently listened and went to bed early the next night so I would be mentally sharp for the moment I had been waiting for: Tony Robbins.

The third day was filled with fantastic training and useful tools to use to explode our business. I got so much out of it, but in the back of my head, I could not wait for Tony to come out. He was the pinnacle of the personal development world. He worked with some of the top performers in the world and helped elevate their game to unfathomable heights.

Typically, he charged thousands of dollars for his events, and I was about to see him live in action for three hours for a fraction of that cost. As the day went by, I grew more and more impatient for him to come out.

Toward the end of the day, my mom brought me up to the section reserved for the top performers in the company, and I got a seat in the seventh row. Right before Tony's segment, Cyndi spoke and shared her story on age. Her influence was skyrocketing in the company, and she delivered a heartfelt and moving training about her trials and tribulations to get where she was. Her speaking up there made the possibility of tremendous success in our business so real.

Cyndi delivered the perfect transition to bring out the next speaker. When she walked off, loud techno music began to roll. A gigantic 6 foot 7 figure came out from behind the curtains jumping and clapping. The crowd of thousands of people jumped to their feet and clapped to his rhythm. The entire conference center was cheering and screaming as they saw this icon in the flesh. After about fifteen seconds, Tony Robbins stopped clapping and raised his right hand. He began to shimmer the hand, then made a sweeping motion with it over the crowd as a signal to stop the clapping. Everyone stopped.

The next three hours Tony guided us through one of the most significant emotional events I have ever experienced. He made us laugh, cry, and get extremely uncomfortable, and most importantly he made us see what was possible. He had a magical way of manipulating the emotions of thousands of people all at once to the beat of his drum.

He was similar to Rod, and I was so fascinated with the influence Tony had on all these people, including me. The way everyone looked at him, the way they responded when he told the crowd to do something, the way that he could change the emotional energy in the entire room like he was simply changing the temperature on a thermostat. It was like nothing I had ever seen before.

Tony was mobile through most of his segment. At least ten times he was just a few feet away from me. Each time he would make direct eye contact with me and hold it for only ten seconds, but at the time it felt like an eternity. I felt like he could see into my soul and understand everything about me as an individual without even directly communicating with me. I was blown away at the magnitude of energy his mere presence gave off. You know when you're in the presence of somebody special, and Tony was one of those people.

By the end of Tony's segment, I had two substantial takeaways. The first was the importance of gratitude. I felt like over the course of the past few years, and especially after Italy, I understood the importance of gratitude, but I realized that there were still blessings I took for granted.

Sure I was grateful for all the traveling I did and my family. But I began to realize with the recent funk I was in, I was even taking my business for granted. I had an automated stream of income, people who were inspired by me, and I helped make a huge impact on thousands of individuals' health and finances.

I was questioning my career and life path just because I hit some turbulence and my plans were not going exactly how I had envisioned.

I felt terrible that I lost sight of the absolute blessing I had and made a promise to myself to never take it for granted again.

Then, there was also so much that never even crossed my mind. My near-pristine health—being disease-free, not being physically impaired, and being able to perform simple tasks like walking. Having access to clean water. Never having had to experience true hunger. Having a roof over my head. Basic luxuries that we don't even think about that some people would trade it all for.

We get so caught up in this comparison game and forget that there are people who do not and never will have the luxury of having the absolute basics. Constantly we are looking at the next person and feel envious or victimize ourselves because they may have a little bit more. A nicer car. A nicer house. A hotter girl. A bigger business. There will always be people who have more than you.

The only person you should ever compare yourself to is the person you were yesterday. Comparison is the thief of joy, and if you cannot find gratitude in the luxuries we are blessed to have that a lot of people do not, you will never find true happiness.

The next breakthrough Tony inspired was my ability to *feel* my own unlimited capability. I've always been aware that human beings have unlimited potential, but I was never actually able to feel that for myself. Tony brought us through a visualization exercise that allowed me to believe in my own unlimited capability.

I could see everything I wanted. Everything I wanted to feel. Everything I wanted to accomplish. It was all there. He stretched my mind much further than the dimensions it had ever gone. He helped me understand that I am here for an extraordinary purpose.

As Tony left the stage, I could tell everyone in the room was impacted in a major way. I also understood that most of these people would more than likely take zero action on this enlightenment. I was not sure exactly what I was going to do yet, but I refused to be one of those people.

As everyone was pouring out of the conference room and saying their goodbyes, Cyndi invited my mom and me up to her hotel room for a glass of wine. We graciously accepted and walked over to the elevator with her. I was still feeling a motivational high from Tony's piece. Just as equally on my mind was evaluating what Tony had just done back there.

The best way to describe it is when you watch a movie with your favorite actor. For me, that is Leonardo DiCaprio. The majority of people watch *Catch Me If You Can* and are viewing it from the perspective of the crazy goose chase Frank Abagnale Jr. brings Agent Hanratty on. Inevitably, everyone is going to see that part. However, for me, I cannot help myself but focus on Leonardo DiCaprio, the prestigious actor performing his craft.

I think about the tens of thousands of hours he put into shaping his acting ability. The countless hours spent in the mirror to nail one scene just right. The amount of sacrifice, relentless pursuit, and pure dedication that he put into becoming the icon that he is today. I watch Leonardo, as an individual, hard at work in his profession that he does better than arguably everyone else.

For Tony, I was studying the same areas. I thought about all of the hours he put in behind the scenes to be as knowledgeable as he is. About how many human interactions he must have had throughout his lifetime to develop the tremendous influence he possesses. I watched as he played the emotion of the people in the crowd like a conductor in an orchestra. I saw him take a crowd from one side of the emotional spectrum and then at the drop of the hat bring them to the complete opposite side. I studied how he used his tone of voice.

I thought deeply about what Tony was actually doing up there and why it had such a profound effect. I was not sitting there as an individual attending a Tony Robbins event. I was there as an individual studying what Tony was actually doing that has resulted in the enormous impact he has made throughout his career.

I had thrown myself into autopilot while lost in my thoughts, and before I knew it, I was sitting in Cyndi's room with a glass of wine.

"So, John, what was your biggest takeaway from this event?" Cyndi asked, as she always loved to do when an event was over.

"Honestly, I am capable of so much more. Tony's piece was absolutely incredible. I know I am playing too small and I need to step it up in all aspects of my life. In fact, I decided that I am committed to winning our Isabody challenge. I am going to start as soon as I get back to California," I blurted out. I actually just decided this at that very moment.

She and my mom both turned their heads and gave me a look of surprise. The Isabody challenge is a sixteen-week transformation challenge within our company. There are over 15,000 entries each judging period. They pick ten honorable mentions and five finalists that narrow down to one champion. The transformations were always incredible, both physically and mentally.

I was already in pretty good shape, but I knew there had to be a new level I could reach that was untapped. Winning this challenge would take every ounce of determination I had.

"I'm committed to winning the challenge. To hold myself accountable, I am going to document the process on social media. Plus, this will be a great way to revitalize my business and get more people on board with me," I announced in another decision I made right on the spot.

I knew that when I put something out to the world, I feel like everyone is watching me. With the spotlight on, I would have no choice other than to give it my absolute all. Half-assing or quitting would not be an option. I also had not really been using social media for my business up until that point, and this would be the ideal transition.

"Wow, I love that idea. Winning Isabody will be extremely tough, but that's the way to stay focused," Cyndi said.

"I love it," my mom said with a big smile.

"It is completely okay if you do not want in, but we are putting a team together for the Championship Cruise Challenge the company announced this weekend. Your mom and the chiropractor on your team, Erin, are in, myself and my husband are in, and my son Tyler is in. He really wants to take this business seriously and get out of his engineering job. We need one more person," Cyndi said. "I would be glad to have you on the team, but I need you to commit. We are in this to win and if you are not all in, we can find someone else."

This challenge the company put out was to win an all-expenses-paid cruise throughout the Caribbean. Our company always went above and beyond to make these once-in-a-lifetime experiences. The challenge would be for teams and individuals, and there was a point system based on recruiting new customers and rank advancing distributors.

The top twenty-five teams would qualify to earn the cruise for free. Already over a thousand teams had entered. The challenge period was six months in total and ended on New Year's Day. Coming off the conference, everyone was pumped to get to work and wanted their spot on the cruise ship. I knew that placing in the top twenty-five would take dedication, hard work, and focus. If one person on the team slacked, the entire team would be toast.

"I'm in," I said. Another decision made on impulse. "And you know what? I am going to get a spot in the top income earners for the year too. I doubted myself because the last few months were slow, but I am going to make it happen." Cyndi and my mom both lit up. I was really digging myself deep. What the fuck did Tony do to me?

The next day, as I hopped in my Uber and crept away from all the flashing lights, energy, and excitement, I started to feel a pit in my stomach. A little bit of unease. I managed to suppress this as I chatted to my driver on the way to the airport about our company and the opportunities it had allowed me.

The voice in my head decided to chime in too. *What the fuck did you just get yourself into*? I almost could not argue with it. Just a week ago, I had no idea what direction I was headed. Now, out of absolutely nowhere, I just committed to three goals that would demand everything I had. I had no plans for any of it either.

All I had was a commitment. A commitment to myself, my mom, Cyndi, and the rest of our team. I knew I could not let them down. Bailing on them was not an option. It was up to me to figure out a way to make this happen.

23

BECOMING A PRODUCT OF THE PRODUCT

THE WHOLE FLIGHT back to California I fought the doubt, uncertainty, and all of the blown-out-of-proportion scenarios in my head. It's insane how your subconscious mind will try to protect your current identity.

I had this image of every person who ever doubted me gathered together, pointing at their phones, and laughing in hysterics as they read the post I put out about committing to my sixteen-week challenge. I was obsessing over the text messages that would be sent about me, the phone calls and conversations people would have, the hate I would receive.

Even worse, I was worried about what would happen if I fell short of my goals. Surely, they would recruit all of their family and friends to the next Roast of Stank so they could laugh even harder and longer about how stupid I looked.

I made every excuse in my head to try and back out: I'm already in good shape, how am I possibly going to compete with over 15,000 people, especially ones who have over one hundred pounds to lose? Or your social media is funny and people like it. You are going to ruin your entire image by doing this.

And this one: I'm already making decent money with the business. Do you really want to put yourself out there like this? People think you're cool and successful. If you do this, they are going to think you are desperate.

The list went on and on.

As my thoughts were drowning me, I got a notification on my phone. Cyndi officially created a group message for our cruise challenge team. It reminded me that I made a commitment, and it was bigger than myself. I could not let them down. Although I had manufactured every reason to back out, I forced myself to put a plan together.

I decided that the sixteen-week transformation challenge would be the basis of the macro change I would undergo. I consulted with Brent about what he thought the most dramatic change I could make would be. He noted that I was already in good shape, so it was going to be a real challenge to have drastic results. We decided I had two options: put on muscle and get big or cut up and get lean.

After weighing the pros and cons of putting on a ton of muscle or getting very lean, I decided that shredding up was the best option. I always wanted to see the extreme of what my body was capable of in this aspect, and I knew the end result would be the most rewarding to me. It would be like the Cabo grind all over again, except this time the purpose behind it was much larger than impressing a beach full of sorority girls.

Next, I set my target weight. I was 190 pounds at the time and wanted to get to 180. I figured that with this goal, I would be able to maintain and grow my lean muscle while shredding off all fat. I then figured out what I would have to do from a nutrition standpoint to achieve this goal. To go from my current weight to my target weight over the sixteen-week period, I would have to be in a slight calorie deficit daily.

I first calculated the exact amount of calories I had to consume (about 2,700 per day). Then, I designed a daily meal plan that would help me reach this goal while maintaining my perfect macronutrient balance. I decided in the beginning that the majority of my nutrition intake would revolve around the products my company offered. They were some of the best on the planet, and if I was going to do this challenge, I wanted to be a true product of the product.

I committed to a strict plan that allowed one cheat meal every Sunday if I so desired it. Once I had the nutrition part in place, I decided what my workout routine would be. I committed to weight training five days per week. The split was chest/triceps, back/biceps, legs, shoulders/arms, abs/cardio, and one day of playing basketball. I would alternate between cardio and abs at the end of every workout as well.

Most of my workouts consisted of moderate weight, high repetitions, short rest periods (less than one minute), and supersets. I changed up my workouts every day to keep my body guessing, so there was no exact plan I followed in terms of exercises.

Now that I had a plan set in stone for my transformation, it was time to put together a social media strategy. I was still so uncomfortable even thinking about this part, but I decided I needed to make a post that announced to the world what I was doing. I knew that this post would get me out of my comfort zone and also make me hold myself accountable.

Posting pictures of traveling the world, getting bottle service, and jackass antics with friends is cool. Posting your goals, dreams, and journey to become the best version of yourself is not nearly as sexy. It also tends to attract hate from people who are unhappy with themselves and who cannot stand to see others outgrow them.

On the other hand, it will attract like-minded people. People who are motivated by you, align with you, and want to join you. Accountability and getting out of my comfort zone were both necessary for me to thrive with this challenge. So I spent about an hour writing a caption that ended up being all of three sentences, took a picture by the pool, and posted on both Facebook and Instagram. This is the exact post:

> Starting another 16-week transformation challenge today! This time I will be documenting on my Snapchat/Instagram stories every day to show people what's going into it and hopefully motivate them. I would like to do this with as many people as possible so please reach out to me if you're interested in making a change! Snapchat: Stankiewicz

That was it. Nothing crazy and nothing over the top, just simple and to the point. However, the second I hit "post," I now felt that the world was watching. This one post, as small as it was, forced me to hold myself accountable. I told the world what I was doing. They were watching, and it was completely on me if I failed to uphold my word.

The final piece to the puzzle was to pull my weight on our cruise team and ultimately crush my business. The sixteen-week challenge and consistent social media posting would be huge for my focus and attracting people to the opportunity. Still, I knew that these variables alone would only keep me focused on the final outcome and hold me accountable.

I would still need to get even further out of my comfort zone to prospect, reach out to past customers who quit, and connect with new people. With my announcement now out to the world, I felt I had no choice other than to follow through with my commitment.

To my surprise, every single follower I had on Instagram did not block me after my first post. In fact, it got a good amount of traction. There were certainly people who made comments alluding to the fact that I was already in good shape, and they did not understand what I was trying to do. There were also people who were pumped to watch my journey and who admired my drive. A few people even reached out to see what exactly I was doing.

In my mind, it was so far, so good. Now it was time for me to start documenting the process.

I decided that I would post part of my workout each day on my story. It could be a quick snap on the stair stepper, a specific exercise, or a recap of my workout with some suggestions. It just had to be content that provided value, motivated, and documented the process. I started putting the process out there and during the first few weeks, I received a variety of responses.

"30's for curls? You're a little bitch!"

"You're so motivating omg" with a very underlying sense of sarcasm.

"You're not really a professional. You are seriously misleading people."

These comments were accompanied by some unfollows. Certain people also stopped talking to me and avoided conversation with me. Did it hurt? For sure. But I decided that if these people did not support my goals and did not want me to thrive, I did not want them in my life anyway.

Besides, there were just as many conversations that started with people asking questions. They wanted to know more about my workouts, my nutrition, and the challenge I was doing. This resulted in a few new customers right off the bat. My plan was working.

As for our cruise challenge, we began to meet as a team for an hour weekly on Zoom. The first call we figured out exactly where we were, where we needed to go, and how we would get there. There were over 2,000 teams participating in the challenge, and we were not even in the top 1,000. We needed to be in the top twenty-five in order to earn the cruise. We had our work cut out for us, but we had faith that it would happen.

We looked at the point system. The main way to earn points was for bringing in new customers, rank advancing distributors, and getting people entered into the sixteen-week challenge I was competing in. Additionally, we needed to each personally sponsor ten new customers to qualify for the challenge, regardless of how many points the team earned.

We already had a large customer base, so we decided to take advantage of the points available for getting people enrolled in the sixteen-week challenge.

For the next week, we contacted all of our customers—current customers and customers who had dropped off the face of the earth. In Network Marketing when some people quit, they literally vanish into thin air. They do not answer your texts, calls, birthday wishes, letter-delivering pigeons, or any other attempt to contact them. It's actually quite impressive how they pull off a disappearing act that could rival Houdini on his finest day.

Overall, I have found that the people are typically not ignoring you over anything that has to do with you. They have failed themselves with the business or products, are disappointed in themselves, and think hiding from you will bring them less pain. By avoiding you, they think they are able to avoid the reality of their failure. You can never take other people's actions personally in this industry.

By the end of the first week, we had all contacted our past and current customers to get them entered into the challenge. Some stayed strong to their vanishing act and showed no signs of human activity on this planet. Some people politely declined. Some people agreed to join the challenge just to help us get the points.

Then, some people thanked me for reaching out and told me they were just about to reach out to me. They had fallen off, felt like shit, and wanted to get their health back together. It was the perfect opportunity for them to get involved again. From this effort alone, we were able to break into the top 200 teams by week two of the challenge.

We met again on Zoom and decided to continue making a push for people to enter the challenge. We also decided it was time to make a big push to start bringing new people on board with us.

My strategy was still to attract people from documenting my challenge, but I also knew I needed to reach out to new prospects as well. This made me very uncomfortable, but the whole team made the commitment, and I could not let them down. We all stated our goals for the week at the end of the call. Mine was two new enrollments. Everyone else had similar goals. Two was the magic number.

As soon as the call ended, I looked down at my phone and my mom was calling me.

"Hey, hun. Great call. I wanted to ask you something real quick," she said.

"Sure, what's going on?"

"So Cyndi forgot to mention this, but she's having a Top 50 event for our team in Ohio in a couple of weeks. You should totally come."

"Yeah, I'd be down to go. What does Top 50 event even mean though?" I asked.

"Rod Hairston puts them on for the top fifty leaders in people's sales organizations. It will be two days—Saturday and Sunday. I haven't been to one yet, but Cyndi said the last one she went to was a game-changer for her business. There are still a few spots left. If you want in, you can come."

"Yeah, I'm down," I said. I really had no idea what would happen there, but I figured what did I have to lose. From my experience with Rod so far, he seemed like an individual who could provide immense value. In this time of drastic change, I could seriously use some help from a man as wise as he.

We hung up the phone and I made my travel plans the next day. Over the course of the next two weeks, I stayed strong with my nutrition and workouts. I could already tell that my body was making a significant change, and I was not even a full month in yet. I kept documenting the process even though it still felt far from comfortable. I continued reaching out to people, but I was not having the results I desired with enrolling.

When the time came to hop on the flight, I was starting to doubt myself. I refused to give up, but I still was not loving the level of results I was having.

24

TO WHOM MUCH IS GIVEN, MUCH IS EXPECTED

I SHOWED UP at the airport for my red-eye flight that Thursday night before the event. My thought process when I booked it was that I would sleep through the flight, wake up in Ohio refreshed, and be ready to rock the weekend. I really do not know how my mind creates these delusions when I am selecting flights. This is how it actually unfolded.

I got to the airport to find my flight was delayed an hour and a half. I don't feel comfortable sleeping in airports, so I stayed up reading a new book I had just gotten, *The One Thing*. When it was finally time to board, I was exhausted and stumbled my way onto the plane and into my seat. I immediately closed my eyes in an attempt to capture every moment of sleep possible.

As soon as my eyes closed, a noise behind me that sounded like someone was reeling in a fishing pole at warp speed caused me to open them back up. The noise would persist for a few minutes, stop briefly, then persist for another few minutes. After a few cycles, I could not help but turn around and investigate what the hell was going on.

I spun around to find a very pasty-skinned male with long red hair arranging a Rubik's cube. However, this was no normal Rubik's cube. This one had gears attached to it that made sure the noise levels given off were maximized as this guy relentlessly practiced for the day that he would get the opportunity to prove that he was, in fact, the world's fastest Rubik's cube solver.

After he did not put the cube down for the entire five-hour flight, I have no doubt in my mind that he is either the current champion or at the very least beyond fit to contest the champion. Needless to say, I arrived in Ohio with no sleep and with the Rubik's cube creator on my hitlist.

I flew into Columbus because that is where Tyler, Cyndi's son, lived at the time. The last time we hung out in person was at the event in San Antonio at the beginning of the year.

After a devastating knee injury, Tyler's football career and dreams of being an athlete were over. Feeling lost, he decided to use his high levels of intelligence to follow the traditional route. Since then, Tyler had gotten so fed up with his corporate engineering job and was ready to make our Network Marketing business happen. He had a desire for freedom and was so inspired by the lifestyle I was able to lead. He was on the cruise team we assembled, so he and I had really started to use each other for motivation and accountability.

As soon as I touched down, I mustered up the energy to call him. For such a simple call, it is one that I can still clearly remember.

"I'm here, man. Physically at least, mentally I could not be further from Ohio."

"Rough flight, huh? I knew when you told me you chose the red-eye that it would suck," he said.

"You have no idea, bro. Anyway, what should I do here? Were you able to get work off?" I asked.

"Nope. My boss was not having it at all. I'm stuck being a cube monkey for the day. My bad, man, I feel awful about it. But what I'm going to do is leave the key under my doormat. You're more than welcome to make yourself at home. I'll be able to meet you for my thirty-minute lunch break. Then we will leave for my mom's house in Sugarcreek tonight."

"Completely cool. We're gonna make sure you aren't a corporate cowboy for much longer. I'll try to go to the gym. Just hit me up when you're good for lunch," I said.

"The cube farm has gotta go, man. I'll see you soon."

To an outside eye, there's nothing crazy about this call at all. In fact, for most people, it's actually pretty normal. People are used to being at the mercy of the man. They feel that life is out of their control. They let other people dictate when they work, when they eat, when they talk on the phone, when they hang out with their friends, and many other areas of their life.

The reason that I remember this call so well is because I knew Tyler desperately wanted out. I knew he was not about to allow someone to control his life anymore. I also knew that he was going to take action to get out. Knowing how much he has accomplished today, I can never forget the moments like that phone call when it was all just a vision.

After I spent the day in a sleep-deprived zombie state, we made the two-hour drive to the Walters' beautiful home in Sugarcreek, Ohio. The house was situated on a golf course in the heart of Amish country. As we approached the house, we passed multiple horse-drawn buggies that were used as the main source of transportation by the Amish.

I was exhausted upon arrival, but it is not possible to maintain low energy when you are in the Walter household. I walked inside and was greeted by my mom who had driven all the way from Connecticut, Cyndi, and her husband, Scott. Cyndi and my mom both ran up to give me a huge hug as I walked through the doors.

Both of them have a magical way of uplifting you and creating excitement out of thin air. Together, they have a synergistic relationship that immediately brings laughs, joy, and inspiration. We all took a moment to catch up and then got straight to business.

First, we talked about our cruise challenge. Five out of six members were present, so we decided to use it as an opportunity to catch up on our progress. We checked our placement in the challenge so far, and we had broken into the top 100 teams. We discussed our strategies to bring in more customers, to get our customers free products, and to maximize our results with the point system.

Beyond that, we discussed the bigger picture and how this challenge was going to serve the visions we had with our businesses. By the end, we were all more motivated than ever to kick things up a notch and take it to the next level.

When discussing our goals, I brought up how I was determined to win the transformation challenge I was in and to earn a spot in the top-ten income earners. Everybody chimed in.

"I just saw your Instagram last week. Your abs already look so defined. You are doing amazing so far," Cyndi said.

I really had put in such an intense effort since I started. Just hearing encouragement like that regarding my progress was huge. It gave me even more belief and determination to get the best transformation possible.

The next morning, we headed to the event with Rod Hairston, which was being hosted in a quaint Amish-style inn five minutes down the road. As the start time approached, many of the top leaders from our organization began to fill the seats in the intimate environment of the smaller room.

It is always gratifying to see everyone in our organization in person. We are always in touch and on virtual calls together, but nothing tops the in-person connection. Everyone has such contagious energy that automatically uplifts the energy of the room as a whole.

We spent a half hour greeting the forty people who came, and then Rod entered the room with his assistant, Molly. As he planted his short and stocky figure in front of the audience, we could feel the energy of his presence, and all focus turned to him as the weekend was officially under way.

"Welcome, everybody." Rod's soothing voice echoed as he scanned the room, made eye contact with every individual, and shot them a huge smile.

"I feel so grateful to be here this weekend. Sugarland, Ohio—" he began as Cindy cut him off.

"It's SUGARCREEK," she corrected him while shaking her head as the room let out a laugh.

"SUGARCREEK. I apologize. I'll tell you what. This is God's country out here in Sugar Mountain. I almost got run over by a horse and buggy this morning while getting my coffee. This place is no joke." He smiled.

All the local people rolled their eyes as the room collectively started to crack up. After a moment of laughter, Rod took the reins.

"On a serious note, thank you for coming out this weekend. The simple fact that you made the effort to be here speaks volumes to your character. I know there are a million other things that you could be doing, right? The fact that you got in your car and came to this event to learn and grow is what will separate you from everyone else in the world.

"We are going to be doing a lot of work this weekend. You're going to learn a lot, you're going to get very uncomfortable, and you are going to grow as an individual because of it.

"If you are not growing, you are dying, and we are here to make sure you are always expanding to the next level. So, first and foremost, let's go around the room. Everybody introduce yourself, tell us where you are from and what you are looking to get out of this weekend."

Rod pointed to a lady in the front to kick it off, and we went around the room one by one. Some people had high energy and massive goals they wanted to achieve from this event. There were a few people who were scared as hell to speak in front of the room, and Rod instructed the room to encourage and cheer them on for their bravery.

A couple of people in the room had been dragged along by their spouses and kept their walls up. They were not open to what was happening at all yet. Rod had a strategic way of getting them to let their guard down. When it was my turn, I had not planned what I was going to say but just stood up and spoke.

"My name is John Stankiewicz. I am from Goshen, Connecticut, but I'm currently living in San Jose, California. To be honest, Rod, I just need a huge kick in the ass," I blurted out. I figured speaking from the heart was the best way to go, and that's what it decided to let out.

"No problem, John. Get up here and I can take care of that," he said as the room chuckled.

I laughed as well. But I was serious. Something needed to change for me, and it needed to change big-time.

We wrapped up the introductions and Rod moved into his first segment for the weekend. This was about the Cycle of Growth. He explained how when we commit to a new goal that requires massive change, such as losing a ton of weight, learning an instrument, building a new business, or anything else that challenges our current belief systems, habits, or identity, we go through the **Cycle of Growth.**

He explained to us how the path of the growth journey is similar to that of a halfpipe. Let's use the example of starting a new business. When you begin, you are in what he refers to as **Inception.** You have this great idea, you are excited, you are thinking about how much money you will make, how many lives you are going to impact, and you might not even be able to sleep.

Your attitude is great, your energy is high; however, your competence is low. In fact, you probably have no idea what you are doing. This is completely normal because it is new to you. In the beginning, the excitement and your attitude are what fuel you to pursue the venture. That is until you hit **Deception**.

Deception is where most dreams go to die. This stage can come as quickly as minutes after Inception. In Deception, you've told your friends about your idea and they think it sucks. You tried to get a business plan together and start realizing how much work it will take. You get rejected a few times and start to wonder if you are wasting your time. This is the first bottom curve of the halfpipe. Your attitude is no longer great, your energy becomes low, and your competence is still next to nothing as well.

Most people decide here that maybe it's best they give up. Throw in the towel and perhaps try something else. They quit. But here's the key. Deception is an important part of the growth process that everybody must go through. No matter who it is, they have experienced Deception in the pursuit of growing and taking themselves to the next level. It is important to celebrate Deception, because it is a sign that you are one step further along the growth process and, more importantly, one step closer to the next step in the process: **Transformation**.

Transformation is where you start to get it. You are starting to feel confident in the action you are taking. You feel as if you are becoming more competent at the actions necessary to build the business you are pursuing. You may have even started to see some results. There is only one thing to be cautious of: you cannot stay in the Transformation stage of the growth cycle. You will either retreat back to Deception or power through to the next stage of **Identity**.

When you hit the Identity stage, this is now part of who you are. The daily tasks to build your business have become second nature and habitual. You are in complete alignment with the person you need to be to succeed in your business venture. Not a word anyone says can veer you from the path you are on. You know what you're doing and why you're doing it. This is an actual part of who you are now. Your beliefs, habits, and lifestyle are all in alignment with building your business.

Rod went on to explain how after you've reached Identity, the cycle begins all over again. You are either growing or dying. There is always another level that you must challenge yourself to grow toward. He explained how your vision must be like a flower growing toward the sun. The flower will never touch the sun; however, throughout its entire life-span, it will always attempt to grow closer to the sun. The sun is the vision and you are the flower. Growth is a never-ending journey.

When Rod explained this, it was like language was being given to feelings and thoughts that I never had words for previously. His teachings made complete sense, and I could actually identify specific portions of my life when I was in the various stages. I was absolutely mind blown at his ability to break it down.

There was so much power to be harvested from understanding this cycle. Especially the concept of Deception. Not only would it help me immensely in growing as an individual, but it would also help tremendously in coaching and guiding my clients through the Cycle of Growth. Right away, he started the weekend off with game-changing content.

This talk along with various exercises carried straight through to our lunch break. For the hour we had, I decided to go to a bakery that was next to the hotel. The bakery was run by the Amish and had the most delectable selection of baked goods that you could imagine. Cakes, pies, pastries, donuts, cookies, and every sweet under the sun that I had to steer clear of for this challenge I was partaking in. It was not an easy decision, but I knew it was for the greater good.

I ordered a turkey wrap, while my mom got her favorite: a vanilla-iced cream stick. I rolled my eyes as I waited for my order to come out.

As I was waiting, Rod came walking into the bakery. He had a big smile on his face and was holding one of our company's energy shots. He walked up to the order counter where my mom and I were standing.

"Rod, this is fantastic so far. Everything you said makes so much sense. I'm so happy we came out," my mom said.

"Thank you, Susan. You are too kind." He gave her a hug.

"What did you guys order here? This pumpkin spice roll looks amazing, but I don't think it's the best choice for lunch," Rod said as we chuckled.

"I went with the turkey wrap. I think it's the only thing in here that won't result in us gaining ten pounds just by looking at it," I said.

My mom walked away, and I took the opportunity. "Hey, Rod. Can I ask you for a favor?"

"Of course, man. What's up?"

"Put me on the spot. At some point this weekend, just make me as uncomfortable as you can," I blurted.

He smiled and nodded. "You got it."

I felt butterflies rush through me, but I knew that I could benefit from whatever was to come my way. I really did not even know what to expect or what I wanted to address, but I knew there was something. If anyone could figure out a way to address it, it would be Rod.

The rest of the day was spent doing group exercises. He brought up a group of volunteers to make people step out of their comfort zones and physically show how our unconscious and conscious minds work. Through his demonstration, he illustrated how the unconscious mind cannot differentiate between what is real versus what is vividly imagined. He went on to explain how this applied to our visions and why it is so important to visualize. Not just to visualize where you are headed but to actually see, taste, hear, and feel it.

He also went on to show us how our unconscious mind is trying to protect us. However, what it is really protecting us from is changing and uncertainty. When you consciously start to change and grow to the next level, your unconscious mind starts to resist. That is the negative self-talk, the doubt, and the worry that we experience.

He related it to the growth cycle and how when we make a conscious effort to change our belief system and take those daily actions for a long enough period of time, those actions become habits; those habits become part of our unconscious mind; and whatever you were working toward becomes your identity. It was incredible how true these theories held when thinking back to all the times I experienced exponential growth in my life.

At one point, my mom shared a story about me, much to my embarrassment. She told about how I totaled two cars (in all fairness, one accident was not my fault). I was sure the entire room thought I was a menace to society.

But her point was this: She pointed to the Cycle of Growth model. She said, "Our job is not to give people handouts (or her son cars). Our job is to help guide people through this cycle." Which explains why I was never given another car or use of a car until I could buy one for myself.

When day one officially came to an end, Cyndi took the microphone and announced that we would be having an authentic Amish dinner that night at a local Amish farm that belonged to her friends. She gave everyone directions, explained what the game plan was for the next day, and congratulated everyone for successfully completing the first day.

After we all changed and got prepared for dinner, we loaded up Cyndi's van to head to the Amish farm down the street. The drive over was short but gorgeous as we made our way down the narrow back roads through the rolling hills of the Ohio countryside. The quiet, peaceful, and serene ride brought me into a beautifully calm state. We discussed how much we were all loving the event so far and how grateful we were that we came. After a quick ride, we pulled into the driveway of the farm.

There were multiple houses on the property, a barn, and segregated pastures with cows, horses, sheep, dogs, and other assorted farm animals. The Amish are entirely self-sustained and all of the basic necessities that they needed to live came from their property.

For us, living in a convenience-driven society where you flick a switch and the room lights up, you open an app on your phone and food is delivered within forty-five minutes, and where you can go online and have any item you want shipped to your doorstep within days, it was perspective altering to see an entire family living off the absolute basics.

Not only were they producing the supplies they needed and living minimalist lifestyles, but individually they all seemed so happy. Their minds were not flooded by the negativity on the news; they were not consumed by cell phones; and they were not living in a place of comparison. They were present, in the moment, and happy with the absolute basics. It really made me take a step back and reframe what is truly important in this life.

After showing us around the farm, the family brought us to a large garage-like room where they had four long tables set up to serve us all dinner. The family brought out large bowls and trays of food to each table.

Before we began to dig in, the father of the family wanted to say a few words. He ended up speaking for about fifteen minutes, and for someone who never did any public speaking, it was beautiful. He shared about what the farm and lifestyle meant to him and how grateful he was to share this experience with us. He spoke on how we, as humans, are united as one. He reiterated his gratitude over and over.

He told us it was an absolute honor for his family to host us and prayed we had the best possible experience under their hospitality. Then he led us through a quick prayer and we began to eat.

Trays of chicken, salad, potatoes, vegetables, and homemade bread were passed around the tables. All of the food tasted like it was professionally catered. Everyone in the room was blown away by how delectable the offerings were. After the appetizer and entrees, they brought out the dessert. This is where it got dangerous. I nearly began to salivate once I saw the mud pie overflowing from the bowl and the moist Ho Ho cake.

Out of respect, I had to at least taste these enticing offerings. By taste, I mean I had a full serving of each. I simply could not pass it up after seeing the look on Rod's face after the first bite he had. Besides, everything is about moderation anyway, right?

After the dinner wrapped up, everyone gathered outside engaging in individual conversations as the sun began to set over the set-back grassy hills. The entire scene was heavenly. The quiet countryside, the overflowing energy of gratitude from our entire group, the scent of field grass, it was all perfect.

Tyler and I decided to walk back to the house, so we said our goodbyes and began the mile walk home.

"So, man, what did you think about today?" I asked him as we walked.

"Fantastic. Rod is amazing. He just understands everything on such a high level. I'm so glad we came."

"I couldn't agree more. This is all happening for a reason. Everything is coming together. So much is aligning and I feel like we are poised for a huge breakthrough. Both of us." I was feeling more certain than ever.

"Absolutely. We just have to make it happen. There's no reason we can't do this," he said.

"One hundred percent. We really need to speak up tomorrow and take advantage of Rod being here. I feel like I have some things to get off my chest. This is the perfect opportunity to lay it out on the table," I said.

"Me too. Yeah, I have some questions for sure. I'm definitely going to speak up in tomorrow's session."

The next day we got up and drove to the Carlisle Inn to get right back into action. Rod and Molly had a full day planned for us. You could feel an energy shift from the day prior as everyone had started to get vulnerable with one another.

Vulnerability has an innate power to connect people and bring them together as a family. Once you let your guard down and let someone in, that is when people build the closest relationships. It is certainly something I struggled with my entire life.

The full morning was spent on the topic of behavior. Rod designed a proprietary model that explained the behavior of individuals based on how they are motivated and where their focus is. When you can figure out how someone will behave based on their focus and motivation, you can do a significantly better job of working with them, coaching them, and influencing them.

After everyone shared their breakthroughs from his teachings, we split for a quick lunch break. I went with the same option from the previous day at the Amish bakery. I spent lunch alone and kept thinking about my conversations so far from the weekend: My asking Rod to put me on the spot. Telling Tyler we need to take advantage of Rod being there and to ask him whatever is on our hearts.

I still wasn't positive what I was going to say to Rod. Even so, I was still nervous from the anticipation of whatever it would be. I clenched my fists and told myself to stop being a little bitch. After I finished the turkey wrap, I decided to go back to the conference room and speak up at the absolute first opportunity that I got. No excuses.

After lunch, we gathered back in the conference room for the last few hours of the weekend. Every single one of us had experienced a spectrum of emotions by that point that opened the door for serious growth. I could tell that the entire room had already gone through a substantial change from these two days alone. As much as we wanted it to last forever, we were ready to go apply the lessons we learned.

Rod walked into the room and began the final segment.

"I really want to make this last segment catered to you. I invite you to share any breakthroughs you may have had this weekend. Ask any questions you may have regarding all of the models we went over. Any questions you have in general. Please speak up," Rod began as if he had been in my mind for the conversation I was just having with myself.

I felt an adrenaline rush throughout my whole body. I got butterflies in my stomach and began fidgeting with my hands. I felt my face turn red. My palms started to get sweaty. I had no idea why I was so nervous. I still did not really know what I needed to address. So I stuck to the motto for the weekend—let it flow from the heart.

I raised my hand. Rod happened to be looking to the other side of the room where another lady already had her hand raised. He picked her. I let out a huge sigh of relief and felt my body return to a much calmer state.

"Well at least I tr—" I cut my mind off before it could finish the thought and shook my head. The lady finished sharing, Rod gave his feedback, and I immediately put my hand back up. Rod gazed across the room until his eyes fell on me. We made eye contact and I felt as if he could see directly into my mind like he already knew what I was going to ask.

"Yes, big man. What would you like to share?" The full attention of the room turned to me.

I went into autopilot and decided to allow whatever words left my mouth to flow out.

"Rod, I don't know. I just—" I started to say as I took a short pause to scour my mind.

"I just feel extremely inauthentic when it comes to this business. My first Network Marketing business failed. I put forth all my effort and everyone I got involved quit and lost money. Now, in this business, I've had a lot of success and I feel like it has nothing to do with me or my efforts. I did not put even close the amount of work I did into my first business, and everything has fallen into place perfectly. I know a lot of it has to do with my mom and how great of a leader she is.

"Overall, I just feel like I did nothing to deserve this. I feel inauthentic when I share with people. I also feel like the people I share with have no hope of succeeding when they join. I just do not know what to do. Every time I try to go all in, I have a mental war in my head because I did not do this all by myself and—" I let the words pour out until I finally cut myself off because I was starting to rant.

Rod simply looked at me for ten seconds. It felt like an eternity as I desperately waited for his feedback. I looked back to him as a slight lip smile appeared on his face and he squinted his eyes to focus in on me.

"John, to whom much is given, much is expected." He widened his eyes and he nodded toward me.

"You have been given a gift. A gift that has completely changed your life. Now you can take that gift, sulk, feel unworthy of it, and sabotage what you are able to do with it because you feel like you did not work hard enough for it. But first, let me ask you this. Do you think an athlete like Lebron, who was gifted with one of the most ideal physical statures to become a world-class basketball player, looks in the mirror and sulks because he did nothing to deserve the body that God gave him? No. He works his butt off and took advantage of that gift to become one of the best players in the history of the game.

"The same goes for you. Look at all the things this gift has done for you. The life you have been able to lead, the people you have met, the freedom you have. You have been given this gift for a reason. It is now your *responsibility* to go out and change the world with it. It is up to you to make sure people are able to experience the things you have because of this gift. Who cares how you got it? You have it, man."

My eyes widened as I felt another adrenaline rush in the back of my head. I looked to my mom sitting next to me who had a huge smile on her face nodding. Everyone else was looking at me the exact same way. One of our teammates, Val, asked Rod if she could chime in. He nodded.

"John, you are one of the most incredible young people I know. I mean, look at what you've done. The fact that at eighteen you saw the vision of this business and took a stab at it in the first place is rare. Even though it didn't go the way you planned, you still stuck with the entrepreneurial route."

She went on: "Look at all the businesses you started in college and had success with. Look at all the risks you've taken, how much you've put yourself out there, how wise you are because of everything *you* have done. Just because you feel like you didn't do 100 percent of the work for this one business does not mean you aren't deserving of it. You've earned everything. Plus, when I hear you speak, I am so inspired. You deserve all of this."

The rest of the room nodded their heads in agreement.

"Wow. Thank you, guys. Seriously," I said to the room. I did not have many words, but they overflowed me with gratitude from what they had to say. It completely altered my perspective. It uncovered an aspect of my situation that I had previously been blind to.

Rod looked at me with a smile and nodded. After a couple of moments, he went on to the next person. As badly as I wanted to be fully present for the next lady sharing, I sank into full self-reflection mode surrounding the advice that had just been given to me.

I started to dig deeper as to why I felt the way I just shared about in the first place. What happened between my first business with the energy drink company where I was laser focused and unshakable to now? How did I go from being so certain about Network Marketing to a place of unease now?

The whole feeling of being undeserving was a piece, but I knew it was deeper than that. What was holding me back from unleashing my full potential? I thought about the Cycle of Growth Rod presented us. I thought about the four stages we go through when making a new behavior part of our identity. All of a sudden, I knew exactly what the problem was. Where does it all start? Beliefs.

At the start of my Network Marketing journey, I was an eighteen-year-old who had just been introduced to the game of entrepreneurship. Network Marketing was presented to me and it was an entirely new concept. I had zero skill in the industry and absolutely no competence in it, but I was excited and saw the vision. I had no idea what the magnitude of hardships, struggles, and challenges were ahead of me. I simply saw what was possible, what could be created, and formed a vision of how I could live the best possible life. I did not overthink anything, I just took my excitement and got to work. I was ignorance on fire as we like to call it in this industry.

After six months of giving it my all and ultimately deciding to leave the company, although I was not aware of it at the time, I developed a set of beliefs. They were beliefs that were not in alignment with the industry as a whole. They were just a product of my specific experience with one particular company. Although I was always grateful for the changes that the first experience brought into my life, there were negatives that came with it and ultimately stuck with me. I was not fully aware of these limiting beliefs until that moment.

The first was that subconsciously I felt as though I was doing people a disservice by introducing them to Network Marketing. My entire customer and distributor experience with my first company was a revolving door. People were quitting just as quickly as they were joining. The products were also not changing people's lives.

Additionally, no one was making any money. Even worse, I was totally out of alignment with the company. They were flashing expensive cars, jewelry, and designer clothes to get people to join. They created this illusion of how easy the lifestyle was to achieve, when in fact it takes a lot of hard work, and most of the people acting like they had it were faking it. By the end, I was so turned off. I still believed in the vision, but I felt slimy sharing it to people because of what I experienced.

With this belief identified, I knew I had to replace it with one that would serve me. I took an objective look at the company I was currently partnered with. We had thousands of people in our organization whose lives were totally transformed by our nutrition systems. People could exercise again, sleep better, have the energy to play with their kids, regain their confidence, and begin to enjoy their lives again. It was incredible what these products were doing for people and even more fulfilling to hear their testimonies.

Another huge difference was the financial impact this was having on people. From earning enough money to get free products all the way to multiple six-figure incomes, this company was changing the financial blueprint of thousands of people. I looked at myself. The products had completely transformed my physical and mental state. The income I was earning allowed me to literally do whatever I wanted in life.

I decided at that moment that I could not let a bad experience ruin this incredible industry for me. I realized that my belief that sharing this with people was doing them a disservice could not be more backward. I was doing people a disservice by *not* sharing this opportunity with them!

Who am I to decide who deserves the best nutrition on the planet? Who am I to decide who could benefit from additional income or replacing their income entirely? Who am I to keep this abundant gift to myself due to selfish limiting beliefs? I decided that it was my responsibility to share this with absolutely everyone, no exceptions. Ultimately what they decided to do with it was up to them, but it was up to me to show them what is possible.

The second belief that hindered me was my belief that I was undeserving. I thought back to all my different business ventures. To all the big risks I took when all of my peers told me my moves were not a smart course of action. The amount of rejection and uncertainty I experienced while in the pursuit of all the ventures I knew were right. No part of my life up until this point was the least bit conventional. I had been living most people's dream lifestyle. I felt ashamed for the statement I had just made. The fact was, this was attracted into my life for a reason.

All of those side ventures I had were building me into the person I needed to become for this. Regardless if they could be considered a failure or success, all of them served me more than I could have ever imagined they would at the time. They gave me a strong business IQ.

They introduced me to the world of personal development that helped me grow to levels that towered over the John who got kicked out of high school. They taught me how to sell. How to communicate with people and build relationships. How to conduct myself when no one else believed in me. They taught me the beauty of sacrifice. They helped me discover my values when it comes to success. They taught me everything I needed to become a person who is in alignment with a true successful identity.

I worked so hard at all my ventures and caught one break. One success came easy relative to the others. How foolish would I be to sulk and feel like I did not earn it? The fact was, I did earn it. I took action and gave my all to every venture. When you put that type of energy out to the universe, you will begin to attract the right things into your life. Sometimes they may not be exactly what you imagined. That's fine. You just need to be able to identify what the things you attract are and receive them with open arms.

What a blessing it was that I attracted this. What a blessing it was that a business model like this exists where you do not need to kill yourself to make a solid income and achieve time freedom. How amazing that my vision of what was possible with this business at age eighteen came to fruition. I deserved this and the world deserved for me to share it with them.

I knew what just happened was special, but it would not be for a little bit of time until I understood the magnitude of the breakthrough I just had. Alongside the breakthrough was one of the most important lessons I have learned in my entire life. The lesson that we decide what our beliefs are.

It is 100 percent up to you to decide what you believe. You decide what religion you believe in, what morals and values you believe in, what you believe to be important or unimportant, what you believe the purpose of life is, and the list goes on. The moment you become aware that you decide what your beliefs are is the moment you begin to take control of owning your life.

There are no rules to life or a manual we must follow. That is the beautiful truth. You can be whatever and whoever you want to be, and you can do it at any time. It all begins with deciding your beliefs of who you are and who you want to be. I was excited to employ my new beliefs around my business and even more excited to take control of every other aspect of my life.

I began to fade back into the room and realized that ten more people had shared during the time I slipped into self-reflection. Rod began to wrap up that segment and moved onto one of the final exercises of the day. He explained that one by one we would be getting in front of the room. When we were up there, we would say with conviction, power, and certainty our biggest goal coming off the event like it already was done. After we said it, everyone in the room was to cheer like their favorite sports team just won the championship.

One by one, everybody went to the front of the room:

"I am committed to building an unbreakable bond with my daughter!" screamed the first guy who went up. Everyone stood up, screamed, clapped, and cheered.

"I am committed to building my Network Marketing business so I can leave my engineering job," Tyler said in front of the room with a bit of hesitation.

"Make me believe it, man," Rod said back to him. "Do it again, but this time make us all believe you."

"I AM COMMITTED TO BUILDING MY NETWORK MARKETING BUSINESS TO A SIX-FIGURE INCOME AND LEAVING BEHIND THE CORPORATE WORLD!" Tyler screamed at the top of his lungs. The entire room stood up and screamed and clapped in encouragement.

This continued with twelve more people until it was my turn to take the floor. I walked up confidently, took a firm stance front and center, and simply gazed around the room for five seconds amid the anticipation and silence.

"I am committed," I began as I took a dramatic pause, "to making sure I never," followed by another brief pause, "total another car ever again in my life!" I yelled as I cracked a huge smile. The entire room broke out in hysterics and cheers. I could not help myself. When I see an opportunity to make people laugh, I'll always take it.

I began to walk back to my seat, but Rod had other plans.

"Wait a minute. You are not getting off that easy. Get back up there. I am proud that you are done wrecking cars, but what is your biggest goal coming off this event?" He motioned me back to the front of the room.

I looked around the room again, but this time I was serious. I felt my heart start beating faster and adrenaline rushing through my head as I yelled, "I am committed to making an ENORMOUS, POSITIVE, and GLOBAL impact with the unparalleled gifts I have ATTRACTED!"

Everyone stood up, screamed, cheered, and applauded. At that moment, my life felt in such alignment. I could actually believe, feel, and envision myself making an impact on the highest possible platform. It all would happen and was already happening. I walked back to my seat with an unshakable level of confidence that I would manifest all that my heart desired.

The rest of the room went up, submerged themselves in full vulnerability, and screamed their goals with the utmost levels of conviction. It was beautiful to watch and incredible to be a part of. I have a concrete bond with each person who attended that seminar to this day.

To conclude the weekend, Rod recommended that we continue this growth following the seminar through his six-week online course. After learning about how important habits are to lasting change, I knew I had to be a part of it. We all enrolled in the program and got ready for the next step.

The next hour was spent having deep, meaningful conversations with all the people who attended, thanking one another, and preparing to step out into the real world to implement what we had learned. We said our heartfelt goodbyes to one another and everyone went their separate ways, prepared to change the world.

We went back to Cyndi's house to recap before we all returned home. We had a catered dinner from the Walters' favorite local restaurant and talked about all of the incredible breakthroughs we had at the seminar. Each of us had been impacted on a deep level, and we could not wait to get into action. As a group, this meant winning the cruise challenge. By doing that, all of our personal goals would be met because we would be required to grow our businesses substantially in order to win.

I was more focused than ever on my sixteen-week challenge, building my business, and ultimately winning the cruise with this team. There were no excuses now. I knew more than ever before that I was in the right place, I had the right opportunity, and I was with the right people. The time was now.

I knew the trajectory of my life had just been severely altered for the best over the past few days. I felt purpose. I felt like I knew exactly what I had to do. I received the kick in the ass that I needed.

25

FOCUSED ON THE MISSION

THIS TIME AS my plane began its descent into California, the feeling was much different. It was not like nine months earlier when I laid eyes on the Bay for the first time with feelings of excitement for a new adventure. It was not like the feeling when I returned from Vegas questioning what the hell I had just gotten myself into.

This time, as the vast lights of Silicon Valley came into sight, I stared out the window with laser focus. I was level-headed. I was not in a state of euphoric excitement. I also did not feel like I was in over my head. I knew my purpose. I knew where I was headed. I knew what I had to do. Now, it was time to do.

Both Brent and Robinson could tell that a big-time change had occurred as soon as I walked through the apartment door. My energy and demeanor had completely shifted. They could tell I had already mentally accomplished all the goals I committed to. There was no talking a million words per minute, hype, or excitement. I was calm, cool, collected, and determined. In my mind, it was already done.

Just a few days after returning, we began the six-week program that we signed up for at the end of Rod's seminar. This consisted of online modules you could go in and complete over the six-week period and two live calls per week. The modules were key for developing the proper habits and beliefs necessary for lasting change.

The calls were crucial for accountability, and Rod and Molly brought next-level value for every single one. I found myself waking up in the morning excited to complete the modules, and I especially looked forward to our calls.

With Rod's program, as with any program, you get out of it what you put in. You could go through this program and half-ass complete the entries or join the call and text your buddies about where you planned on drinking that weekend, then ultimately finish the program without having a single change in your life.

A lot of people will do this and say, "Yeah. I tried that program. It was a waste of money and didn't work." I knew that to make the change I wanted, I had to be all in.

I put forth my full effort to complete the modules. I logged onto the calls, put my phone aside, took notes, and used the forum as an opportunity to ask questions. More importantly, I applied the concepts to my real life and goals I had set for myself. It took serious discipline and focus. I put my full focus toward building the habits necessary for success like the habits were a muscle I was training in the gym.

I embraced Rod's model for the Cycle of Growth. Being consciously aware of what it would take to get where I wanted to go made the process an entirely different game. I could identify exactly where I was in the process every step of the way. I separated my emotions from my actions. The process became a lot more fun, and I was in complete control.

The gym and my nutrition were the categories where I was met with the least amount of resistance for change. For the most part, I was already disciplined in those categories. A healthy lifestyle was part of my identity.

At that point in the challenge, my cravings for junk food barely existed. I felt so amazing from the nutrition I was putting in my body, I was sleeping better, had more energy, and my physical stature was changing. My muscles were growing while fat was shredding off my body. Even so, I still applied Rod's principles which kept me more focused than ever.

My second goal of documenting the process on social media was more mentally challenging for me. I had been putting my workout clips up, but I still did not feel comfortable. I now knew that putting my healthy and active lifestyle on social media was not part of my identity yet. That was okay because now I knew how to get there.

Going forward, I coordinated the majority of my workouts with Brent. We both pushed each other in the weight room and felt accomplished after we finished training. Brent also recorded clips of our workout daily, which I posted to my Instagram stories without a second thought.

To enhance the value I was able to provide, I had the idea of getting certified as a personal trainer. I had this idea on the phone while I was brainstorming with my mom. The next day, I enrolled in an online course to get my certification. Within one month, I had my license. My goal was never to work as a personal trainer, but I knew it would come with enhanced credibility, knowledge, and, more importantly, value to give to my followers.

I started posting more workout suggestions, explanations for proper ways to complete specific exercises, nutrition ideas, and much more. People began to get accustomed to finding value on my page. This resulted in many more people reaching out to me for my expertise.

My third goal was to win this cruise challenge and ultimately build my business. I also still had the top-ten earners in my sights. I knew it was going to take a lot of work, but success was possible. My ongoing transformation and documentation were developing into effective tools for bringing on new customers and distributors. However, they were just that. Tools.

To really level up, I needed to be intentional. This made me the most uncomfortable out of all the goals I was working toward, but I knew that outside of my comfort zone was where I needed to be living in order to manifest the change I desired.

I first committed to adding three new people to my network daily. They could be in person or through social media. The rule was that we both had to follow each other and have some sort of conversation to initiate the relationship.

Next, I committed to inviting three new people per day to take a look at our business plan or products. I also committed to following up with three people daily whom I already had a conversation with to see if they were ready to enroll. Finally, I committed to having three people watch a video, presentation, or get on a three-way call daily. My plan: 3x3x3x3.

The first few days were not fun at all. I dove right back into rejection and getting ignored. I had to stay laser focused on the Cycle of Growth and the fact that it was my responsibility to share this with people. I kept reminding myself of what Rod said to me: To whom much is given, much is expected.

After about a week, I was still a little uncomfortable, but I was having some success. Inviting three people per day resulted in twenty-one invites. One of the people I reached out to told me he had been following me and had been meaning to reach out to me. He started with one of our systems. These small victories made me stay focused on the mission.

One month in I had invited nearly one hundred people. At that point, the process was becoming clockwork. I had a list of people, sat down with a coffee, and did my 3x3x3x3. I could feel the habit starting to form and was no longer feeling uncomfortable. Like eating healthy and working out, this was just a part of my daily action. It was a part of how I operated. It was action that served my purpose and vision.

All of these habits were leading to a big contribution to the cruise team. We skyrocketed through the ranks and were hovering around fifteenth place on the leaderboard. The top teams were constantly shuffling positions, and we stayed in the money consistently. The vision of our Caribbean getaway was getting closer and closer to becoming a reality.

We continued our online meetings and grew an unbreakable bond as a team. We constantly pushed and motivated one another while holding each other accountable. The level of teamwork made us family, which was necessary. The competition was real. If one of us did not pull our weight, we would all miss out on this once-in-a-lifetime experience.

I had been going through the motions for a few months when one day it hit me. Results were starting to happen. I was consistently bringing new people into my business from the 3x3x3x3 action plan. My income was growing. My leadership was developing. I was in the best shape I had ever been in. My social media felt in perfect alignment.

More importantly, I felt in alignment. Our cruise team was still among the top teams with only a month left before the challenge ended. The mental conditioning paired with the consistent action was moving me in the right direction toward my vision.

Around this time, I made the decision that after our lease was up that I would return to the East Coast. I felt as though my goals, business, and vision would be best served if I returned home. California was a cool place, but I was not in love with the Bay Area and did not see myself being there for the long term. Once I made the decision, I wanted to explore the places I had yet to see in California. At the top of that list was Los Angeles.

Originally, I was going to go alone. Brent had school, Robinson had a new job selling cars, and our friend Colt who moved out there during the summer had a demanding job and was still healing from a recent ACL tear. I was cool with it. It turned out that Sanjay lived just outside of LA. We had yet to link back up in person since our college days, and that alone would have made the trip worth it to me.

Before accepting a solo trip, I figured I would put forth a Calipari-esque recruiting effort to see if I could get the boys to accompany me. I spent an entire week preaching how this would be the last opportunity to go to LA as a squad. After I moved back to the East Coast, there was no possibility of this happening again (very false). I explained how, after I moved, they would never make the collective effort to go down there either. I nagged, persuaded, tantalized, and even bribed.

After I gave it my all, both Robinson and Colt decided that they were down for the trip. As we solidified our plans for the weekend in our living room, Brent was on the couch.

"Dude, this is your last chance. Are you in, or are you out?" I asked him. He was sick and tired of hearing about it.

"I told you, man. I have an exam on Monday. I need to study for it. If I go, there's just no way I'll study. I'm out."

I pulled up the drive from San Jose to LA on my phone and showed him the screen.

"Five hours each way, buddy. That's ten hours of study time. Plus, if you need to stay behind in the hotel room and study a bit, that's completely cool. Heck, bring your notes to the beach. You will be uninterrupted, and all of your study efforts will be respected," I said.

He started to shake his head. "Regardless of that, I've spent way too much money this month. I'm a student. I barely have any income. I know that you guys are going to spend a ton of money down there and I can't swing a hotel room," Brent said.

I thought for a moment. Good point, but not good enough.

"Your portion of the hotel room is on me. Plus, the second night we will be staying at Sanjay's. They are hosting a Friendsgiving so there will be a ton of food as well. Other than that, you only have to pay for food, which you would be doing anyway, and drinks if we go out. Basically, the only extra cost you will have is gas split among us and a few drinks. That's not gonna break the bank, is it?" I said. I knew I was getting closer.

He sat there staring at the textbook in his lap.

"Damn, man. You're really going to bail, huh. Hollywood. The place that's been calling for us our entire lives. The City of Angels. The City of Brotherly Love," I rambled.

"That's Philly," Robinson chimed in.

"That's beside the point. This is the opportunity of a lifetime, and you are going to let the team make the trek down to the promised land without a key player. This is crazy." I kept going.

Brent slammed his textbook shut and jumped off the couch. He stormed into the kitchen.

"Where are you going?" I asked him.

"I'm going to the lounge to study. Now that I'm going to LA with you guys, I'm going to have to pull an all-nighter. Unbelievable." We all began to cheer.

Now that the whole squad was assembled and my recruiting campaign was victorious, we were ready to take on the city.

26

THE CITY OF ANGELS

THE NEXT MORNING, we all reconvened in the kitchen. Brent came stumbling down the stairs like he had just risen from the dead. He was wearing the same gym clothes from the night before and his eyes looked like he dumped two full salt shakers into them.

"Damn, man. You look like shit!" I said as we started to crack up.

"Didn't sleep," he replied as he opened up the refrigerator.

"No kidding. Well, you'll have to get some rest in the car. We have a long weekend ahead of us," I said.

"I can't wait until you move back to Connecticut." He smacked his head into his hands in pure agony.

For some reason, we decided to take Robinson's gas-guzzling war tank that was on the brink of explosion. It made no sense at the time we made the decision, and it still makes no sense now. Nonetheless, we loaded it up, aimed south, and started the trek to LA.

The five-hour drive was actually a great experience. I had been so focused on my business and transformation that I was barely taking any time to unplug. The entire ride down we were bumping the widest variety of music and jamming out. Although most of the scenery was vast farmland, the drive was still a cool way to see a large portion of California.

When the music was not on full blast, we were joking around with each other in full jackass mode. A few hours in, everyone agreed that they were extremely happy that we decided to make the trip. I was thanked for my relentless recruiting effort.

Inevitably, whenever we got into the groove of smooth sailing, we got clobbered with a tidal wave. Just as we entered LA, Robinson's car started to make a thumping noise.

"Dude, do you hear that?" Robinson said. We all did, we just did not want to address it out of fear that it would postpone our arrival time.

"You're fine. We are twenty minutes from the hotel. Full speed ahead," Brent said.

"No, dude this definitely is not fine," Robinson replied as he let out a nervous laugh. "I'm stopping at the next gas station."

Colt, Brent, and I all collectively sighed and threw our arms up at the same time.

We ended up finding a gas station and pulled off the road. Robinson got out to investigate, and sure enough, his tire had an egg-sized bulge on it.

We convinced Robinson that we could at least make it to the hotel, and then from there we could use Ubers and figure out the tire situation the next day. He reluctantly agreed. It felt like we were riding on horseback, but after a delicate drive, we made it to the hotel.

On the way in I could not contain my excitement that LA was already exactly what I imagined it would be. Women that looked like they belonged on magazine covers were casually strolling the streets at every turn. Luxury sports cars zoomed by our ready-to-detonate tank one after another. The California sun radiated perfectly warm beams, and the energy in the air felt like we were in a rock star kingdom.

The hotel was stunning, with palm trees lining the entrance and sparkles of extravagance radiating from the glass lobby. We hopped out of the car and let the valet know that the tire could blow at any second. He took the keys, and we thought we were in the clear. Little did we know we were about to be slapped with the next whammy.

I went to the front desk to check in, and the concierge could not seem to locate my reservation. After about ten minutes, the whole squad had given up hope on the hotel and me.

"Looks like we will be sleeping on the beach tonight," Robinson mumbled. "Way to go, Stank."

"I know I booked it, man. Hold on, I'm going to pull it up," I said as I took out my iPhone. I scrolled through my emails and pulled up the reservation. I smacked myself in the forehead.

"Well, we have a slight problem, boys. You see, I must have accidentally selected the wrong date when I made the reservation. It appears as though I booked the hotel for New Year's Eve."

"Damnit, Stank," Brent said as they all threw their arms up in the air.

"Well, the good news is that at least we have New Year's Eve plans now," I joked. It was not well received.

I explained to the concierge what happened, and they were accommodating. They canceled my future reservation and allowed me to make one for that night. The price was a bit higher, but at least we had it figured out. We all walked over to the elevator in hysterics at how much had already gone wrong. A lot of people would have let those two setbacks ruin their entire trip. For us, it simply added to the story.

Upon entering our room, Robinson hopped in the shower while Colt and Brent went down the street to get some food. I stayed behind and posted up by our window in a perfectly positioned lounge chair. This was one of the cities I dreamed about visiting my entire life, and I was finally there.

It sort of felt surreal as I thought about how much I had already seen and experienced in life so far. I was feeling elated as I absorbed the beauty of the skyscrapers, mountains, and obscurely engineered staircase structure on the ground level. For me, not much can match the feeling of experiencing somewhere new, and I could tell LA was going to be a place that won a special spot in my heart.

I was so lost in the moment that I almost did not even notice my phone ringing. I picked it up and looked at the screen. It was an Arizona number. I thought about declining but decided to answer.

"Hello?"

"Hello, John?" the lady on the other end of the phone said in an extremely friendly voice.

"Yes, this is John. May I ask who is calling?" I replied.

"This is your Corporate Team. We are calling you to congratulate you on earning a spot in the TOP-TEN WORLDWIDE INCOME EARNERS FOR AGES TWENTY-FIVE AND UNDER," she said as the entire team she was with broke out into applause and cheers.

I sat there in silence as chills began to run through my body.

"This is a huge deal. Thank you so much for your servant leadership and the contributions you are making to the START community. You are making such a huge impact and we are so proud of you. Keep inspiring and changing the world. Congratulations again and we will see you at New Year's kickoff where you will be recognized on stage," she said.

"Wow! Thank you so much." That was all I could say. I was actually speechless. I hung up the phone and stared out the window at the city for ten seconds until the news really set in.

"LET'S FUCKING GOOOOOOOOOOOOOO!" I screamed as I began running around the room. I started launching pillows and jumping back and forth between the beds like a child.

"Is everything all right out there, you maniac?" Robinson yelled from the bathroom.

Words can hardly describe how I was feeling at that moment. My Network Marketing journey had been an absolute roller coaster. My *life* had been an absolute roller coaster. I thought back to when I got kicked out of high school. How lost I was and how at first I thought I would never be able to make something out of myself.

I thought back to when I first was introduced to the industry. Eighteen years old, hungry, and determined to achieve a lifestyle like the top performers in my company. Deciding to quit after six months and my upline telling me that I would never amount to anything in Network Marketing.

My hesitation for years to fully jump back in. The scrutiny, the rejection, friendships lost, the self-doubt, the doubt over the industry as a whole, the highs associated with periods of exciting momentum, and the lows when it was all falling apart. All of it was so worth it.

Less than a year before I was sitting in the audience watching the young entrepreneurs whom I aspired to be like walking across the stage. I decided at that moment that I would be up there the following year. There were times where I had full confidence in making it happen. There were times where I did not think it was possible anymore.

There were ups, there were downs, but ultimately I stuck it out. No longer was being a part of the group an aspiration—it was a reality. I needed to call the person who was there when I made the commitment to make this happen. I picked up the phone and called my mom.

"Hey, Honey, what's going on?" her high energy voice said as she answered.

"Hey, Mom! Just got to LA and settled into our hotel room. Kind of a mess getting down here, but we made it. And guess what?" I said.

"I can only imagine. What's up?"

"I just got a call from our Corporate Team. I made the top-ten earners," I told her as I awaited her response.

"OH MY GOSH! That is freaking amazing. Congratulations, John. I am so proud of how much you've accomplished in life already. You are so young and have so many amazing blessings coming your way. I am especially grateful that you are finally committed to building this with me. It only took about five years after you spent all your money on those stupid energy drinks," she said as we both laughed.

"Seriously though, this is just the beginning. You are going to do huge things, John. I am so excited to watch it all. I am so proud of you, and we will have to have a celebratory drink when you are home for Christmas," she said.

I sat staring out the window until Colt and Brent busted down the door with food and a handle of London's finest gin.

"What's the huge smile for, man?" Brent asked. "And why are there pillows everywhere? What the hell did you do while we were gone?"

I laughed and told him and Colt the news.

What are accomplishments if you don't take a moment to celebrate them. We all started cheering as we made a toast to the weekend ahead. We threw on some music as we continued to have a few more drinks. Then we all got dressed up in V-necks and blazers for a night on the town. We called an Uber to begin our tour of the city and to have a night for the books.

A night for the books is absolutely what it was. On our way to dinner, we drove by the iconic Hollywood sign staggered on the mountainside. It felt so cool to see this in person after going through life seeing it in every movie, TV show, and magazine. We hit up Hollywood Boulevard, checked out the star walk, and discussed the legends who earned a spot among its legacy.

After dinner at the Hard Rock (basic, I know), we started to hop between different bars and clubs to live out the hype of the LA nightlife scene. We ended up at an outdoor club next to the Santa

Monica pier. We partied the night away next to the ocean feeling like absolute movie stars.

I remember looking around feeling so fulfilled and so grateful for the moment. I was with some of my best friends, in a beautiful city that I had always wanted to experience, and I just hit a major milestone in my business and life. This is what it was all about.

My last memory from that night was staring out at the ocean while taking a sip of my drink. The next memory was waking up in the hotel knowing that the night and celebrations were a success.

The next day we spent the morning exploring the Santa Monica beach. We walked the beach aimlessly and allowed the day to bring us wherever it pleased. One of the coolest parts was the skatepark with large concrete bowls located next to the beach. Some of the guys looked like pros; others were taking an absolute ass-whooping.

One guy kept falling and rolling on the ground, taking his skateboard to the shin, and overall eating shit every single time he tried a trick. I had to give it to him, though, he kept getting back on his board.

In the end, that's all that matters. I've always had a ton of respect for skateboarders because everyone we were watching that was good was at one point the disaster man we were watching. They fell, bled, and endured severe pain, but they kept getting back on the board.

After exploring for a few hours, we realized we had to get Robinson's car tire fixed. We rolled slowly through the hood until we found a tire shop that carried the specific model of tire his steamboat needed. Once it was replaced, we went down to meet up with Sanjay.

I had not seen Sanjay since he graduated one year before I did. We stayed in touch, but we had so much to catch up on. It felt crazy to me how close we were, how many moves we were making, and then how life got in the way and we ended up pursuing different paths. When we pulled up to his apartment complex, it was like we never even skipped a beat.

He was standing in the parking lot and waving us toward the proper parking spot.

"STAAAAANK!" he yelled to me.

"Sanjay, baby!" I yelled back as we brought it in for a hug. Brent and Colt already knew him and greeted him with a hug as well. I then introduced him to Robinson.

"So, you're the one who started a textbook empire with Stank, huh?" Robinson said.

"Ah, man, that's old news. I'm focused on what's next," Sanjay replied.

"So you're over that lifestyle?" Brent asked.

"Nah, man. It was cool for sure. But that's the past. It's over. I'm onto making moves for the future."

"Sickening. I respect it for sure," Brent said.

I loved it. To be honest, I was the same way. I never liked talking about the past too much. What happened happened. It shaped us into who we are today. I was grateful for all my amazing experiences. But it was done. Too many people get stuck there, whether it's in terrible memories or the glory days.

I've always believed you should stop and take a moment to celebrate your accomplishments, but after that, it was over. You have to live in the present and take action on what you can control and constantly strive for more. Getting stuck in the past is one of the worst cages you can put yourself in.

Sanjay brought us into his apartment and introduced us to all his roommates and friends he had over for Friendsgiving. We immediately submerged ourselves and started connecting with every person there. I've always loved how, as a friend group, we were able to hop into a social situation where we knew nobody and proceed to thrive within it.

We were telling stories and jokes that had everyone there in hysterics. We convinced this kid Charlie to start doing backflips in the middle of the room and empowered him to pursue his career as a skateboarder. By the end, he was determined. At one point, we formed a dance circle around a four-year-old girl who stole the show and put us to shame. It was all so simple, but we were having an absolute blast.

After we ate dinner, I stepped aside with Sanjay.

"How's life, man? It seems like you're killing it down here. I would expect nothing less," I said.

"Yeah, I love California. My job is cool too. I'm making a lot of money and have an awesome schedule. I just feel like I need to find a way to start helping people, that's the only thing lacking. I love that you've created something where you are making a true impact. Everything about what you're doing is so inspiring," he told me. "Now you're in the top-ten earners in your company? You've been killing the game ever since I met you."

"I'm so grateful for it," I said. "There have definitely been challenges, but everything has come together perfectly. And honestly, I'm so grateful for you, bro. You played a huge part in the entrepreneurial aspect of my life. All of the ventures we had led to this. As for you, I know you're going to find your way. You are a special person."

"I'll find it, man. I love what you are doing with your business, but I just don't think that's the route for me. I definitely love the products, though. They make me feel superhuman. On top of that, I've been so in touch spiritually and mentally. Everything really is great, I just want to start helping other people," he said.

"You know I always got you. If you ever are ready to take another look at this business, I'd be more than happy to help you crush it. In the meantime, just keep working on yourself and figure out a way you can provide value to people. You're going to do huge things, I'm sure of it." I said.

We went on to have another fantastic night. The whole group went to an outdoor tiki bar where we kicked it back and had drinks. Again, I felt so happy and so grateful. The whole weekend came together perfectly.

I was sitting at a table thinking about how far I had come, but was even more excited for how much more was left to accomplish. The few days spent in Los Angeles with some of my best friends could not have played out better. Receiving the news of the top ten was the icing on the cake, making it inevitable that this would be a weekend I'd remember for my entire life.

I soaked in the moment and enjoyed every second. The celebration was great, but upon return, I was ready to get back to work. I stuck to the motto: Always grateful, never satisfied.

27

MY PURPOSE IN LIFE

OUR TEAM STARTED to blow up the news on social media that I earned a spot in the top ten. I was receiving tons of messages from team members, friends who were not involved in my business, and random people in the company I never met before.

I felt as if people were watching closer than ever. I felt responsible to show them what was possible. I hopped back into the grind harder than ever as soon as we returned to San Jose. I've always prided myself on my ability to completely unplug for a few days, then at the flick of a switch immerse myself into full grind mode. Balance is key.

As the time was dwindling down until New Year's, the competition in our cruise challenge became more intense than it had been the entire challenge. Teams who were in the top ten the entire time were dropping out of the top twenty-five. New teams surfaced that were bringing on ten to fifteen new customers per day. We remained around twelfth place and we were more focused than ever. We worked so hard to get this far, we could not let it slip now.

During this time, I was coming to an end in my sixteen-week challenge. I was ecstatic with my results. My abs had never been as chiseled as they were. My arms were the leanest they had ever been. My energy levels were through the roof. When the day came to take my after pictures, I knew what I accomplished was special.

I sent the pictures to my cruise team, and every single person was positive I would be a finalist in the challenge. I felt extremely confident in my physical transformation, but that was only half of the challenge. The other half was based on an essay that described my experience and change during the challenge.

I did my best to construct a five-hundred-word essay that depicted the transformation this challenge had on me mentally. I could have written an entire book, but I felt confident about the essay I produced. I uploaded my after pictures and essay on the company website and clicked submit. I had put forth my best effort, and now it was up to the judges to decide if it was good enough. That night, I had a Five Guys burger with a strawberry milkshake to celebrate. I deserved it.

My before and after pictures from the sixteen-week transformation challenge.

A few days later I flew back to Connecticut for Christmas and New Year's. Being with my mom at home kicked us into overdrive as our challenge came to an end. Through the holidays, we continued recruiting new customers and business builders to make sure our team's position was safe. On New Year's Eve, we were in thirteenth place. We had one last team call, and most of us felt comfortable with our position. Cyndi was slightly worried people would make a last-ditch effort, but I thought we had a comfortable enough lead.

I had plans to celebrate with my friends down in Stamford. We booked out a block of hotel rooms with all our friends from college and our dates. Colt ended up driving me, and on the way down he stopped at his mom's house.

While he was in the shower, she and I started to have a conversation about my business and the solutions we provide. I showed her my recent transformation and she was blown away. She told me that the night before she had won $500 at the casino and wanted a transformation of her own. I got her enrolled on a starter pack by the time Colt was ready to leave the house. I figured that would secure our spot even further.

After a night of New Year's celebrations, I woke up in the hotel room and immediately checked my phone. I logged onto our website and checked the cruise challenge leaderboards. I looked at the top-ten teams.

We were not there, and half of the teams were different than the day before. That was okay. I did not expect to be in the top ten anyway. I clicked the next page that showed us the top twenty teams. Almost all of the teams were different. I did not see our name anywhere. My heart sank. I could not believe it.

I took a deep breath, clicked to the next page, and closed my eyes. Once I opened them, I saw our fate. There we were. Twenty-first place. We made it by the skin of our teeth. I hopped out of bed and shouted at the top of my lungs.

"WOOOOOOOOOO! HELL YEAH, BABY!"

I woke up everyone who was in a groggy hungover state.

"What the hell is wrong with you, man?" Brent mumbled.

"We're going to the Caribbean, baby. You're coming with me," I yelled as I started launching pillows at his bed. I had to stop getting the news of my accomplishments while in hotel rooms. At this rate, I was going to have an incidental damages bill that was through the roof. Brent laughed and held his fist up in the air.

A few weeks later, I was in Phoenix for our New Year's kickoff event. I checked in for the event and was given a backstage pass plus a reserved seat in the top earner's section at the front of the room. After check-in, it took me three hours to complete the fifteen-minute walk back to my room. Countless people on our team, friends within the company, and people I had never even met were stopping to congratulate me. It was like nothing I've ever experienced before.

The amount of praise I received. The number of people who shared how big of an inspiration I have been to them and their family. People who wanted to know how I've achieved the level of success I've had at such a young age. People who were genuinely so ecstatic to see me thrive. When I got back to my hotel, I was so full of gratitude. I knew I was exactly where I was supposed to be.

The next morning, I was up at 7:00 a.m. to report backstage for our recognition segment. I threw on a white V-neck, gray blazer, black jeans, and one of the pairs of black Gucci sneakers I secured in Italy. I put on my shades and threw my Air Pods in. I scrolled through Spotify and pulled up "Pound Cake" by Drake and Jay-Z. I took one last look in the mirror, put on a huge smile, and began my walk over.

I stepped out into the street and looked around as the song played. The warm Arizona sun was shining on what was a perfect January day. Chills kept running through the back of my head and down my spine. I felt excited, I felt in alignment, and I felt right.

I entered the convention center and walked past the thousands of seats that were already beginning to fill up for the day straight to the backstage entrance. I flashed my badge to the two guards who greeted me and let me through.

When I rounded the corner, I was greeted by the corporate team who ecstatically welcomed me and handed me the trophy I would walk across the stage with. After chatting with them, I started to mingle with all of the other young people who had earned a spot in this elite group. I had seen a lot of them on social media and from being recognized by the company, but I had not yet met them in person.

To say I was blown away by the high level of human beings the group contained would be an understatement. The young people in the group were some of the purest, most genuine and purpose-driven humans I have ever met. Sometimes with high levels of success comes arrogance and an inflated ego. There was a reverse effect on all of these individuals. The more success this group of people had, the more grounded and genuine they became.

One of the first couples I connected with was Jared and Sharaya Maples. Coincidentally, they both were a part of the energy drink company I was partnered with years back. Sharaya hit one of the elite ranks but started to feel as if the company was treating her like a dollar sign. Feeling totally out of alignment, she decided to step away before the company came crashing down.

Jared's mom was one of the top leaders in our company and earned a seven-figure income annually. Jared never went to college and did whatever was necessary to make ends meet while in the pursuit of building his Network Marketing business. He was driving for Uber until his business exploded exponentially. It was unbelievable how many similarities there were in our stories.

The main theme in both of them was perseverance. We had every excuse in the book to leave the industry, but we stuck with it and made it happen. To this day, both Jared and Sharaya have been so abundant and helped me tremendously with their servant leadership.

Another girl I met was Chelsea Miller. She attended one of the top colleges for entrepreneurship, finished top in her class, and after graduation decided to become a professional network marketer. At the time, she was living in Bali and building her business full-time from her phone and laptop. We connected because I used this vehicle to travel the world as well. She was such an intelligent, confident, and real individual who was making an astounding impact.

One of the people I was most interested in was Morgan Nelson. He was from Australia, and prior to building this business, he was a full-time carpenter. Morgan changed my perspective of the business so much after his explanation of the industry.

"Yeah, mate. I was a carpenter, working sixty to seventy hours a week, and it fucking sucked. I hated it. Worked my ass off, barely got any time off, and was miserable. My buddy introduced me to this company, and I couldn't understand why everyone wasn't doing this. So I went all in, built this business, and now I'm living full-time in Bali. Why in the fuck would I ever want to do anything else? There's not a chance in hell I would ever go back to a nine-to-five. Fuck that!" he explained to me in his Australian accent.

I started to laugh, but he was so right. I was so interested in how raw and real he was. Morgan was 100 percent unapologetically himself. He did not sugarcoat his words or worry about what people thought about him. His belief was unshakable. That is why he is the success he is today.

Then there was Mackenzie Arball. She was a powerhouse leader who had the entrepreneurial spirit running through her veins since her midteens.

Before being introduced to our company, she was running a brick-and-mortar business in San Diego. One of her recurring clients had attempted to recruit some of Mackenzie's staff, but never actually approached Mackenzie herself. She overheard these attempts, and since she was always staying open to new business opportunities, Mackenzie reached out to her on social media to learn what it was all about.

Coincidentally, one of our biggest company events was happening in San Diego, so she decided to check it out. She only attended for two hours, but during that time she listened to a top leader share her story on stage. Being extremely well versed in business, she saw the incredible advantages of the Network Marketing business model and decided on the spot that she would run with our opportunity.

She faced tremendous adversity and rejection but ultimately stayed true to her commitment and built a multiple six-figure income.

James and Audrye McLeod were another couple who radiated positive energy and inspiration. Audrye was the nanny for two of the top leaders in our entire company and observed their life, work ethic, and Network Marketing lifestyle daily. After two years, she could no longer deny that Network Marketing and our partner company were the real deal, so she finally said yes to the opportunity.

While building the business with relentless dedication, she met her future husband, James. They began building together, and that year, they were the number one income earners for our age category.

I could have spent days backstage with that group of people just listening to their stories and learning more about them. The more I talked to everyone, the more I realized that they were all just normal people who saw the vision, made no excuses, and put in the work to get to where they were.

"Let's line up and take a few pictures. After that, it's time to take the stage," said the coordinator. We took a bunch of pictures and then made our way to the entrance for our stage segment. I grabbed one of our energy shots off the table of products and gulped it down.

The company owner's son began with his introduction of what this young community was all about. It was like deja vu from last year, except this time I was where I envisioned I'd be—among the group of extraordinary individuals, not watching from the audience.

I turned around to Morgan.

"Dude, you have to do a dance move," I said with a grin.

He started to "floss" as we all cracked up.

"If you do that, I'll do my signature move," I said.

"Oh yeah? What's that mate?"

I broke out into The Hurricane. We all burst into laughter.

"If you do that, I will buy you a box of our energy shots," Allison, another one of the top earners, said to me.

"Hah. Done," I said.

"Let's see it," she said shaking her head.

The upbeat music began to roll as they started to announce names. The couple who earned the number ten spot was called out. The crowd cheered as they took the stage. Then, the couple in front of me was called. The crowd cheered and applauded. The lady coordinating the segment signaled me over to the bottom of the stairs to take the stage.

"Coming in at number eight, JOHN STANKIEWICZ!" boomed the company owner's son's voice over the stereo system as the lady tapped me on the shoulder to go. I looked back and smiled at everyone as I began to walk out.

I walked up the stairs and came onto the stage. I noticed the backdrop had a billboard-sized picture of me and as I looked outward toward the crowd, I could barely see past the first row of the sea of over 5,000 people due to the blinding lights. Everyone clapped and cheered, especially the section where a large portion of our team was sitting.

As I walked toward the front of the stage, I stopped midway and broke out into The Hurricane. Three full storm-like motions and I continued on as if nothing happened. Both the owner's son and the other lady on stage were dying in laughter. I approached them, gave them both hugs, and stood up front with my trophy to get my picture taken.

I looked down and saw my mom in the front row. I shot her a huge smile. She stood there with her arms folded and a lip smile on as she shook her head. It was the perfect mixture of being proud of her son while at the same time continuously embarrassed by my actions when I got the spotlight. I know she would not want it any other way.

I only stood up there for five seconds, but it felt like an eternity. I saw people taking pictures and videos that would serve as an inspiration to them that they could achieve their wildest dreams from this business. I noticed millennials who were looking up at me with the same level of determination I had one year before to earn a spot on that stage. In that instant, I knew my purpose in life shifted to something greater.

From the moment I got expelled from high school, all I ever wanted was to become somebody. To become a successful person that people held in high regard. Somebody that people respected, looked up to, and admired. I do not think there is ever a specific point where someone can say they made it, but while I was standing on that stage, I felt I had finally become that person I was so hungry to grow into.

Ironically, it was exactly then that I had the epiphany that allowed me to grasp the most important lesson of my life. This was no longer about me.

This journey was for the kid who made a big mistake when he was young and now thinks he can never amount to anything.

It was for the teenager who received subpar grades in school and now believes he is stupid and can only exist as a minimum wage worker.

It was for the college student who was scared to death of a nine-to-five, had huge dreams, and had them shot down by their family and friends.

It was for the people who dream of calling the shots and getting every last drop of juice out of the one shot we have at this incredible life.

It was for the people who simply wanted more. All of my mistakes, failures, successes, experiences, and lessons were for *them*!

As I turned my back to the crowd and they called the next name, I knew my life had become bigger than I was. I knew that if I could just show my journey to the masses, I could bring light to millions of people as to where they must place their focus in order to succeed in our new world.

It would show them where true education begins and where the people who have succeeded on the highest level placed the majority of their focus. They would begin to concentrate on learning from the greatest teacher of them all: experience. They would find a new path where nothing is promised yet anything is possible. A path where their wildest dreams and an abundance of fulfillment waited for them to take into their grasp.

I knew that it was my responsibility to pick up the pen and show society the path that exists beyond the classroom.

Being recognized on stage in 2019 for achieving a spot in the top-ten income earners for twenty-five and under for the second year in a row.

The 2019 START top-ten income earners for ages twenty-five and under. Back row, left to right, Sharaya Maples, Natalia Mulieri, Mackenzie Arball, Aubrey Mable, Whitney Beers, Cameron Biafore, and Chelsea Miller. Front left to right, Jared Maples, Morgan Nelson, John Stankiewicz, and Tyler Walter.

The Championship Cruise Challenge Team on the ship: back row,
left to right, John Stankiewicz, Cyndi Walter, and Tyler Walter. Front row,
from left to right, Scott Walter, Sydney Mullet, Mattie Walter, Zoe Scott,
*Susan Wheeler (mom), and Brent Young. *Not pictured, Dr. Erin Peck.*

Speaking at a 2019 company training event in Columbus, Ohio.

FINAL THOUGHTS

As I sit here writing the final words of a book that encapsulates my entire life, so far, and that I have obsessively worked on for an entire year now, the spectrum of emotions I am experiencing can hardly be articulated.

I think back to the gut-wrenching feeling of getting kicked out of high school. Those feelings of uselessness and despair I would not wish upon any individual on this planet. No fourteen-year-old should ever have to feel like a disgrace and fuck up every time they step out of their bedroom. Yet, if I could go back, I would not change a thing.

I think back to every person who tried to jam me into a mold where I simply did not fit. The teachers who tried to tell me who and what I could or could not be. The ones who told me to rethink my dreams because of the letter assigned to me from my ability to circle letters on a piece of paper. The people who tried to deter me from chasing extraordinary dreams because of their own extraordinary self-imposed limitations.

I think back to some of my very first business ventures. The feeling when people you consider to be some of your best friends laugh in your face. When you walk into a room and everyone cracks jokes and calls you a con artist. I remember some of my first business presentations, speaking in front of a room to show people a life-changing opportunity, and watching them sneer as they walk out and never talk to you again.

I think back to the rejection. The hate. The uncertainty. The painful growth. The self-doubt. The frustration. The fear. The feeling of being alone.

Guess what? I would not change any of it. Each and every one of my past negative experiences served as a brick to build the foundation of who I am today. I could not be more grateful.

Although I may have been bitter at the time, I now understand. I understand that people tend to project their insecurities and shortcomings in negative ways upon people they feel threatened by. I know that most of the people who tried to deter me from pursuing my dreams were trying to protect me. They themselves have been tainted by society's "way to live life" virus. I understand that people are programmed in a way that severely limits their unlimited capability.

I am so damn grateful that I was able to see past this epidemic at a young age. I am so grateful my rebellious mind refused to follow the beaten path and instead whipped out a machete and started chopping my way through the pricker bushes. I am so grateful I stayed true to myself, because if I had not, I would not be here to share these lessons with you.

I hope that out of all the lessons in this book, the one that sticks with you is to always be true to yourself and your intuition. People will always give you their two cents about your dreams and aspirations. When they tell you what you should be doing, simply smile, nod your head, and when they leave, go right back to taking massive fucking action on what you know is right.

It will suck at first. You will deal with similar obstacles that I and every other person who has decided to design their own destiny has. But trust me when I say, it's better than the alternative. That is, play it safe, make the people around you happy, go through the motions, then look at life when it's over drowning in regret.

As I have repeated over and over, I learned few applicable skills in school that have gotten me to where I am today. When I realized school and the traditional life were not for me, I put all of my focus elsewhere and got an education in experience.

I did what felt right, and you saw where it got me. And let me be clear, I do not feel like I am some beacon of success. There are so many people out there who have accomplished much more than I have in a shorter period of time. I do, however, feel that I'm an example of what is possible.

My advice to you is focus on real-life experiences. Get out in the real world and take action. I have always been a believer that if an idea lingers in your mind, it's there for a reason.

Do you have a business idea you can't get off your mind? Take action to get the ball rolling. Have you wanted to start an Instagram page to showcase your workouts? Stop thinking and start posting. Do you have a passion for vegan cooking? Go find a vegan chef who is willing to let you work for him or start experimenting in the kitchen. Getting out there and doing will always be the ultimate form of learning.

I had no idea what it would take to write a book, but I noticed that for three years I thought about my book idea daily. If that's not a sign to take action, I don't know what is. I proceeded to listen to other authors, watch YouTube videos, and take action to get my words on paper for a couple hours a day. You will figure out the process as you go.

Above all else, do what makes you happy. Through trial and error, you will figure out what lights you up inside. At the end of the day your happiness is all that matters. Place your happiness first and protect it with everything you have.

I will be forever grateful that I stayed true to myself and focused on my passions. I'll forever be thankful for the willful John who refused to listen to his teachers or society's advice and followed his heart. Every one of his actions and decisions led us here. And now, I feel like we are only just getting started.

Since the final scene in my book, so many surreal things have happened.

For my sixteen-week challenge, I did not end up winning; however, I was selected as one of ten honorable mentions out of over 15,000 entries.

As for my business, I have now earned a spot in the top-ten income earners for three years in a row. I also have been able to travel to even more amazing places this world has to offer. In fact, while spending a month in Colombia and Costa Rica, I had my highest paid month to date from my Network Marketing residual income.

I have been able to use the income from Network Marketing to invest in other business opportunities, including one with my mentor Rod Hairston. I went through an extensive training to become certified in mindset coaching, and we are now creating online personal development programs that are changing lives around the world.

In addition, I have been blessed with the opportunity to speak in front of thousands of individuals to share my story and train on entrepreneurship and mindset.

As I have said, everything I am doing is now bigger than I am, and I could not be more excited for what is next—helping you.

As a Certified Growth Leader with over eight years of personal development experience, I know that the foundation for success all begins with the right mindset and beliefs. I am confident in my ability to set you up for success by helping you build a mindset that will serve you, your goals, and your vision. Please apply on my website to see if you are eligible for my one-on-one coaching.

Nothing lights me up more than sharing my story and pouring value into a room full of hungry individuals who want more out of life. I love speaking at events and would welcome the opportunity to speak at yours. If you would like me at your next event, please submit an inquiry on my website.

Network Marketing will be a platform that I stand behind and preach about for life. It changed my life, and it could very well be the vehicle that changes yours. If you are not yet involved, please visit my website (www.JohnStankiewicz.com) so I can show you how you can be a part of this incredible industry.

If you are involved in Network Marketing already, it is important to know that we are all in this together. I am committed to making this industry a profession that is discussed as a career path the same way people talk about being a doctor, engineer, accountant, nurse, banker, or candlestick maker.

I would love to pour the knowledge I have learned along my seven-plus-year journey into your team. Please reach out on my website to inquire about booking me for your team call, for an in-person event, or for one-on-one coaching.

Now, I want to take one last moment from the bottom of my heart to thank you for picking up my book and reading it until the very end. I was able to see this through because I felt that I needed to get this book into your hands, and it is my hope that you found at least one nugget within these pages that will propel you to a better life.

If you did, I want to hear directly from you. Please send me a DM on Instagram @johnstankiewicz and let me know how this book impacted your life.

Also, stay tuned. I have a feeling this book is the beginning of so much more to come.

ACKNOWLEDGMENTS

I thank my mother, Susan Wheeler. Without her love, support, and belief in me, I could not possibly be where I am today. Thank you for being the best mom on the planet, I love you so much!

Speaking of moms, I would like to give another shout-out to my second mom, Cyndi Walter. Thank you for your abundance and positivity and for introducing us to the vehicle that changed our lives. You have played an enormous role in helping me get where I am today.

I thank the guy who introduced me to the world of entrepreneurship—Christian Anderson. Whether you realize it or not, you opened my eyes to a new way of living that I never turned back from. Regardless of the life you choose to pursue, you will always be a brother to me.

Sarab Kukreja and John McInally—I don't even know where to begin. I'll forever be grateful for all of our ventures together. You guys each challenged and pushed me to grow in ways that formed me into who I am today. Our different business endeavors, which extend far beyond what I was able to fit in this book, are some of the memories I cherish the most from college.

Another huge shout-out to one of the sickest to ever do it—Brent Young. Although we have much different goals in life, you are the hardest working individual I know and are always blowing my mind with what you are able to accomplish. Keep shining, my brother.

Brian Sow, thank you for making my experience in Italy what it was. I learned so much from you that shaped the way I view the world today. I will forever appreciate your huge heart and abundance and for taking me in like a brother.

Tyler Walter—NYKO in San Antonio, the Top 50 event, and the cruise team changed my life, and I'm honored that I was able to go through that growth with you. Thank you for the accountability and determination to succeed on the highest level. From the cube farm to using the world as our playground, I appreciate you and am blown away by everything you have accomplished.

Thank you, Rod Hairston, for giving me the kick in the ass I needed. Your wealth of knowledge and ability to help people grow to the next level has been crucial to my journey. I am so grateful that we crossed paths and am excited to change the world together.

Jim, Kathy, and Erik Coover—you guys have changed my life. Not a single day passes where I am not grateful for your relentless work and tremendous sacrifices. Thank you for your servant leadership and for creating a vision that so many of us have been blessed to be a part of.

To the rest of the Isagenix corporate team, thank you for always going above and beyond to make this company a family. Your professionalism, genuine care for distributors, and unparalleled energy have made Isagenix a home for me.

The START family—you guys inspire me daily and have become some of my closest friends. This Network Marketing journey has been enhanced tenfold because of the greatness each of you brings to the table. Shout-out to Tyler Walter, Morgan Nelson, Jared and Sharaya Maples, Mackenzie Arball, Chelsea Miller, Sydney Lich, Cameron Biafore, Whitney Beers, Natalia Mulieri, Zoe Scott, Chelsea Cepeda, Casey Plouffe, Eric Chen, Alexe Rainville-Barzey, Sandra Tartaglia, Malena and Glen Schrauben, Ciji Siddons, James and Audrye McLeod, Elle Martinette, Zach and Eden Slobin, Emily and Hayden Vavra, Joanna and Mike Cavalcante, and the thousands of other amazing eighteen- to thirty-five-year-olds representing this incredible movement.

To my Network Marketing family, there are thousands of you, and each of you individually are the reason for my success and why I am committed to serving the world. Your transformations, encouragement, belief in me, support, and positive energy serve as my daily motivation. The words you have shared with me after hearing me speak at events, the messages I received after calls, and the praise you have given me in person served as the fuel I needed to complete this book. I am forever grateful and thankful for every single one of you.

Mike, Cliff, Pat, and Jay—you guys have been some of the best friends I could ask for. I am honored that I was able to grow up with all of you and am so appreciative for the memories we have made together.

The UCONN squad—Brent, O, Willie, Lex, Max, Trey, B, Tino, Noory, Carson, Jeff, Scoob, Odi, Rano, Perimenis, Robinson, Ross, Tucci, and the rest of my brothers that I was blessed to share this period of my life with—what a time.

Smart Lit—Chimmy, Andrew, Decker, J-Bone, Drapes, Poggi, Pretty Face, Jacqueline, Aurora, Hannah, Caitie, Dearth, Lindsay, Jackie, Lila, Ryan, Brian, Doug, Matt, Justin, Chloe, Jordan, Alex, Alaina, Klus, and everyone else whom I was not able to form a relationship with because they were fired within their first week—thank you crooks for your friendship and making Italy as amazing as it was.

To Jaclyn, James, Stephanie, and Jennifer—thank you guys for being such supportive siblings. I am so grateful for all of our laughs together and am always here for you no matter what. Love you guys!

Dad—I know that we never spent a ton of time together when I was growing up, but I value and appreciate all the moments we did have together. It's crazy how similar our personalities are and I know that nothing ever came from a bad place. Love you, man.

Mat, Cliff, Cathy, Adam, Kristin, and Amy—thank you guys for taking me in and becoming my family. I could not thank you all enough for everything you guys have done for me over the years. The dynamics of Sunday dinners have certainly evolved over the years; however, they will always be memories I appreciate dearly. I love you all.

To the team that made this book possible. Thank you so much for the work you put in to make this dream come to fruition: Sandra Wendel (editor); Elizabeth Saharek (Cover Photo); Mom, Katie Walter, Ryan Parker, Tyler Walter, Cyndi Walter, and Zack Etter (proofreaders).

Jim Keller, you were one of the first people to ever believe in me. You have no idea how much that meant and still means to me. On the surface it was just baseball, but you unlocked an ability to believe in myself that has transferred to every other area of my life. To this day I still am unsure why you picked me to pour that level of belief into; however, I am grateful for it daily. Thank you. And remember, "Armpits and down."

Now, this part is slightly unconventional. Although I do not know these individuals personally, they have made an enormous impact on my life through their work. Thank you to Drake, Kanye West, Jay-Z, J. Cole, Tony Robbins, Ed Mylett, Andy Frisella, Eric Worre, Floyd Mayweather, Robert Kiyosaki, Lebron James, Kobe Bryant (RIP), Brendon Burchard, Alex Banayan, John Maxwell, James Lawrence, Gerard Adams, Mark Cuban, Daymond John, The Weeknd, Kevin Hart, Gary Vaynerchuk, Grant Cardone, Ace Hood, Leonardo DiCaprio, Will Smith, The Rock, and Dean Graziosi.

To the rest of my friends and family, I wish I had room to mention you all in here; however, my editor already wants to kill me for how long I've made this book. Just know that every single one of you that I have encountered in my life has played a part in changing me in some way, shape, or form. I could not possibly be who I am today without all of you. Thank you all.

ABOUT THE AUTHOR

John Stankiewicz is an entrepreneurial phenom—a Network Marketing three-time top-ten income earner for ages twenty-five and under. He has built a sales organization of thousands of people that has generated seven figures in product sales.

Although this twenty-something earned a bachelor of science degree in applied mathematics and economics from the University of Connecticut, John preaches about how the most important skills to success come from focusing on an education rich in experience outside of traditional schooling.

After getting kicked out of his small-town high school, John was lost and desperate to do whatever it took to get on the path to success. He reluctantly followed the traditional route until he found a better way via entrepreneurship.

Since then, John has gone on to build a mega-high-dollar-earning sales organization, become a certified mindset coach through Growth-U, speak in front of thousands of people on the topics of business strategy and mindset, and emerge as a top income earner in his Network Marketing company for distributors in his age group.

In addition, John has been able to become his own boss where he has designed a life of time freedom, works from anywhere, and has traveled to over twenty-five countries. He travels the country coaching individuals and audiences about his passion surrounding mindset and entrepreneurship.

Connect with John and follow him on Instagram @johnstankiewicz.

For business or speaking inquiries, please visit his website: www.JohnStankiewicz.com.